ASSESSMENT IN NEUROPSYCHOLOGY

Assessment in Neuropsychology is a practical and comprehensive handbook for clinical psychologists and other professionals who use neuropsychological tests in their everyday work. There is comprehensive coverage of assessment procedures for specific functions such as sensory-motor function, visual perception, speech and language and memory. Leonora Harding and John R. Beech also explore new developments in neurological and neuropsychological assessment and clarify legal issues.

The detailed analysis and case examples point the reader towards the most relevant assessment to use for a particular client's needs. The book is an excellent source of reference for assessment procedures, and where and how they can be acquired.

Assessment in Neuropsychology will quickly become an invaluable source-book for clinical psychologists, neurologists and other professionals as well as those in training.

Leonora Harding is a Clinical Psychologist at the Royal Aberdeen Children's Hospital and an Associate Fellow of the British Psychological Society.

John R. Beech is Senior Lecturer in Psychology at the University of Leicester and a Fellow of the British Psychological Society.

ROUTLEDGE ASSESSMENT LIBRARY
Series editors: Leonora Harding and John R. Beech

The *Routledge Assessment Library* is the definitive collection of reference books on assessment. Written by professionals from a wide range of different disciplines, the books are multi-disciplinary in their approach. Each contains a comprehensive discussion of all the important issues relating to assessment in the area specified, and a critical review of the main assessments in the field.

TESTING PEOPLE
A Practical Guide to Psychometrics
Edited by John R. Beech and Leonora Harding

ASSESSMENT OF THE ELDERLY
Edited by John R. Beech and Leonora Harding

EDUCATIONAL ASSESSMENT OF THE PRIMARY
SCHOOL CHILD
Edited by Leonora Harding and John R. Beech

ASSESSMENT IN SPEECH AND LANGUAGE THERAPY
*Edited by John Beech and Leonora Harding
with Diana Hilton-Jones*

ASSESSMENT IN NEUROPSYCHOLOGY

Edited by Leonora Harding and John R. Beech

London and New York

First published 1996
by Routledge
11 New Fetter Lane, London EC4P 4EE

Simultaneously published in the USA and Canada
by Routledge
29 West 35th Street, New York, NY 10001

Typeset in Times by Datix International Ltd, Bungay, Suffolk
Printed and bound in Great Britain by
Biddles Ltd, Guildford and King's Lynn

British Library Cataloguing in Publication Data
A catalogue record for this book is available from the British Library

Library of Congress Cataloging in Publication Data
A catalogue record for this book has been requested

ISBN 0–415–09390–2
0–415–12953–2 (pbk)

CONTENTS

BOXES

FIGURES

CONTRIBUTORS

David M. Anderson Head of Physiotherapy Service, Dundee Healthcare NHS Trust, Dundee.

Elizabeth Beardsworth (deceased) Principal in Child Neuropsychology, The Radcliffe Infirmary and Park Hospital, Oxford.

J. Graham Beaumont Head of Department of Clinical Psychology. Royal Hospital for Neuro-disability, London.

Elizabeth Fairgrieve (retired) Head Occupational Therapist (Children's Service), Dundee Healthcare NHS Trust, Dundee.

Jamie Furnell Consultant Clinical Psychologist (Child Health), Department of Child Clinical Psychology, Stirling Royal Infirmary; and Advocate, Faculty of Advocates, Edinburgh.

John C. Marshall Neuropsychology Unit, University Department of Clinical Neurology, The Radcliffe Infirmary, Oxford.

Graham E. Powell Senior Lecturer, Psychology Department, University of Surrey, Guildford.

Alistair G. R. Rennie FRCS, FCOphth, Consultant Ophthalmologist, Aberdeen Royal Infirmary.

Clive Skilbeck Consultant Clinical Neuropsychologist, Academic Unit, Hunters Moor Hospital, Newcastle upon Tyne.

Christine Skinner Lecturer/Clinical Co-ordinator, Speech and Language Sciences, Queen Margaret College, Edinburgh.

Barbara Wilson Senior Scientist/Clinical Psychologist, MRC Applied Psychology Unit, 15 Chaucer Road, Cambridge.

Sarah L. Wilson Lecturer, Psychology Department, University of Surrey, Guildford.

Andrew W. Young MRC Applied Psychology Unit, Cambridge.

SERIES EDITORS' PREFACE

The word 'assessment' conjures an adverse emotional reaction in many people. We have all at some stage undergone an assessment in some form – for instance, when sitting an examination – and many of us have found it a distinctly unpleasant experience. Why should we make assessments of people, and even more to the point, why launch a series of volumes on the subject?

Assessment is usually to do with making a judgement about an individual in relation to a large group of people, based on the acquisition of a body of knowledge concerning that individual. The professional believes that it is necessary to make such an assessment as a basis for deciding a particular course of action. This activity is considered to be predominantly in the best interests of the person being assessed, but at times will also protect the interests of society, or an organization, such as a company. Whether or not one agrees with the concept of making an assessment, the practice continues in our society, even if it waxes and wanes in some professional sectors. Our own view is that assessment is here to stay and in many cases is beneficial to the individual.

It is important that the best available means of assessment are used by professional workers to provide an accurate body of knowledge on which to base decisions. Errors of diagnosis can sometimes have serious consequences. The national press seems to report almost every day on situations in which diagnosis has been problematic, such as releasing a violent prisoner prematurely, or making erroneous accusations of child abuse, and so on. Less dramatic situations would be ones in which a child is inaccurately assessed and is then put on a training programme which is not appropriate for his or her needs, or where an elderly person is inaccurately considered as unable to live in his or her own home and transferred to another environment. Given that many of these assessments are essential, improving their accuracy is a worthwhile goal. If this series of volumes is instrumental in improving accuracy to some degree, we shall be well pleased.

As well as inaccurate use of tests, breakdown of communication between professions can lead to wrong decisions and inappropriate therapy or placement plans. Any one client may be treated, assessed or discussed by a number of professionals with different training, areas of expertise, approaches to assessment and vocabulary. (The term 'client' itself suggests one particular approach to care.) This series is explicitly directed towards the sharing of knowledge and the breaking down of barriers between professionals. We believe multi-disciplinary co-operation and information exchange can only benefit the subjects of assessment. It should be borne in mind, however, that certain tests which have been reviewed in these volumes can only be applied by professionals with the appropriate qualifications. We hope that there will be a certain amount of liberalization of these strictures in the future in order to facilitate co-operation between professionals.

When planning the series we decided early on that we were not going to produce exhaustive manuals, giving thorough reviews of all possible assessment techniques. There are many books of this nature already available. We thought that it would be a much better idea to produce fairly short books targeted at a particular category of person requiring assessment, such as the elderly, or those with speech and language difficulties. Our readership would be the professional workers involved with such groups, either directly as assessors or indirectly as those who use test results in their decision-making. Students training for these professions, or professionals undergoing in-service training, will also find these useful. Therefore, we have set our writers a very difficult task. Each contribution has to be easy to read, but at the same time provide information which the current professional worker will find useful when deciding on an assessment strategy. The writer might point to a new test which has been developed, or highlight the inadequacies of one currently used. The chapters do describe the application of tests within a particular area, but they also provide a range of other useful information; for instance, check-lists, case studies, points to bear in mind with certain types of patient, and so on.

Most of the volumes contain a final section of reviews on the main tests currently applied in that area. Because the subject of neuropsychological assessment is so wide ranging (from straightforward IQ tests to pilot tests used in research), we have decided not to include the usual test review section for this volume. Rather (and partly because many tests are not available from the usual test publishers) we have decided to give a list of the tests cited in the chapters, together with the name of test authors and address of publishers. We hope this will be a useful source of reference. Several of the tests and assessment procedures described in the volume are of an experimental nature and have not been widely standardized. Others have wide validity, reliability and application for assessing the usefulness of a test for a particular purpose. The reader should be aware of issues such as standardization, simple validity and reliability.

The interested reader is referred to our book in the series entitled *Testing*

People: A Practical Guide to Psychometrics, which goes into the statistical basis of testing in more depth. This is a corner-stone volume in the series, which is intended for professional people who wish to update their statistical knowledge in order to understand the basis of the tests. It does not assume any previous statistical knowledge.

Turning briefly to the contents of the current volume on neuropsychological assessment: the first three chapters are of an introductory nature, setting the scene regarding assessment and recent developments and covering pertinent issues and problem areas in the assessment of children and adults. Chapters 4–9 are an assessment of the functions, including motor and perceptual impairments; speech and language impairment; and written language and memory. The last section of the book reviews further and future application in the use of neurological assessment for legal cases, in recent developments in neuropsychology, and in ethical issues.

We would like to thank the contributors, Vivien Ward of Routledge, and many others for their enthusiasm and support in producing this volume. In particular we would like to honour Elizabeth Beardsworth, who warmly co-operated to produce an excellent survey of children's problems whilst (unknown to us) suffering a terminal illness.

Leonora Harding and John R. Beech

Part I

1

INTRODUCTION
The aims of neuropsychological assessment

J. Graham Beaumont

The essential aim of any neuropsychological assessment is an improvement in the condition of a client who has suffered some form of damage to the nervous system. However, within that general intention there are a number of ways by which the improvement might be achieved and in consequence a variety of forms which the assessment may take. Although there is a range of current practices within neuropsychological assessment, it is important to maintain a clear idea of the precise goal of a particular assessment procedure and the appropriate form which it should, as a consequence, take.

There are two basic forms of the neuropsychological assessment. They are often confused, but it should be recognized that they are fundamentally different, and have different applications with respect to the specific goals of a particular investigation. They are the generation of structural descriptions, and that of functional descriptions, of the client's present status.

STRUCTURAL DESCRIPTIONS

The object of a neuropsychological assessment which generates a structural description is to provide a report of the changes in the client's nervous system in neurological, anatomical terms. Until recently this was the more important of the two forms of neuropsychological investigation.

The history of scientific neuropsychology over the past century shows that the principal concern during much of that period has been the discovery of brain–behaviour relationships. The techniques of clinical neuropsychology (see below) have primarily provided evidence about the association between anatomical structures and behavioural functions. The obvious application of this scientific knowledge was to observe the dysfunctional changes in specific behaviours and draw inferences about the gross neuroanatomical changes which can be presumed to have produced them.

Applications of this principle are still of some value, but they had greater importance before the introduction of computerized axial tomography (CAT scans) in the 1970s and the subsequent development of more refined techniques of imaging the brain. In that period the physical investigations open to neurologists and neurosurgeons were of inferior validity, and psychological evidence could make a significant contribution to the localization of a tumour, the assessment of the degree of cortical atrophy, or the topography of the effects of a stroke. Neurosurgeons might also be concerned about the lateral representation of psychological functions when deciding, for example, how radical the resection of the anterior temporal lobe might safely be made in a case of unilateral anterior lobectomy (Beaumont, 1983).

FUNCTIONAL DESCRIPTIONS

An alternative form of description can be generated in purely psychological functional terms. Such a description is without reference to neuroanatomical structures, and forms an account, employing psychological models, of the client's relative abilities across a spectrum of behavioural functions.

Functional descriptions have assumed much greater importance in the last ten or fifteen years, for three reasons. The first, already discussed, is the decline in the importance of psychological evidence in the structural identification of a client's lesion. The second is a growth of interest, long overdue, in behavioural approaches to management and remediation. The third, and most significant, is the development of cognitive neuropsychology as a distinct approach within neuropsychology. The generation of cognitive models of normal and abnormal performance has facilitated the description of a client's functional status in terms which need make no reference to anatomical localization.

These two forms of description are rarely so clearly separated, and of course there are logical interrelationships which permit some degree of mapping from one to the other. Possessing a structural description allows inferences to be made about the relative status of different behavioural systems; a functional description will often permit some assessment of the neuroanatomical basis of the various dysfunctions. Nevertheless, each form has its own peculiar merits and application to specific assessment goals.

SPECIFIC ASSESSMENT GOALS

There are five main goals in neuropsychological assessment by which clinical improvement in the client's status might be achieved.

Medical intervention

Appropriate medical intervention, whether by surgery, drug treatment, or other forms of physical management, depends upon accurate diagnosis of the client's neurological state. Psychological evidence can contribute to this by assisting in the localization and identification of the client's lesion. While this role may have declined in recent years, psychological test results are still relevant to many medical decisions. With this goal it is structural descriptions which are generally more important.

Psychological intervention

Psychological interventions are less well established but there has been a rapid expansion of these techniques in recent years. They include: specific remedial therapeutic approaches; ways in which the client's orientation and concentration can be improved; techniques to assist clients to overcome handicaps in, for example, memory; and the modification of general behavioural disorders. It is clearly not possible to apply psychological interventions aimed at specific behavioural problems unless the therapist possesses a good description of the client's functional psychological state. Functional descriptions are therefore of prime importance.

Management

The general management of clients with a neurological disorder involves a variety of forms of support, some specifically medical, some nursing, some psychological, with contributions from other specialisms. Each of these may benefit from a neuropsychological description of the client's status, and structural and functional descriptions may contribute differentially to the management of the client's disorder.

Prognosis

A particular aspect of the management of the client is the formulation of a behavioural prognosis. Depending upon the disorder, this may be the eventual level of function which might be regained, or it may be the likely course of a disease as it progresses. The prognosis may be relevant to management decisions, and is also of great importance to the client and to relatives and carers. Functional descriptions are likely to be of greater value.

Monitoring change

A particularly valuable goal of neuropsychological assessment is the regular monitoring of behavioural changes, often conducted as a contribution to management, to the evaluation of interventions, or to the refinement of prognosis. Although not necessarily formulated in functional terms, the description of behavioural changes is likely to be more precise and useful if constructed as a functional description.

There are, of course, other reasons for conducting neuropsychological assessments. Scientific enquiry is a valid reason for the investigation of clients providing that the client's individual interests are respected; there may be medico-legal reasons for determing the client's functional status; and the legitimate concerns of relatives and carers must also be taken into account, as well as, occasionally, those of a wider community. However, these reasons normally share features with the goals of assessment which have already been identified, and which form the basis of contemporary practice in clinical neuropsychology. (For general reviews see: Beaumont, 1983; Crawford et al., 1992; Golden and Vicente, 1983; Walsh, 1985.)

APPROACHES IN NEUROPSYCHOLOGY

The current conceptual basis of clinical neuropsychology is complex, and is rarely stated explicitly. It is complex as a result of the variety of influences which have acted upon it over the last century, and it is still in rapid evolution. Much is implicit in the clinical and research procedures which neuropsychologists employ, and close examination of the conceptual assumptions which underlie these procedures would fail to reveal a consistent or coherent underlying philosophy.

The most fundamental problem stems from a failure to take a clear position on the essential issue, which is that of the relationship between mental and physiological events: the 'mind–body problem'. Most contemporary neuropsychologists adopt, by default, the position of 'emergent psychoneural monism': accepting that mental properties in some way emerge out of neural events and can be correlated with them, but reserving the possibility that mental properties may have an existence which is to some degree independent of physiological events.

This compromise allows neuropsychologists to accept the relevance of anatomical and physiological data to neuropsychological states, but avoids the reductionist trap of shifting the focus of attention to ever more elementary biological mechanisms. It permits, for instance, the sensations of taste to be explained by neural mechanisms, but the taste as perceived to be a mental property which is associated with, but not wholly determined by, the neural apparatus. The detection of sugars in biting an apple is carried out by the brain, but the sweetness is in the mind.

This is not an entirely satisfactory position, and there are obvious philosophical objections to it when it is stated so baldly. It is also inconsistent with much that neuropsychologists actually do: for instance, by discussing the localization of higher mental abilities such as gnostic functions. (For an unusually clear discussion of these issues see Bunge, 1980).

Models of neuropsychological function

Historically, neuropsychology began by adopting a localizationist approach. The early neuropsychologists, in the second half of the nineteenth century, believed a particular part of the brain to be responsible for a specific psychological function, and set about identifying the localization of each function.

However, from the start, there were opponents who supported the alternative equipotential theory: that while sensory input is localized, perception involves the whole brain, and that the effects of brain lesions depend upon their extent and not upon their location.

Both approaches fail, in some way, to account for the relevant evidence. It is certainly possible to demonstrate some degree of localization of higher functions, but not with the precision which is demanded by localization theory. The outcome has been that most neuropsychologists now ascribe to a third, intermediate, approach known as interactionist theory. This theory probably originates from the work of Hughlings Jackson, who argued that 'higher' abilities are built up by combining a number of more basic functions. Damage to the brain affects the more basic level of component skills and so has an effect upon various higher functions to the extent that they depend upon the more basic skills.

Generally accepted findings that no function or learning process is entirely dependent on any particular area of cortex, and that each part within the brain plays an unequal role in different functions, support the interactionist position. In practice, interactionist theory is linked to the concept of 'regional equipotentiality': that at the level of neuropsychological analysis relatively specific functions can be assigned to regions of the cortex, but that a degree of equipotentiality operates within this region. This is a pragmatic, rather than a scientifically justified, position.

The research strategies adopted by neuropsychologists, and the clinical procedures which are derived from them, are based upon the interactionist approach. Clinical cases are observed for the functional deficits which they demonstrate, and these deficits are correlated with the nature of the lesion, including its location. A typical research design selects groups of patients with particular lesions which can be classified along a series of dimensions (location, size, diffusion, chronicity, pathology), and these groups are contrasted with respect to performance on a particular function.

A particular refinement of this approach is the use of 'double dissociation' (Weiskrantz, 1968). Double dissociation is demonstrated where lesions of area A affect function X more than function Y, while lesions of area B affect function Y more than function X. This is a useful analytic concept, but relies upon relatively strict and stable localization, and is often difficult to apply in a complex clinical situation.

Although the logic of these approaches is simple, there is a variety of methodological difficulties in putting them into practice. Their success is also dependent upon the adequacy of the interactionist theory which is itself a slightly uncomfortable compromise between competing conceptual approaches.

7

Cognitive psychology and neuropsychology

There has inevitably been a close association between neuropsychology and experimental psychology, more latterly as cognitive psychology. The information and models derived from the study of psychological abilities in normal states is of obvious relevance to the study of these functions in abnormal states.

The dominant approach incorporated in information-processing models has been transferred into clinical neuropsychological models and procedures. In its most general form, what we might call the 'telephone exchange model', it assumes that sensory information comes into the brain in primary (highly localized) cortex, from where it is routed to secondary cortex for the processes of perception and elaboration, and then on to tertiary association cortex, where higher functions are performed. This is consistent with the interactionist approach, and allows information to be routed among different basic processing modules which are combined to generate higher-level functions. The effect of lesions is supposed both to impair the function of specific basic modules and to interrupt the connections among them.

The development of more sophisticated models in cognitive psychology in recent years has both benefited from clinical neuropsychological data, and provided more elaborate conceptual structures by which individual clients may be assessed (Ellis and Young, 1989; McCarthy and Warrington, 1990; Shallice, 1988). It is currently having a profound effect upon clinical neuropsychology because it has shifted the research emphasis from studies of groups of similar patients to the intensive study of individual cases. A clear example is a recent lengthy monograph which deals exclusively with the single-word processing deficits of an individual client (Howard and Franklin, 1988). This shift is generating a vigorous debate about the relative merits and applications of group versus single-case studies in neuropsychology. It is too early to assess the full impact of the cognitive neuropsychological approach in clinical applications, but it will undoubtedly involve some radical revision of the kinds of assessment procedure which clinical neuropsychologists of the next decade will employ.

A quite separate, and even more radical, challenge to the general contemporary approach comes from connectionism, or 'neural networks' 'parallel distributed processing' (PDP). This approach is based upon the modelling of nerve-like elements in computational matrices which learn and perceive and remember. It is fundamentally different from the contemporary cognitive psychological approach in that the processes and the semantic information are entirely distributed throughout the network (Morris, 1989).

These connectionist models are attractive in that they appear capable of performing higher-level psychological functions and possess certain properties which make them brain-like. They have been applied to clinical neuropsychological states (Patterson *et al.*, 1989). Again, it is too early to

8

assess their impact on clinical neuropsychology, but if the approach proves successful it would have radical implications not only for neuropsychological practice, but also for a theoretical understanding of neuropsychological processes.

Practical approaches in clinical neuropsychology

At a more mundane level, there are three traditions which can be identified in the practice of clinical neuropsychological assessment. These three approaches are: behavioural neurology, the neuropsychological battery approach and the individual-centred normative approach (see Beaumont, 1983; Walsh, 1985).

The behavioural neurology approach derives from the highly influential work of the Russian psychologist Alexander Luria (Christensen, 1975). It is individual-centred and clinical in nature. The goal of neuropsychological assessment is not a quantitative measurement of the client's difficulties, but a qualitative analysis and description of the client's problems. Rather than employing psychometric procedures to identify abnormal performance by statistical means, with reference to a normal population, the emphasis is on behaviours which any normal individual of the age, background and general ability of the client should be able to perform. When such behaviours cannot be generated a deficit has been demonstrated. Attention is paid to *how* the task is performed as well as to the absolute level of performance attained.

The approach has the advantage of an explicit theoretical foundation and is flexible, but it demands a very high level of clinical skill and its validity has never been explicitly demonstrated.

The neuropsychological battery approach has been most popular in the United States, partly because of the strong psychometric tradition in American psychology. Two batteries are of current major importance: the Halstead–Reitan Neuropsychological Battery and the Luria–Nebraska Neuropsychological Battery. Each of these batteries attempts to sample a broad range of the client's functions and to apply actuarial procedures to the determination of the location and type of a given lesion (Bleiberg and Kaplan, 1992; Golden, 1979; Incagnoli *et al.*, 1986).

In favour of this approach is its systematic organization and the explicit statistical foundations upon which it is based. It demands relatively low levels of clinical skill and is amenable to computer-aided support. The batteries, however, are relatively time-consuming and are to some degree inflexible. The approach is a valuable one, but may be insensitive to the need to explore particular aspects of the client's cognitive pathology.

The individual-centred normative approach has been generally associated with British neuropsychology. It relies to some extent upon a formal psychometric approach, but emphasizes the need to tailor the assessment to the nature of the particular client's difficulties. The aim is to formulate a psychological description of the client's deficits which goes beyond a simple diagnostic classification. Individual tests, preferably with associated normative data, are applied flexibly to an investigation of the client's problems.

This approach relies heavily on the skills and insight of the individual clinician. There is the risk that areas of function may be neglected or that complex functional interactions may be missed. Nevertheless, many consider it the most intelligent approach to neuropsychological assessment if practised by a capable and sensitive clinical neuropsychologist.

THE INVESTIGATORY CONTEXT

Neuropsychological assessment is not carried out in a vacuum; it is one of a number of investigatory approaches which are applied to the client. Usually, by the time that the client is referred to the neuropsychologist a number of other investigations will have been completed. A more or less rigorous neurological examination will have been carried out, as will certain routine physiological examinations. It is increasingly common for a CAT scan to have been performed, and the results of other ancillary investigations may be available. The clinical neuropsychologist must learn to make use of this information (and not to be misled by it) in making the psychological assessment. (For a further introduction to these topics see Brain, 1978; Lishman, 1978.)

The neurological examination

The neurologist or neurosurgeon will generally carry out a standard neurological examination. This comprises taking a history of the illness, and making a clinical examination of the patient.

The history will normally involve enquiring about mental state, patterns of sleep, difficulties of speech and writing, attacks of loss of consciousness, headaches, disturbance of the special senses, muscular weakness and possible loss of voluntary and involuntary motor control, difficulties of balance and gait, disturbances of sphincter control and normality of reproductive functions, and any changes in body weight. A history of previous illnesses will also be taken, together with a social and a family history. Information may be taken from relatives or carers as well as from the patient.

The clinical examination of the patient involves an assessment of the patient's state of consciousness, functions of the cranial nerves, sensibility and functions of the trunk and limbs (paying attention to muscular power and co-ordination and to sensory acuity), the state and tone of bodily reflexes, sphincter functions and trophic disturbances. The head will be examined, with external examination of its vascular function, and gait will also be tested.

The clinical examination will also include assessment of intellectual function, emotional state, and speech and articulation. Intellectual functions are, however, rarely tested beyond crude tests for orientation, everyday memory, knowledge of current events, and the presence of delusions or hallucinations. Similarly, language functions are rarely tested beyond simple comprehension, expression, repetition and the ability to name objects readily to hand at the bedside.

Ancillary examinations

Examination of blood, urine and CSF

Routine physiological examinations will be carried out on samples of body fluids taken from the patient. Standard haematological tests will be performed and serological tests for neurosyphilis. Serum electrolyte, serum protein and liver function tests are likely, and serum B_{12} and foliates may be measured. The urine will be examined for sugar, albumin and its specific gravity. These tests will reveal the presence of systemic diseases and physiological imbalances.

A sample of cerebrospinal fluid (CSF) may be taken by lumbar puncture for the examination of proteins and the possible presence of blood in the CSF, or of abnormal cells associated with cerebral tumours. The pressure of the CSF can be assessed at the time that the sample is taken.

Electrophysiology: EEG and evoked potentials

While EEG (electroencephalogram) recording is less central to neurological investigation than it once was, it is still commonly performed as a routine examination. The electroencephalographer will examine the relative power of the standard frequency bands and inspect the EEG record for specific abnormal features. This will provide an assessment of the patient's state of consciousness, as well as evidence of epileptic activity and localizing abnormal signs which may be associated with focal pathology, such as a tumour.

Evoked potentials are also used to assess the state of sensory systems, particularly in patients unwilling or unable to co-operate. Brain stem evoked potentials can provide evidence of the function of sensory afferents. Evoked potentials may also be used to assess the possibility of hysterical reactions.

Plain X-ray

Plain X-ray of the skull is carried out in cases of head injury for the possible presence of fractures, but it can also be of value in other cases by providing evidence of raised intracranial pressure, and of calcification within the brain, which is evidence both of certain types of tumour and of certain other cerebral diseases. Altered bone density can also be a diagnostic sign.

Computerized axial tomography

The CAT or CT scan was the first of the new generation of imaging techniques. It involves the use of a rotating X-ray beam, which circles the head in combination with a paired detector while a computer calculates the densities of the tissue being imaged and presents the information in the form of a series of slices through the brain. CAT scanners show good bony detail and delineation of CSF spaces, and may show some differentiation of grey and white matter and changes in brain density.

The CAT scan has become the standard method of localization of lesions in both clinical neurology and neuropsychology. It is widely available, is without discomfort or significant risks, and has a relatively good validity. (For an introduction to all modern imaging techniques see Andreasen, 1989; Bigler, 1992; Kertesz, 1989.)

Positron emission tomography

A more recent development is the PET scan. It involves the measurement of oxygen and glucose metabolism using a positron-emitting isotope and a computerized tomography scanner. It is not widely available, as it demands the presence of a particle accelerator and a highly specialized clinical team, which means that it is also expensive. It has poor anatomical resolution but has the advantage of measuring cerebral metabolism and therefore function.

A less expensive version using single photons (SPECT) is likely to become more generally available and may have a greater clinical impact.

Magnetic resonance imaging

MRI or NMR (nuclear magnetic resonance) imaging is the latest development and shows the greatest promise in accurately locating lesions without the use of radiation. It uses the inherent magnetic properties of spinning atomic nuclei. The head is placed in a large magnetic field so that short-wave radio pulses generate a resonance signal that can be quantified and computerized. The technique produces images of startling anatomical detail, which can be in sections not just restricted to the horizontal plane of CAT scans. It can safely be used with normals. MRI scanning is in a rapid state of development and will almost certainly come to complement CAT scanning in clinical application.

Angiogram, air-encephalogram

These techniques were important before the introduction of computerized tomography. In angiography, a contrast medium is injected into the cerebral circulation so that sequential plain X-ray images of the head reveal the dynamics of vascular circulation, and the topography of blood vessels. Air-encephalography involves the insertion of a quantity of air into the CSF so that by rotating the patient the outlines of the ventricular system may be imaged. Both techniques involve some risk and considerable discomfort to the patient, and have been largely supplanted by the modern imaging techniques.

The neuropsychological assessment

This is, of course, the subject of this book, and subsequent chapters will describe various aspects of the neuropsychological assessment in some detail. There are, however, two general points to be made in conclusion to this chapter.

The first is the growing introduction of computer-based support in clinical neuropsychology. Although its utility may not be as extensive as in certain other areas of applied psychology, it is nevertheless having an impact in two ways. The first of these is the computer-aided administration of assessment procedures, and a number of tests are now available in computerized form (Beaumont, 1990; Beaumont and French, 1987; Norris *et al.*, 1985). The second, and more widespread, of these is the use of computers for analysis and interpretation of the results of psychological assessment. This has been a notable development in association with the battery-based approach more common in North America (Adams and Heaton, 1985; Kay, 1992).

The second and final point is to remember that all neuropsychological assessment has an ultimate goal of improving the client's status, whether by diagnostic assessment or in connection with management and rehabilitation. But this goal can only be attained by operating within the context of a clinical team. Not only the purely medical specialists contribute to this clinical effort, but also a variety of other professionals: particularly speech and language therapists, medical social workers, physiotherapists and occupational therapists. Each profession has its own expertise and its own, sometimes very formal, methods of assessment. The effective neuropsychologist will learn to work within this team, and to take account of the contribution of other specialities, so that the psychological descriptions which an assessment generates may be more valid and of greater benefit to the client.

REFERENCES

Adams, K. M. and Heaton, R. K. (1985). 'Automated interpretation of neuropsychological test data.' *Journal of Consulting and Clinical Psychology*, 53, 790–802.

Andreasen, N. C. (ed.) (1989). *Brain Imaging: Applications in Psychiatry*. Washington, DC: American Psychiatric Press.

Beaumont, J. G. (1983). *Introduction to Neuropsychology*. Oxford: Blackwell Scientific.

Beaumont, J. G. (1990). 'Expert systems and the clinical psychologist'. In A. Ager (ed.), *Microcomputers in Clinical Psychology*. Chichester: John Wiley.

Beaumont, J. G. and French, C. C. (1987). 'A clinical field study of eight automated psychometric procedures: the Leicester DHSS Project'. *International Journal of Man–Machine Studies*, 26, 661–82.

Bigler, E. D. (1992). 'Utilization of brain imaging techniques in neuropsychology'. In S. L. Hanson and D. M. Tucker (eds), *Neuropsychological Assessment*. Philadelphia, PA: Hanley and Belfus.

Bleiberg, J. and Kaplan, D. (1992). 'Evolution of neuropsychology using the Halstead–Reitan Neuropsychological Test Battery'. In S. L. Hanson and D. M. Tucker (eds), *Neuropsychological Assessment*. Philadelphia, PA: Hanley and Belfus.

Brain, Lord (1978). *Clinical Neurology*. 5th edn (rev. R. Bannister). Oxford: Oxford Medical Publications.

Bunge, M. (1980). *The Mind–Body Problem*. Oxford: Pergamon Press.

Christensen, A. L. (1975). *Luria's Neuropsychological Investigation*. Copenhagen: Munksgaard.

Crawford, J. R., Parker, D. M. and McKinlay, W. W. (eds) (1992). *A Handbook of Neuropsychological Assessment*. Hove: Lawrence Erlbaum.

Ellis, A. W. and Young, A. W. (1989). *Human Cognitive Neuropsychology*. Hillsdale, NJ: Lawrence Erlbaum.

Golden, C. J. (1979). *Clinical Interpretation of Objective Psychological Tests*. New York: Grune and Stratton.

Golden, C. J. and Vicente, P. J. (eds) (1983). *Foundations of Clinical Neuropsychology*. New York: Plenum Press.

Heilman, K. M. and Valenstein, E. (eds) (1985). *Clinical Neuropsychology*. 2nd edn. New York: Oxford University Press.

Howard, E. and Franklin, S. (1988). *Missing the Meaning?* Cambridge, MA: MIT Press.

Incagnoli, T., Goldstein, G. and Golden, C. J. (eds) (1986). *Clinical Application of Neuropsychological Test Batteries*. New York: Plenum Press.

Kay, G. G. (1992). 'Advances in computerized neuropsychological applications'. In S. L. Hanson and D. M. Tucker (eds), *Neuropsychological Assessment*. Philadelphia, PA: Harley and Belfus.

Kertesz, A. (1989). 'Anatomical and physiological correlations and neuroimaging techniques in language disorders'. In A. Ardila and F. Ostrosky-Solis (eds), *Brain Organisation of Language and Cognitive Processes*. New York: Plenum Press.

Lishman, W. A. (1978). *Organic Psychiatry*. Oxford: Blackwell Scientific.

McCarthy, R. A. and Warrington, E. K. (1990). *Cognitive Neuropsychology: A Clinical Introduction*. London: Academic Press.

Morris, R. G. M. (ed.) (1989). *Parallel Distributed Processing: Implications for Psychology and Neurobiology*. Oxford: Clarendon Press.

Norris, D. E., Skilbeck, C. E., Hayward, A. E. and Torpy, D. M. (1985). *Microcomputers in Clinical Practice*. Chichester: John Wiley.

Patterson, K., Seidenberg, M. S. and McClelland, J. L. (1989). 'Connections and disconnections: acquired dyslexia in a computational model of reading processes'. In R. G. M. Morris (ed.), *Parallel Distributed Procession: Implications for Psychology and Neurobiology*. Oxford: Clarendon Press.

Shallice, T. (1988). *From Neuropsychology to Mental Structure*. Cambridge: Cambridge University Press.

Walsh, K. W. (1985). *Understanding Brain Damage*. Edinburgh: Churchill Livingstone.

Weiskrantz, L. (1968). 'Treatments, inference and brain function'. In L. Weiskrantz (ed.), *Analysis of Behavioural Change*. New York: Harper and Row.

2

DEVELOPMENTAL NEUROPSYCHOLOGY AND THE ASSESSMENT OF CHILDREN

Elizabeth Beardsworth with Leonora Harding

A recent spate of publications of child neuropsychology textbooks attests to the increasing interest shown in this area of assessment. Unfortunately, the interested clinician is faced with a large and often conflicting literature but few reliable tools. In the face of these difficulties one approach may be to adopt the battery approach so popular in America (Hynd *et al.*, 1986); but another is to encourage the pursuit of the exact nature of deficits by selecting individual tests to explore underlying processes. A fuller description of the functional architecture of skills is more likely to lead to successful remediation efforts.

The most obvious difference between the assessment of children and of adults is that, in the case of the child, one is assessing an ever developing organism. The effects of insult will vary according to the child's stage of development, and subsequent development may be distorted. If a child receives an insult that results in problems of verbal learning and memory at the age of six years, both subsequent vocabulary acquisition and general semantic development may be undermined. Depending on the timing of the assessment, test results will reflect both the initial insult and its later effects. However, the developmental stage of the child is just one aspect of the age variable; experience and expectations are others. Deficits may only become obvious when a child reaches a stage where he or she is expected to rely less on parental supervision.

Despite a choice of tests available for assessing intelligence in children, there are few well and recently standardized tests of more specific functions (see Spreen and Gaddes, 1969, for norms on certain tests). This is no doubt due to the fact that the development of skills throughout childhood requires that tests be standardized on children of all ages so that they should be developmentally sensitive.

The purpose of the present chapter is to highlight those aspects of the literature that are relevant to the interpretation of results in the individual case, to review briefly and far from comprehensively the literature on some commonly occurring disorders, and to pinpoint which tests are useful and readily available in the assessment of those disorders.

BRAIN DEVELOPMENT AND PLASTICITY

The differential effects of lesions according to age at insult is one of the main concerns of developmental neuropsychology. The view that there is better recovery in childhood is widely held and it is important to review the evidence for this. Recovery in patients of all ages is fortunately a common occurrence (see Finger and Stein, 1982). However, there are many cases which suggest that the immature brain is more vulnerable to insult than a mature one.

The effect of congenital infections (such as the rubella virus) is the most startling example of this, but malnutrition and environmental deprivation can also have strong and more pervasive effects on cognitive functioning when they are allowed to attack an immature brain, either *in utero* or in early infancy. Furthermore, there is also evidence from normal children suggesting considerable early cerebral specialization (see Hahn, 1987), which would seem to limit plasticity. However, other findings suggest some flexibility in the system as a direct response to early injury. There is the reduced incidence of and marked recovery from aphasia in childhood (but see Satz and Bullard-Bates, 1981), the relative robustness of language in hemispherectomy cases after early insult (Basser, 1962; Beardsworth and Adams, 1988), and the evidence of increased incidence of right-hemisphere-based language after early left-hemisphere lesions in temporal lobectomy patients (Milner, 1975). Terms like 'transfer' and 'switching' are commonly invoked to describe the processes involved, but how far do such terms capture the essence of what may be going on in brain development after early brain injury?

In order to understand the nature of early neurological disorders and their effects, and in particular to understand the notion of plasticity, it is important to consider briefly current ideas of brain development (see Volpe, 1987, for full account). The basic external form of the brain is established by the end of the first six weeks of embryonic life. Neuronal proliferation is at its height at twelve to eighteen weeks, as the cortical layers are established. Disorder at this time may result in a brain that is either under- or over-sized. From three to five months of gestation, cells migrate from their site of origin in the ventricular and sub-ventricular zones to their final loci in the cortex. A disorder at this stage can affect development of the gyri or folds of the cortex, or of connecting structures like the corpus callosum. The period from six months from conception to several years after birth is called the period of organization. During this time several processes are being completed: the alignment, orientation and layering of cortical neurones; the elaboration of dendrites and axones; contacts

17

between synapses; selective elimination of many cells; and glial proliferation and differentiation. Relatively little is known about the primary disorders at this time, with the exception of response to trauma (such as birth injury). The final stage is myelination. This is most rapid immediately after birth but continues to adulthood. Again, primary disturbances of this stage are little documented, but certainly some of the effects of malnutrition in early infancy can be attributed to interference with this process.

An important question is whether brain development is pre-programmed or whether it develops in response to external forces. Of course, if development were pre-programmed the brain would be very vulnerable to early injury. In fact, evidence from a variety of sources suggests some 'reserve capacity' or redundancy in the system, largely because of projections of the developing nervous system due to overproduction of cells and connections. In normal development, remodelling can occur during the period of organization with the death of unneeded cells. Rates of cell death have been estimated as from 15 to 85 per cent in different brain regions. It is thought that it is the modification of the pattern of cell death that allows some preservation of function after some forms of early brain injury, rather than a real transfer of abilities as such.

There is another way of looking at differential response to injury according to age, which describes children not as less vulnerable, but rather as affected differently. In childhood onset cases, one tends to find a general lowering of abilities regardless of whether the insult is to the right or left hemisphere, and even when the insult is quite localized. When injuries occur later in life, one tends to get more specific deficits. Hebb (1942) suggested that more cerebral efficiency or 'intellectual power' is needed in early childhood for intellectual development than is needed to sustain later functioning at the same level. Thus lesions in early childhood result in less severe effects for particular skills but have a more global effect and depress functioning all round.

At this stage it is perhaps useful to point out that the distinction between developmental and acquired disorders is also being questioned (see Temple, 1991a). It has been demonstrated that cases of developmental dyslexia, for example, have a neurological base (Galburda et al., 1985). For the clinician attempting the assessment of children's current levels of understanding, this suggests that test results, even age-old favourites like Verbal-Performance discrepancies on IQ tests, should be interpreted with caution. In patients with early-onset lesions, irrespective of age at assessment, test results are rarely a reliable guide to the lateralization or the localization of lesions.

GETTING STARTED ON TESTING

Since the 1970s there has been a heated debate between factions continuing to support the psychometric tradition (who upheld the value of norm-referenced testing) against a new approach drawing on the methodology of behaviourism that favoured detailed task analysis or criterion-referenced testing. This controversy was most prominent among psychologists working with learning-disabled children. It clearly arose because such psychologists are frequently asked by teachers or parents for very specific advice about how to proceed with children who are not learning effectively with the usual school approach.

Although norm-referenced tests (such as the Wechsler Intelligence Scale for Children III) can highlight a child's relative strengths and weaknesses and can give some idea as to how general or specific his or her problems are, it is still a considerable leap from assessment to guidance on remediation. One need take only one look at the vague suggestions in recent neuropsychology textbooks, and at the depressing literature on diagnostic-prescriptive teaching (see Ysseldyke and Mirkin, 1982), for confirmation. Criterion-referenced testing held out the hope that even complex learning processes such as learning to tell the time or even learning to read could be submitted to task analysis like simpler tasks such as learning to put on a teeshirt. If the learning process could be broken down into smaller steps and success at each step consistently rewarded, then one only had to identify how many stages had already been mastered and it would be obvious what should be tackled next. Criterion-referenced testing has not fulfilled its promise, largely because of the complexity of the skills to be learnt and our comparative ignorance about the relevant processes and stages of development.

Of course, both approaches have a lot to offer. The approach chosen with any particular child will depend on the purpose of the assessment along the continuum from 'Why is this child failing?' to 'What should we be trying next week?' The assessment will include not just an exploration of within-child factors but also some appraisal of the appropriateness and sensitivity of the teaching method.

When a child with a neurological condition is referred for assessment, the test results can be used in a variety of ways. In addition to highlighting cognitive strengths and weaknesses, reviewing the appropriateness of current school placement and guiding teaching methods, test results can also be used as a medical 'barometer' to monitor the child's clinical condition. Series of test results can be used to chart the recovery or (sadly) the decline of cognitive functioning. Specific tests can be used to evaluate the effects of treatment (such as medication or surgical interventions) and tests can be used in conjunction with other investigations (such as EEG [electroencephalo-gram] monitoring) to explore the undermining effects of the neurological condition.

However, test results, particularly IQ results, have to be interpreted with considerable caution. This is not simply because of the discussion already covered about the inappropriateness of using guidelines derived from adults in the interpretation of the test profiles of children, but also because social factors may be as important as medical factors in determining test results. In a large study of 407 patients from the Hospital for Sick Children in Toronto, Dennis (1985) found that, despite comprehensive and highly informed consideration of potentially relevant medical factors, these accounted for only 25 per cent of the variance in IQ. Unaffected siblings can be used as controls for family circumstances when this is thought to be relevant.

Although single measures of 'g' are being revived, the usual practise is to choose IQ tasks sampling a wide variety of abilities. The tasks may have been organized according to the nature of the material (for example, verbal or non-verbal with the Weschler Scales; WISC–III and WPPSI); according to the process involved (for example memory or matching, as in the British Ability Scales [BAS]-R); or according to style of processing required (for example, successive or simultaneous, as in the Kaufman battery). Most IQ tasks, when they do reflect theories of intelligence, tend to enshrine theories current several decades ago, simply because of the time it takes to launch a new test. Choice of test can depend on a variety of factors: the age of the child; the recency of standardization; the range of abilities sampled; and the availability of back-up information which will allow informed interpretation of the results. Often it is necessary to go beyond making an assessment of the general level of abilities by identifying specific difficulties. For children with neurological problems, a thorough assessment often includes some exploration of memory and attention. A lack of age-appropriate tests makes this difficult to do, especially with children under 12 years of age.

Intact verbal memory skills are clearly very important to a developing child. This is recognized in the common inclusion of digit-span tasks in most IQ tests. However, other aspects of verbal memory also need to be considered. Clinical tests usually involve some form of story recall and word-list learning. Normal children as young as 8 years of age can obtain scores as high as those of young adults on paired associate learning (for instance, from the Wechsler Memory Scale), but data on normal children on age-appropriate story recall tasks is needed (Curry et al., 1986).

On the face of it, the situation in the testing of non-verbal memory is better, with several tests available with some norms for children, such as the Benton Visual Retention Test BAS-R Recall of Designs, and the Rey–Osterreith Complex Figure, for which there is the original normative data (Osterreith, 1944) and more recent information (Waber and Holmes, 1986). All these tasks simply test recall of visual design information. The Rivermead Behavioural Memory Test (Wilson et al., 1992) has recently been adapted for use with children and includes items on pictorial and facial recognition as well as memory for everyday events such as route finding and remembering a message (Box 2.1).

Box 2.1

A child with a specific spatial-memory problem

Andrew was a right-handed, 7-year-old boy who suffered generalized tonic-clonic seizures following a series of prolonged febrile convulsions at fifteen months of age. Regular seizures had started at age 5 years. Recent EEG recording suggested a focus in the left temporal region, but the CT scan was normal. Andrew was coping with mainstream schooling but he had been referred to an epilepsy centre for full investigation of his epilepsy, and in particular for some explanation of puzzling periods of disorientation. For two days Andrew was monitored with an EEG ambulatory monitoring device. The aim of this was to exclude any possible role of seizure discharge contributing to any period of disorientation. This was not started until Andrew had spent at least two weeks in the centre. The nurses observed that surprisingly, even for a boy of this age, he was still unable to find his way round the centre without adult help. Moreover he frequently mislaid his possessions, could not remember his place when playing board games, and games like Pelmanism that require a good recall of spatial location would reduce him to tears.

He was assessed formally on a day when he was wearing an ambulatory EEG monitoring device. IQ was within the normal range (WISC-R VIQ [Verbal IQ] = 113, PIQ = 92, FSIQ = 103). The lower PIQ was largely due to a slow performance on the coding subtest. Andrew found it difficult to find his place after he had looked up at the key to identify the necessary symbol. Attainments were on the whole reasonable, with a Neale Reading Accuracy age of 7.9 years and a Vernon Maths age of 8.6 years. The Schonell spelling age at 6.9 years was a few months below age expectation. Verbal memory seemed good, with average scores on a story recall task, paired associate learning, and for digit span. This contrasted with performance on non-verbal memory tasks. The Rey test was too difficult for him; his copy contained so many omissions and distortions that it failed to serve as an adequate model against which to compare recall. Again, observations suggested that Andrew was getting 'lost' in this complex design, and this undermined any attempt at systematic checking that would allow him to identify any omissions, and also contributed to the distortions. Therefore Andrew had to be tested using simpler stimuli.

On the BAS-R copying test he obtained a score at the seventy-fifth percentile; by contrast his score on the BAS-R Recall of Designs fell below the first percentile. During the assessment Andrew needed to go down to the toilet and was taken down to the corridor where his bedroom and the toilet were situated. It was quite clear that he had no idea which door of the six on the corridor led to the toilet. As his need for the toilet became urgent he became increasingly agitated, running up and down the corridor, opening doors, but not in a systematic way, and unluckily for him failing to open the right door, which had to be pointed out to him. This sort of behaviour with its strong emotional content was later described to his parents, who said that it was

21

familiar to them and was what they would describe as disorientation.

Examination of the EEG record during the assessment and the visit to the toilet indicated that no seizure activity had been recorded at all. It was therefore suggested on the grounds of the test results, and of observations during the assessment and during the whole of Andrew's stay at the centre, that he had a specific non-verbal memory problem that undermined his ability to find his way round, and that this sometimes resulted in considerable agitation. Given Andrew's young age it was felt that rehabilitation was most likely to succeed if an approach was taken whereby his environment was structured to reduce the load on memory. It was suggested that doors should be clearly labelled in school, that he should be paired up with another child who would be prepared to act as guide, and that all his possessions should be carefully labelled so that others were more likely to return them to him, and so on.

Children with neurological problems are commonly described by their parents and other caretakers as having a disorder of attention. However, attention is far from a unitary concept and covers distractibility, failure to persist, restlessness and failure either to divide or to select attention. Not surprisingly, therefore, poor correlations are usually obtained between different measures of attention (such as parent or teacher ratings, observations and neuropsychological measures). These latter may include vigilance-type tasks (Children's Paced Serial Addition Task; Johnson *et al.*, 1988), speeded tasks like coding on the WISC-III, and tasks involving listening skills (such as digit span of the WISC-III) or several learning trials like Paired Associate learning (Taylor, 1986). With children with grosser forms of attention difficulties, such as those seen in cases of hyperactivity, simple observation of time 'on task' or even time 'on seat' can be very useful (Slee, 1988).

Children with frontal lesions often have attentional problems. Other cognitive aspects of frontal-lobe function are difficult to isolate in younger children, and even normal children find traditional card-sorting tasks (such as the Wisconsin Card Sort or the Children's Category Test) difficult until 10–12 years of age (Chelune and Baer, 1986).

ASSESSMENT OF INFANTS

Traditional infant tests have three main features. The first is a reliance on parental report, with many items concerning behaviours that occur naturally in the home setting (such as self-help skills). A high proportion of other items involves behaviours that occur naturally in the clinic situation (such as whether the child is interested in the task materials). Finally, there is a heavy reliance on motor responses. This is due partly to Piagetian influences and partly to the fact that motor responses are easily observable. It is unfortunate that more cognitive items are not included, since motor responses are often impaired in the children that tend to be referred at an early age.

Prediction in at-risk infants is perhaps the most important information that parents hope a developmental assessment will produce, as, in addition to providing information on current functioning and identifying possible means of intervention, the assessment should also be able to predict later functioning. Unfortunately, results from infant scales correlate very poorly with later tests results and have very little predictive power except in the severely handicapped.

Gaussen and Stratton (1985) suggest wider use of psychophysiological measures to reduce the reliance on intact motor responses in infant assessments. Visual or auditorily evoked responses could test the integrity of sensory modalities. Measures of heart rate or orienting response could provide measures of attention or of memory. These measures might tap the behaviours underlying the alertness, responsiveness and communicative intent on which experienced clinicians and parents base their judgements of potential in even severely physically handicapped infants, and might increase the predictive value of the assessment.

Gaussen and Stratton (1985) also suggest that prediction of later functioning could be more reliable if one abandoned the medical status model of development and looked beyond the current capacity of the child to include some assessment of the caretakers' abilities to further future development. One would be looking for the sensitive, contingent and predictable responses which characterize the adult contribution in an optimal interaction between a parent and infant. Even with potentially normal babies, early parenting styles can have a deleterious effect on development. In a prospective and longitudinal study of 267 mothers, Egeland and Erickson (1987) found that the children of mothers described as 'psychologically unavailable' experienced a significant decline in scores on the Bayley scales between the ages of nine and twenty-four months. It is, however, important to remember that many handicapped children are not able themselves to contribute the sorts of signal or response that parents are naturally looking for; babies with sensory deficits are the most obvious example, where either partner in the interaction may adapt in a more or less beneficial way.

A more comprehensive and wide-ranging assessment of infants is needed. However, these new ideas are not yet framed in easy-to-use and standard tests as such (but see Fagan, 1988). Psychophysiological measures and even assessment of caregiver responsiveness require a degree of technology and additional personnel not usually found in developmental assessment centres. Some progress could be made even under existing conditions using naturalistic observations (see Slee, 1988, for a full review of observational techniques with children).

ACQUIRED DISORDERS

Early insult

Children with early insult and general delay are more likely to be referred to clinical psychologists who work with children rather than neuropsychologists. Assessment is then more likely to concentrate on overall functioning rather than specific cognitive tasks or factors affecting IQ over time. Also, the interpretation of tests of specific cognitive abilities like memory and even language ability becomes very difficult when IQ is below average, because of a lack of normative data. Even in children of normal intelligence, one cannot be sure how close the correlation between intelligence and memory function should be.

Sudden insult

By contrast with the greater numbers of children whose development is distorted from birth or pre-natally, some children develop normally and then suffer cerebral insult. In these cases, particularly where the child has reached school age, the findings bearing on plasticity suggest one should be able to predict the degree and nature of impairment in a reasonably lawful way as in adults, at least in the early days after injury.

Head injuries

These are the most abrupt of injuries. Paediatric versions of the Glasgow Coma Scale are available for early assessment (Raimondi and Hirschauer, 1984), but there is very little information available to guide assessment of post-traumatic amnesia (PTA) in young children in a standardized way. Consequently the relationship between length of PTA and later cognitive sequelae in young children has not been addressed. However, some assessment of the period of unconsciousness and of PTA should be made in the individual case, if only because in adults these measures have been found to correlate with later cognitive sequelae. Most research studies in children have concentrated on severely injured children; but there are also studies of more minor injuries and post-concussional syndrome (see Casey *et al.*, 1986). Reports indicate that motor, visual-motor, speech and language, cognitive and memory functions are frequently impaired. These effects are linked to the severity of damage (Livingstone and McCabe, 1990) and to length of coma (Andrews *et al.*, 1993). Recovery in the young brain is not necessarily better than that of the older brain (Levin *et al.*, 1982) and more pronounced deficits may occur with maturation (for example, severely head-injured children on reaching adolescence have difficulty with inference and meaning: Dennis and Barnes, 1990). Emotional and behavioural problems are also evident (Dalby and Obrzut, 1991) and adaptive behaviour and self-esteem may be affected (Andrews *et al.*, 1993).

The assessment of any child with acquired neurological problems must begin with the collection of information about pre-morbid status, since part of the aim of the assessment is to identify changes in the child as a result of injuries or illness. This will involve contact both with parents and with schools for older children.

Once a child has regained consciousness, some simple assessment to monitor what may be slow progress can be useful (the Brazelton neonatal scale has been used: Bagnato *et al.*, 1988). It is not clear yet whether this approach is justified with either adults or children, since not enough is known about the natural history of recovery (that is, whether functions return in a developmentally predictable way). It is likely that one would observe deviant patterns as well.

It can be difficult to know when to go beyond observation. A compromise is to have a small collection of bedside tasks that require a minimum of co-operation and take less than fifteen minutes to administer. Such tasks might include a few simple instructions to assess verbal comprehension, some pictures to elicit some spontaneous speech (such as Renfrew's Action Picture Test), a sentence to repeat as a test of verbal memory and, if motor function is not too affected, a pegboard task for both hands (Annett, 1970).

As the child becomes more accessible he or she can cope with tasks requiring more sustained co-operation. WISC-III Full Scale IQ (FSIQ) before discharge has been found to be the best single predictor of outcome in a study including a wide variety of other investigations. Deficits in FSIQ are largely due to a lowering of Performance IQ (PIQ). This is rarely because of any real loss of spatial ability, but because the child is slowed down, and so is penalized for this on non-verbal tests which are timed. Recovery in IQ can continue for several years post-injury. Although many aspects of neuropsychological test scores after head injury can be accounted for by a general loss of ability and slower information processing, specific deficits in verbal memory (the Buschke selective reminding task) and in other measures of verbal ability, such as verbal fluency and naming, have been reported (see Ewing-Cobbs and Fletcher, 1987, for review).

Therefore, when the child appears well enough to comply with a longer assessment, and certainly before complete return to school, a full assessment should be made. This should include a fairly comprehensive test of current intellectual level, full attainments, some measure of verbal and non-verbal memory skills (involving measures of performance at both immediate and delayed recall), language tasks (see Skinner, Chapter 7, this volume) and possibly motor. It is sometimes useful to be able to demonstrate in these cases that slowness in responding is not entirely due to motor weakness alone. Speeded tasks are therefore needed that require a minimum motor

Box 2.2

A head-injured child

Matty was a 13-year-old boy who was riding his bike on the pavement and fell into the road, where he was hit by a car. He suffered a severe head injury, was unconscious in ITU for four days, and experienced post-traumatic amnesia for two weeks. Speech was very effortful for him and he had a right-sided hemiparesis that at first made independent ambulation impossible.

School and his parents described him pre-morbidly as a quiet child who needed some 'pushing' to get him to work and whose literacy skills were weak. On routine tests in school two terms before, he had obtained a score of 100 (that is, average) for verbal reasoning, and reading and spelling scores at a 10–11-year level.

He was discharged four weeks after the accident. At that stage he could just walk around the house holding furniture, he still needed some supervision with self-help skills, and speech was very slow and tended to be single words only. He spent long periods of the day asleep and when required to make sustained effort (that is to do his physiotherapy exercises), he became very tearful. At this stage he obtained scores indicating severe impairment of both comprehension and expression of language on the shortened Token Test, the Renfrew Action Picture Test and the Renfrew Word Finding Test. He was gently phased into a half-daily programme of physiotherapy, speech therapy and education at a rehabilitation centre. After a month, home tuition was also provided.

Three months after injury he was able to return to school in the company of his educational therapist for a few mornings each week. By this stage Matthew was looking physically stronger and was less tired and 'fragile', but he was realistically concerned that his unusual speech and jerky gait would lead to adverse comments from his peers. Assessment at that time indicated some continuing impairment. Although scores on language tasks returned to average levels, initiating a response both on tests and in spontaneous conversation was clearly still a problem. FSIQ on the WISC-R was 83, in comparison with the score of 100 obtained for verbal reasoning pre-accident. Some memory difficulties were evident on story recall (in an experimental Oxford test), paired associate learning and the Rey. Right-sided weakness in a previously right-handed boy undermined performance on paper-and-pencil tasks. (He achieved an age-scaled score of only 1 on the Coding subtest of the WISC-R, and he took three times longer than he should have done to sign his name.) However, motor slowness was not confined to one side, and this resulted in slow scores for both hands on the Annett pegboard (10 standard deviations below the mean). It was demonstrated that not all the slowness could be attributed to motor weakness alone, since both Picture Completion (age-scaled score = 6) and Speed of Information Processing (below the first centile for age) were impaired, despite the fact that these tasks required little motor involvement. Finally, reading and spelling were only at a 7-year level.

It was concluded that although Matthew was making a very good recovery, three months after injury, test results indicated that he had suffered some probable fall in the general level of his abilities (that is, in his intelligence), there had been a definite loss of reading and spelling skills, his physical mobility had been compromised, and in particular he was not writing easily with his right hand. Finally, he showed a cluster of memory and attention difficulties as well as a marked slowness in responding that is characteristic of performance in the early months after severe head injury. Although it was expected that there would be continuing spontaneous recovery for at least a year, it was necessary to make arrangements in school to support him, and in particular he would need individualized specialist teaching to boost his literacy skills.

In this particular case it was especially useful to have obtained from school the results of their own tests pre-accident, since the teachers were maintaining that they saw little change in him on his first few mornings back in school. This made it easier to persuade the divisional education officer and the educational psychologist to arrange for additional resources and to monitor his progress.

response (the BAS-R Speed of Information Processing is useful in this respect). See Box 2.2 for an example of an assessment.

It is very important to consider the effects of head injury on school performance. Acquired problems with hearing or more commonly vision, motor problems affecting writing, and, most important of all, attentional, memory and other cognitive difficulties can all undermine functioning. Outcome studies suggest that reading and spelling skills are undermined in younger children (Ewing-Cobbs and Fletcher, 1987). A likely explanation is that skills in a rapid stage of acquisition are likely to be more vulnerable than previously well-learned skills. Mathematical ability has also been reported as impaired in groups of head-injured children.

As far as possible the discussion of the results should illustrate the probable connection between deficits on the formal tests and observed difficulties in everyday life, and can also spell out the educational implications of the results by pointing out those skills that are taken for granted in normal children that may be undermined (the Rivermead Behavioural Memory Test will be useful here), albeit temporarily, in an injured child; that is, anything from being able to find one's way without adult help around a school site to being able to write notes at speed or to remember homework assignments. Behavioural and emotional problems are also likely to be in evidence (Ewing-Cobbs and Fletcher, 1987; Perrot et al., 1991) as well as general irritability and fatigue (Dalby and Obrzut, 1991). Those children who have seemed impaired at the full assessment should be briefly reviewed after one month in school to check that any additional educational arrangements made are working satisfactorily, and the assessment should be repeated in six to twelve months' time to monitor recovery.

It is in the child's best interest if the clinical services work closely with professionals from the education authority, and in particular close co-operation between the clinical psychologist and the receiving school's educational psychologist is mandatory. The clinical psychologist will have more experience of head injury, its effects and the sorts of test that can be used to illustrate deficits; the educational psychologist offers his or her specialist knowledge of the best arrangements that can be made in schools to facilitate recovery and will usually take on the role of long-term monitoring.

Thousands of children each year are admitted to hospital with head injuries and most are discharged after a night or two in hospital with no sequelae. The lengthy assessment detailed above is only relevant to those children with more severe injuries. A useful criteron would be for children to have been unconscious for at least half an hour, or to have been apparently less severely injured but still to have difficulties reported when they returned for medical or surgical follow-up.

Ideas for rehabilitation of head-injured children are available, but where interventions have been evaluated (e.g. Light *et al.*, 1987), it has been difficult to improve the level of cognitive functioning, although gains in adaptive behaviour can occur.

Tumour

Brain tumours account for 20 per cent of all paediatric cancers. In children cortical tumours are less common than brainstem tumours (such as medullablastoma). Most of the effort of neuropsychologists working in this area has gone into assessing the effects of treatment variables, in particular cranial radiation therapy and intrathecal chemotherapy, on cognitive functioning in all forms of cancer (see Fletcher and Copeland, 1988). Younger children, especially those under 5 years, are more vulnerable to adverse effects. Research has been largely restricted to general measures of intelligence.

There are only a few reports of assessments of children with cortical tumours. As in other areas of the cancer literature, children are rarely tested before treatment is started and it is difficult to identify what aspects of neuropsychological function are attributable to the tumour and which aspects are the results of treatment. The testing of localized functions is hampered by a lack of sensitive tests for use with younger age groups. Moreover, test results in individual cases with apparently similar pathology may vary according to the stage of presentation among other factors. Three cases are given to illustrate this (see Box 2.3). Many cortical tumours have a general effect on a wide range of functions and, in the less malignant tumours at least, testing after surgical removal may suggest some recovery in contralateral functions.

Box 2.3

The effect of tumours in the left-temporal lobe

Jamie first presented at the age of 7 years with a short history of seizures uncontrolled by medication. At assessment IQ was within the average range, and non-verbal memory and verbal memory, with the exception of paired associate learning that was arguably a little low, seemed adequate. Attainments were at about an 8-year level, with the exception of spelling, which was about a year below expectation for age. Pegboard speed was average for both hands. On a range of language tasks performance was average for age; his only noticeable problem was some word-finding difficulty.

Matthew also presented at 7 years of age but he had a three-year history of seizures resistant to medication. His IQ was also within the average range. Non-verbal memory was poor on the Rey, adequate at immediate recall of simpler stimuli (BAS-R Recall of Designs), but poor again for maze learning (an experimental Oxford test). Verbal memory was weak on both story recall (another experimental Oxford test) and Paired Associate learning. Attainments were at age expectation. Both hands were slow on a pegboard task. Language was mildly aphasic with relatively low scores on tests of comprehension and of expression. In this child, therefore, although language problems were more obvious, some tests of non-verbal and motor abilities also indicated impairment.

Michael presented at the age of 12 years with an uncontrolled seizure disorder and mental deterioration. At the age of 9 years he had been coping with the demands of mainstream school; by 12 he had failed to attend school for more than twelve months and he presented as almost mute. Few tests were possible because of Michael's difficulties in initiating speech and because of the low level of his general abilities. Those that were administered all resulted in scores indicating severe impairment.

All three children had CT scan evidence of tumour in the left temporal lobe. At operation (temporal lobectomy), the pathology in all three cases was of astrocytoma. Jamie and Michael were seizure-free two years post-op. Jamie underwent radiotherapy. Seizures recurred six months after operation in Matthew. Post-op., Jamie and Matthew experienced some initial verbal memory problems. Michael's verbal fluency improved and other areas of function showed some recovery, with FSIQ rising from 41 at six months post-op. to 52 at two years post-op.

Infections

CNS (central nervous system) infections are a major cause of mortality and neurological sequelae in children. Estimates of mortality and serious neurological sequelae (that is, mental retardation, epilepsy, seizures and hearing loss) vary, with more recent surveys reporting lower figures due to more effective treatments. There is little reliable information on more subtle long-term effects. One study using sibling controls (Taylor *et al.*, 1984) identified

---

Box 2.4

The consequences of a severe infection encephalopathy

Jonathon experienced a severe attack of mumps encephalitis at CA (chronological age) 2.11 years. Consciousness was affected for several days. As he began to recover it became clear that he had lost some skills; in particular his expressive language, which had been considered advanced prior to the illness, returned to the single-word stage. During the next two years his language ability recovered but he never returned to the chatty and interesting child he had been previously. Moreover, his family had great difficulty in managing his behaviour; he was very fearful of new situations and reacted aggressively to being left in the company of other children. The family's suspicions that Jonathon had memory difficulties were brushed off. He was assessed several times on tests of general intelligence, and since he scored at a high average level it was assumed that his behaviour was due to the stress of a traumatic illness necessitating hospital admission, and his mother was given general behavioural advice about management. The situation improved somewhat after school entry and Jonathon coped with the demands of mainstream school without additional support. Although he eventually made friends he always appeared anxious, even in the company of close family. He was referred to a neuropsychologist at the age of 14 years with 'spatial orientation' problems after a crisis when he had remained in bed for several days, saying that he would never be able to find his way round and consequently would never grow up.

At assessment he obtained scores on the WISC-R giving him a FSIQ within the high average range. Severe memory problems resulted in low scores for retention of both verbal and non-verbal information (tested on the Wechsler Memory scales, the Rey–Osterreith, Benton Visual Retention test, and two experimental tasks, namely a stylus maze and a paired faces task). A rehabilitation plan was devised with a particular emphasis on teaching Jonathon the skills necessary to find his way round independently in unfamiliar places; that is, map reading, drawing simple maps and approaching other people to elicit help. His schoolwork was reviewed and he was allowed to give up those subjects requiring a heavy load on memory and a lot of reading, such as history, in order to concentrate on more skills-based subjects (such as science). Both Jonathon and his family appeared to find it a great relief that the nature of his difficulties had at last been recognized, and united in devising ways of reducing the need for continued adult supervision and for constant reminding at home.

significant differences in IQ scores in a range of neuropsychological tasks in a group of children six years after infection, and lower scores and coding in some performance tasks such as Object Assembly (WISC-III) and grooved pegboard have been reported in cases of meningitis (Taylor *et al.*, 1984). The incidence of these infections is highest in those under 1 year of age, and again younger children are more at risk for sequelae (see Box 2.4).

Neurodegenerative diseases

There are 750 neurodegenerative diseases of childhood (Dyken and Krakiecki, 1983). Fifty per cent of these are familial, but other common causes are persistent viral infections or ongoing exposure to toxins which may include medication. The two most common are subacute sclerosing panencephalitis (SSPE) and neuronal ceroid lipofuscinosis (NCL). It is likely that in the near future cases of human immunodeficiency syndrome will be a more frequent diagnosis (Epstein *et al.*, 1986).

Because in children the disease process is attacking a developing organism, clinical presentation and the course of the disease may vary according to age. When dementia is a feature, neuropsychological assessment is important to delineate the course of the disease, identify remaining strengths and evaluate treatment efforts. Since development may maintain some momentum, a child may present less as losing skills than as only capable of slow progress.

There are some methodological difficulties in monitoring such children over time, mainly centring on having to change from one test to another, either because the child has become too old for a scale already used, or because, due to serious loss of ability, he or she is too incapacitated for a test to be administered that he or she had previously succeeded on. Correlations between tests are too poor to allow precise comparison of performance.

In the final stages of disease, test administration is neither appropriate nor feasible. Swift *et al.* (1984), devised a Psychological Disability Scale with six levels which indicated disability in gross motor skills, self-care and social skills, language and verbal IQ, visual motor skills and performance IQ, and finally academic skills. Information was collected from interview, observations, an adaptive behaviour scale and intelligence tests, or developmental scales and attainment tests. General use of such a scale, particularly if there is an increase in numbers of children with HIV, would allow comparison between centres and multi-centre research.

Common symptoms of neurological problems

Epilepsy

Seventy per cent of people suffering from recurrent seizures manifested their first attack during childhood. Tharp (1987), gives an excellent overview of paediatric seizure disorders, and Hermann and Seidenberg (1989) includes papers on neuropsychological and psychosocial effects. Children with epilepsy are frequently referred for assessment because of poor achievement or memory or concentration difficulties.

Clinicians are usually faced with the severe cases: Farwell *et al.* (1985) identified in a clinic sample a high rate of difficulty, with only 37 per cent of children tested scoring about Full Scale IQ 100, and 70 per cent scoring in the impaired range on the Halstead–Reitan battery.

Many different features of a child's epilepsy history make it more or less likely that cognitive function will be adversely affected. Few of these are mutually exclusive (see Lesser *et al.*, 1986, for review). Age of onset, seizure type, and drug-related variables can all be important. Perhaps the most salient finding is that age of onset, regardless of seizure type or duration of seizures, undermines ability. Children who present with seizures before their fifth birthday are more at risk than older children.

Serial testing in the same individual can reveal considerable variation. In Bourgeois *et al.*'s study (1983) of seventy-five children over a four-year period, only 31 per cent showed less than 10 points difference in FSIQ scores obtained from one assessment to another. However, only 11 per cent (eight) of children showed persistent decline, and young age of onset and periods of drug toxicity account for five of these patients. Falling IQ scores may well prove reversible with better control of seizures and should not be taken as a necessary sign of progressive pathology. IQ tests are usually considered too insensitive to changes in functioning that may be attributable to drug effects. Motor and speeded tasks are often more useful than cognitive ones, but see Box 2.5 for an illustration of the difficulties of demonstrating drug effects.

Selective neuropsychological deficits according to lateralization and localization of lesions in those patients for whom there is evidence of underlying focal pathology are sometimes, but not always, reported. Most studies carried out in the States have used a battery approach, the results of which are limited in the pursuit of the exact nature of a child's difficulties. Careful studies of the precise correlation between errors in performance and seizure activity (see Seidenberg, 1989) hold out more promise. Although there have been few recent studies of school functioning in children with epilepsy, what evidence there is indicates wide-ranging problems in the spheres of behaviour, attention and achievement. Attainment measures are reported to be generally a year below what one might predict from IQ.

Finally, any assessment of a child has to take account of the fact that seizures can undermine test performance, any overt seizures occurring during the assessment should be carefully noted and described, and some evaluation of their impact on test scores should be made.

Box 2.5

A young person with epilepsy

Philip was first seen for assessment at the age of 12 years during his admission to an epilepsy centre. He had a high frequency of seizures. His behaviour during the assessment was typical of that since his admission, with a high rate of physical restlessness, a low threshold for distractibility, and a tendency to give up easily in the face of difficulty. Although he did not have any overt seizures during the assessment, it seemed likely that he was experiencing subclinical seizure activity. He obtained a VIQ of 82, PIQ of 69 on the WISC-R, giving him a FSIQ of 74. Paired associate learning was impaired (initial learning score = 7.5) and his Rey–Osterreith copy was unscorable. Speed of information processing was below the first percentile, and Coding was slow and inaccurate (age scales score = 4). Philip was seen again for reassessment after changes in medication which resulted in less overt seizures. He was wearing an ambulatory EEG monitoring device which confirmed the absence of seizure activity during the assessment. He was less restless, had better orientation towards the tasks, and was more compliant. Four subtests of the WISC-R, Recall of Digits, Comprehension, Picture Arrangement and Coding, were repeated with no significant change in score. Speed of Information Processing was again below the first percentile, and although Philip was able to copy the Rey figure so that it was at least recognizable, the score obtained (Copy = 21, Recall = 10) was still in the impaired range. The only test on which there was a marked improvement was Paired Associate learning (of the Wechsler Memory Scale) where Philip obtained an average score on an equivalent form (initial learning score = 13.5). These results were disappointing in view of the obvious improvement in his clinical condition, and also somewhat puzzling, since one might have expected high scores from practice effects alone on those tasks without equivalent forms, namely WISC-R.

Philip was seen again three years later. His clinical condition had remained steady on the drug regime introduced at the earlier admission and he was in mainstream school preparing for GCSEs. On this admission he was still slow at Coding (age-scaled score = 4), and obtained a low score for Rey recall (10), but Rey copy was average (30), and Paired Associate learning was also unimpaired (initial learning score = 18). Most importantly, however, there was a marked improvement on all subtests of the WISC-R (except for coding) and FSIQ had risen by 27 points to 101.

On many counts one could argue that the tests chosen to demonstrate the efficiency of the changes in drug regime were not successful in doing so. In particular, tests of speed (Coding and Speed of Information processing) were not helpful. The only test that did show an immediate improvement was Paired Associate learning. However, this probably represented a real improvement in learning ability, which was reflected in the higher IQ scores obtained three years later.

Hydrocephalus

Hydrocephalus can arise for a variety of reasons, both congenital (such as dysraphic conditions of the spine or skull) and post-natal (such as infantile haemorrhages). It is usually treated by insertion of a shunt to remove excess fluid and reduce pressure. Since hydrocephalus thins and distends the brain, such children are at risk for lower intelligence (Dennis *et al.*, 1981).

One of the more important issues for clinicians working with children with hydrocephalus is how useful and reliable measures of cognitive functioning are in the detection of subtle deficits that might respond to shunting, particularly in the rare cases of 'normal pressure' hydrocephalus, where the usual symptoms like lowered level of alertness, ataxia and so on are not the presenting signs. Opinions vary as to the wisdom and efficiency of surgical intervention in this group. Neuropsychological measures (such as tests of memory function) often change immediately after shunting, and in some cases IQ recovers with the passage of time. Academic achievement scores do not seem to be sensitive to the same degree.

Cerebral palsy

Cerebral palsy is a chronic disability characterized by aberrant control of movement or posture. It can be the result of pre-, peri- or post-natal insult, but movement disorders resulting from known progressive disease are usually excluded from this classification. On the basis of neurological findings, three diagnostic groups are recognized: first diplegia, tetraplegia and hemiplegia; second ataxic syndromes (congenital ataxia and ataxic diplegia); and finally dyskinetic syndromes like athetosis and dystonia. There is risk to cognitive function (see Stanley and Alberman, 1984, for further information).

Neuropsychologists can contribute to this field by helping to develop reliable assessments to identify the impairment, disability and handicap experienced by children with cerebral palsy. In particular, the development of objective measures of motor function that are not unduly affected by IQ level is necessary. In recent surveys the dynamometer (Fleishman, 1964) has been used to measure hand grip, the Purdue pegboard for manual dexterity (Costa *et al.*, 1964) and selected items from the Oseretsky test (Bruininks, 1978) for looking at the function of lower limbs. The Annett pegboard (Annett, 1970) has been extensively used with hemiplegic children.

In the individual case, the psychologist is often faced with the problem of obtaining a reliable assessment of cognitive ability that is not unduly undermined by motor or speech impairments. At present in severe cases one has to fall back on tasks that are untimed and involve a minimum or no speech response (such as Raven's Progressive Matrices or British Picture

Vocabulary Tests with forced choice format). The use of habituation measures and the development of specialized computer-based tests allowing minimum responses are also recommended.

THE DEVELOPMENTAL DISORDERS

The developmental disorders are an interesting and somewhat mysterious group. Some might argue that their inclusion in a book about assessment of neurological disorders is inappropriate. In all of them a child evinces a cognitive impairment, often every bit as serious or disabling as if he or she has had an acquired impairment, but without any evidence of obvious neurological trauma or any definite evidence at present about a possible underlying neurological basis. However, recent post-mortem studies of people with developmental dyslexia have demonstrated neurological abnormalities (Galburda *et al.*, 1985). The other criteria that are generally accepted in this country are that: first the possibility of a psychiatric or social explanation for the disorder must be ruled out – so, for example, elective mutism or autism are excluded from the developmental language disorders, although they are included in many American classifications (Raspin and Allen, 1983); and second the child's difficulties must also be specific, that is, there must be good evidence that his or her difficulties are not explicable in terms of a general delay in functioning.

The status of the developmental disorders is being hotly debated at the moment, particularly in the fields of specific learning disorders. A developmental psychology view considers that a developmental disorder arises when there is a delay or an arrest in development. It follows from this that one can predict that only certain sorts of deficit can arise. For example, it should not be possible that a child may fail at an early stage without mastery of certain key skills but go on to show himself or herself capable of later developing skills (although some sorts of drilling might make it look as though he or she has continued to make some progress). Another view arising from cognitive neuropsychology suggests that the developmental view underestimates individual differences and the independence of cognitive systems, and that, just as in adults with acquired impairments, one can with children with developmental disorders demonstrate double dissociations. Such a child may be capable of using one strategy to help him or her read or manipulate numbers but might find another strategy very difficult. Cases of both reading difficulty (Temple and Marshall, 1983; Temple, 1988), and mathematical difficulty (Temple, 1991b) have been given as examples.

Developmental language disorder

Impaired language development (developmental dysphasia) is relatively common. Different studies of incidence in the general population give figures varying from 3 to 15 per cent depending on the comprehensiveness of the assessment, the cut-off points chosen for classification, the age of children surveyed and, most importantly, whether children with general delay are excluded.

Communication disorders are usually divided into two broad categories: speech disorders, where damage or dysfunction impairs the ability to transmit meaning into sound; and language disorder, where meaning is undermined.

Two forms of language disorder are usually described. In one the child experiences specific problems with language form both phonological and syntactical but with normal and appropriate content (Raspin and Allen, 1983); in the second, the semantic-pragmatic (Raspin and Allen, 1983), the child uses superficially sophisticated and complex language which is clearly articulated, but the use and understanding of language is defective.

Assessing a child with language delay necessitates an estimate of the child's non-verbal abilities to exclude mental handicap. Then the assessment of language must include measures of both expression and comprehension, and take account of phonology, syntax, morphology, semantics and pragmatics (for full discussion of speech and language assessment see Beech *et al.*, 1993).

Obtaining a sample of spontaneous speech for analysis can be difficult in a clinic setting in a limited period of time and on a first meeting, and there are no universally accepted ways of analysing the data. Transcribing can be costly in time and requires a practised ear and training. However, there are two simple tests with some British norms that are useful for eliciting at least some expressive speech, and require only a minimum of co-operation from the child. Unfortunately information on their reliability and validity is sparse. The Renfrew Action Picture Test requires the child to answer questions about eight individual pictures, such as 'What is the woman doing?' A score for content (semantics) and for syntax (grammar) can be obtained. Renfrew has also produced the Bus Story Test, which requires the child to tell a story with a series of pictures for cues having once heard the therapist do so; from this a mean length of utterance and content score can be obtained. Word-finding difficulties can be identified on several tests (Renfrew Word Finding, BAS-R naming). For those wanting to make a formal assessment of pragmatics, a test with American norms has recently been published (Wiig and Secord, 1987).

Language comprehension can be assessed with forced choice format, with choice of pictures for single-word vocabulary (Peabody or British Vocabulary tests: Dunn and Dunn, 1981) or for syntactic structures (Test for Reception of Grammar: Bishop, 1983), or in tests where the child is required to manipulate toys according to verbal instructions of increasing difficulty (BAS-R Verbal Comprehension subtest).

As a general rule it is probably safe to consider a child to be specifically delayed in language development if he or she is of average intelligence non-verbally but is scoring below the third percentile for age on several language tasks.

What about prognosis? Bishop and Edmundson (1987) found that at age 4 years, that is, at the initial referral, the Bus Story as a sole predictor (score of six or below at 4 years) identified the outcome of 83 per cent of cases. Poorer prognosis was also related to lower non-verbal ability. Since almost half of the children had a good outcome at $5\frac{1}{2}$ years, regardless of whether or not they received speech therapy, it seems that for a reasonable number of children the notion of 'delay', which allows for the possibility that the child may 'catch up' spontaneously, is appropriate. Of course, the proportion of children recovering in this way in any sample will depend on the age at ascertainment, since the older the age group the larger the number of children representing the 'hard core' with very serious impairment that will require specialist intervention.

Development dyslexia

Many children who have delayed language development go on, not surprisingly, to have difficulty acquiring basic literacy skills. The incidence of reading failure from whatever cause (and causation must be multi-factorial) is relatively high at 10 per cent of the school population overall. The term 'developmental dyslexia' is used here loosely to refer to the failure to acquire literacy skills at an appropriate rate in the absence of neurological insult as a known precipitating factor.

Arguments continue as to whether children who have difficulty reading are on a continuum with normal readers or whether they are a distinct group. The single-case studies that have dominated the neuropsychological literature assume that individual cases can stand as prototypical examples of a subtype. There is some evidence that children with reading difficulties in fact fail for a wide variety of cognitive reasons, and that there exist verbal and visual-spatial subtypes (see the Boder Test of Reading–Spelling Patterns) or surface and deep dyslexic subtypes (Temple, 1991a) similar to that occurring in adults.

Classification has gone beyond the simple distinction as to whether reading ability is in line with general ability, and attempts have been made to distinguish children according to their psychometric profile or according to the strategy used in reading.

A major problem with the psychometric profiling approach is that it is impossible to determine whether any idiosyncrasies in test performance are the cause or the effect of reading problems. Moreover, the relative failure of diagnostic-prescriptive teaching suggests there is little practical advantage to this approach. Despite this, it can be argued that a complete reliance on error analysis may be too limited, partly because children with different neuropsychological profiles often make the same sorts of error, presumably for different reasons, and remediation should address this; partly because dyslexic children make many of the same sorts of error as normal readers who may be younger but are at the same reading level.

Our understanding of how normal children read is far from complete and must limit our ability at present to account for reading failure. A fully comprehensive model should encompass both 'bottom-up' processes, that is, the acquisition of basic word-recognition skills, and 'top-down' processes like the utilization of context in facilitating the reading process. Furthermore, it has to be compatible with models of skilled adult reading. See Stuart and Coltheart (1988) for discussion of current 'stage' theories of reading.

What sort of assessment is appropriate in developmental dyslexia? For the sake of brevity, only the direct assessment of the child will be considered. The assessment of the other important feature of a learning situation, namely the sensitivity of the teaching process, will be neglected.

It can be useful to establish whether a child's reading age is in line with the general level of abilities. Yule *et al.* (1982) provides information to allow one to predict for 6–12-year-olds what reading age on the Neale test could be, given chronological age and FSIQ on the WISC-R. Although it has been argued that the correlation between IQ and achievement is too poor for this to be a valid manoeuvre and that there are considerable statistical difficulties, the regression equation is often used in clinical practice.

There is a wide range of test material available (see Vincent *et al.*, 1983; Harding and Beech, 1991) for establishing reading and spelling level. It is useful to include measures of both text and single-word reading. Text reading gives a measure of everyday reading ability, but single-word reading allows a pure estimate of real decoding ability, since the reader cannot utilize contextual cues. However, all the recent approaches to assessment stress the need to go beyond simply looking at level of competence, that is, deriving a reading age, to identifying the cognitive processes underlying reading. This is done by comparing the accuracy and speed of responding to different classes of word, such as regular or irregular, real or non-words, homophones, etc. Errors are another potential source of information about strategy. See Marshall (Chapter 8, this volume) for examples from dyslexics, and Stuart and Coltheart (1988) and Read (1986) for evaluation of errors in beginning readers and spellers (Box 2.6).

Assessment should lead to effective remediation. Unfortunately, although there are plenty of single-case studies where remediation produces dramatic improvement, there are also many disappointing group studies (see Rourke *et al.*, 1986, for a brief review). Early intervention and further research on techniques of remediation are obviously very important.

Box 2.6

A young person with reading and spelling difficulties

Simon was referred by his GP at his parents' request. He was 13 and in mainstream school. His parents, who were both teachers, described him as a bright, lively and verbal boy whose written work, which was minimal, poorly presented and of poor quality of content, in no way reflected his real intelligence. They had been told by school, however, that Simon's difficulties were not severe enough to warrant referral to the school psychologist. There was no concern about his early development, except for the first few hours after birth when he was taken to the special care baby unit.

Simon showed me his school books with an understandable lack of enthusiasm. He co-operated well with testing but was clearly fed up and slightly embarrassed in the assessment situation. On the WISC-R he obtained a score at an above average level (VIQ = 125, PIQ = 108, FSIQ = 118). Word recognition was poor (Neale reading accuracy 'age' = 8.8 years, BAS-R Single Word reading = 7.9 years). He had almost no phonetic skills, finding unfamiliar yet regular words like 'panic' impossible. The majority of errors were visual errors, such as 'their' for 'then', 'processed' for 'proceeded', 'altogether' for 'although'. However, although text reading was far from fluent, with many hesitations and inaccuracies, somehow he managed to extract enough information to answer questions about the text at a more age-appropriate level (Neale comprehension).

On the Vernon Spelling test he obtained a spelling age of 8.6 years. Some of his errors were familiar and suggested an attempt at a phonetic route, such as 'strat' for 'straight', but others were visual; for example, his first attempt at 'young' was 'unger' and his second attempt 'yonig'; his first attempt at arrive was 'away' and his second attempt 'arave'.

Simon's parents were encouraged to approach the school psychology service on his behalf themselves. They were advised that he needed a remediation programme that not only tackled basic spelling skills but also helped him with planning essays verbally before writing, or any other technique that might prevent him from becoming so bogged down in the mechanics of written expression that he failed to write what he knew.

Developmental dyscalculia

Interest is now turning from the neuropsychology of dyslexia towards children who may have specific difficulties with acquiring calculation skills and mathematical concepts. However, there is very little information to date on such difficulties, be they developmental or acquired (see Grafman, 1988). Moreover, there is such a wide range of ability in the school population that it is difficult to imagine how one might identify which children one might be tempted to dub acalculic. For example, in a study of 10,000 11–15-year-olds it was discovered that half of the children could only perform the basic operations (+, −, ×, ÷) on small whole numbers under ten (Ward, 1979).

Nevertheless, there is some evidence for types of developmental dyscalculia (procedural and number-fact) in line with adult acquired dyscalculia (Temple, 1991b). In cases where it might be important to make some assessment of ability in this area, it is often useful to administer both a sheet of simple calculations, like the BAS-R basic number skills, to check on ability with basic mechanics, and also a test that requires both some verbal interpretation and identification of the operations necessary, like the Vernon Graded Arithmetic test. Again, error analysis can be useful. Reversals, failure to grasp the significance of place value, inaccurate counting, and uncertainty about what symbols represent are easily identifiable. Perfect performance tells one little; it is the nature of a child's errors that reveal his or her personal theories about how numbers are manipulated. (See also Ridgway and Harding, 1991.)

Developmental movement disorders

There is even less agreement on the underlying difficulties in children who are described as developmental apraxic than there is in the other developmental conditions. Such children are often referred to as 'clumsy', which is a perjorative term best avoided, but is used of a child whose ability to perform skilled movement is impaired despite normal intelligence and normal neurological findings.

There is considerable room for confusion in the fact that developmental apraxia, unlike the other developmental disorders, refers to different abilities and is consequently differently assessed from apraxia in adults (see Chapter 5 in this volume). The assessment of children not only includes familiar motor items like whether the child can hop on one foot, but also covers everyday purposeful activities and amounts to a check of what a child can or cannot do for himself or herself in comparison with his or her age peers; for example, the Test of Motor Impairment (Stott et al., 1984), and the Movement ABC (Henderson and Sugden, 1992). These items may include doing up buttons, handling scissors, and so on. Scores on such tests are often averaged to give a motor 'age', although poor correlations between different aspects of motor performance suggest this manoeuvre is not useful. Henderson (1987) points out that such tests are essentially descriptive; they simply sample the sorts of behaviour that gave rise to parental or teacher concern in the first place (see also Henderson, 1991). Henderson recommends some analysis of the quality of action. The success of this will depend on the experience and competence of the observer, and few psychologists will know enough about normal development of motor skills to detect minor immaturities.

There is some interest in the analysis of processes which underlie the impaired performance (see Lord and Hulme, 1987, for review). Presumably such children do not form a homogeneous group. In adults certainly a distinction can be made between those with a problem at the planning phase and those with a problem at the executive phase. Hulme points out that at least three perceptual systems underlie adequate motor skills (Lord and Hulme, 1987). Visual skills are necessary to guide movements in relation to the environment. The child must as well be able to discriminate the position of parts of his or her body, and the amplitude and direction of movements even in the absence of visual and auditory cues; this is kinaesthetic perception. There also has to be some integration between the visual and kinaesthetic modalities. Although research in this area has identified differences in the perceptual abilities of normal children of the same age and those referred to physiotherapists as 'clumsy', the findings have not stood up to the more rigorous comparison between impaired children and controls matched for motor skill. In addition, recent attempts to discriminate 'clumsy' children from normals using the Kinaesthetic Sensitivity Test (Laszlo and Bairstow, 1985) have been disappointing.

CHILD NEUROPSYCHOLOGY AND REAL LIFE

Any neuropsychological assessment has to include consideration of the ways in which the child's neurological condition and the impairments he or she experiences directly or indirectly undermine daily living and distort the child's natural development. This involves asking parents, teachers and the child himself or herself about problems in everyday life. One can try to judge how far difficulties described by parents are illustrated in test performance. Indeed, one can start with reported real-life problems and use this information to guide test selection, so that one can elucidate further the nature of the underlying impairment and also confirm areas of strength. A child who is reported to be careless or inattentive may in fact be better described as having memory problems. Attempts should be made to reduce the impact of any cognitive difficulties, either by side-stepping deficits with the provision of aids or by helping the child to use a different approach or strategy. In this connection it would be useful to know more about strategies that children spontaneously use at different developmental stages.

Cognitive impairments also undermine social functioning, and there is a clear relationship between the degree of cognitive and of social impairment. Although some of this is due to CNS involvement, indirect effects like distorted parental management, restricted opportunities, anxieties, sadness and frustration also play a part. It is difficult as well to separate out possible neurobehavioural problems such as attention deficit disorder (hyperactivity: see Barkley, 1982). It is important to delineate as clearly as possible those aspects of impaired social functioning that are not necessarily an inevitable consequence of the disease process; for example, those aspects that may be due to an unnecessarily restricted lifestyle, or to a lack of understanding or of appropriate support for a child who is struggling.

There are many published scales (Rutter *et al.*, 1970) for the assessment of social and behavioural functioning in children, but most of them have drawbacks. The commonest is that the most scientifically rigorous and most recent are those devised in America, the norms of which have to be interpreted with caution in a British population. As far as use of these scales with neurologically impaired children goes, most recent work has been largely confined to children with epilepsy, although further work on children after head injury is now being done.

FINAL COMMENTS

Child neuropsychology is in its infancy itself. Much of the work done to date has perhaps unfairly been concentrated on the developmental disorders. There has also been more emphasis on assessment than on rehabilitation, and little work on the practical implications of neuropsychological impairments for everyday functioning. In all areas of neuropsychology we are having to accept the challenge of moving away from the traditional role of diagnosis and lesion spotting towards providing more coherent explanations for impaired performance. In order to develop both the necessary age-appropriate assessment tools and interventions with neurologically impaired children, links with developmental psychology need to be as strong as those with adult neuropsychology.

REFERENCES

Andrews, T. K., Johnson, D. A. and Rose, F. D. (1993). 'Social and behavioural problems following clinical head injury in children'. Paper presented at the Neuropsychology Conference, Scottish Branch of the British Psychological Society, St Andrews.

Annett, M. (1970). 'The growth of manual preference and speed'. *British Journal of Psychology*, 61, 545–58.

Bagnato, S. J., Mayes, S. D., Nichter, C., Domoto, V., Hamman, L., Keener, S., Landis, C., Savina, J. and Teleko, A. (1988). 'An interdisciplinary neurodevelopmental assessment model for brain injured infants and preschool children'. *Journal of Head Trauma Rehabilitation*, 3, 75–86.

Barkley, R. (1982). *Hyperactive Children*. Chichester: John Wiley.

Basser, L. S., (1962). 'Hemiplegia of early onset and the faculty of speech with special reference to the effects of hemispherectomy'. *Brain*, 85, 427–60.

Beardsworth, E. D. and Adams, C. B. T. (1988). 'Modified hemispherectomy for epilepsy: early results in 10 cases'. *British Journal of Neurosurgery*, 2, 73–84.

Beech, J. B., Harding, L. M. with Hilton-Jones, D. (1993). *Assessment in Speech and Language Therapy*. London: Routledge.

Benton, A. L. (1980). 'The neuropsychology of facial recognition'. *American Psychologist*, 35, 176–86.

Benton, A. L., Hamsher, K. de S., Varney, N. R. and Spreen, O. (1983). 'Test of Facial Recognition'. In *Contributions to Neuropsychological Assessment: A Clinical Manual*. Oxford: Oxford University Press.

Bishop, D. V. M. (1983) Test for Reception of Grammar (TROG). Available from the author at MRC Applied Psychology Unit, 15 Chaucer Road, Cambridge CB2 2EF.

Bishop, D. V. M. and Edmundson, A. (1987). 'Language impaired 4-year-olds: distinguishing transient from persistent impairment'. *Journal of Speech and Hearing Disorders*, 52, 156–73.

Bourgeois, B. F. D., Prensky, A. L., Palkes, H. S., Talent, B. K. and Busch, S. G. (1983). 'Intelligence in epilepsy: a prospective study in children'. *Annals of Neurology*, 14, 438–44.

Bruininks, R. H. (1978). *The Bruininks–Oseretsky Test: Examiners' Manual*. Circle Pines: American Guidance Service.

Buschke, H. (1974). 'Components of verbal learning in children: analysis by selective reminding'. *Journal of Experimental Child Psychology*, 18, 488–96.

Casey, R., Ludwig, S. and McCormick, M. C. (1986). 'Morbility following minor head trauma in children'. *Paediatrics*, 78, 497–502.

Costa, L. D., Scarola, L. M. and Rapin, I. (1964). 'Purdue Pegboard scores for normal grammar school children'. *Perceptual and Motor Skills*, 18, 748.

Chelune, G. J. and Baer, R. (1986). 'Developmental norms for the Wisconsin Cardsorting Test'. *Journal of Clinical and Experimental Neuropsychology*, 8, 219–28.

Curry, J. F., Logue, P. E. and Butler, B. (1986). 'Child and adolescent norms for Russell's revision of the Wechsler Memory Scale'. *Journal of Clinical Child Psychology*, 15, 214–20.

Dalby, P. R. and Obrzut, J. E. (1991). 'Epidemiological characteristics and sequelae of head injured children and adolescents: a review'. *Developmental Neuropsychology*, 7, 35–68.

Dennis, M. (1985). 'Intelligence after early brain injury 1: predicting IQ scores from medical variables.' *Journal of Clinical and Experimental Neuropsychology*, 7, 526–54.

Dennis, M. and Barnes, M. (1990). 'Knowing the meaning, getting the point, bridging the gap and carrying the message: aspects of discourse following clinical head injury in childhood and adolescence'. *Brain and Language*, 39, 428–46.

Dennis, M., Fitz, C. R., Netley, C. T., Sugar, J., Harwood-Nash, C. F., Hendrick, E. B., Hoffman, H. J. and Humphreys, R. P. (1981). 'The intelligence of hydrocephalic children'. *Archives of Neurology*, 38, 607–15.

DeRenzi, O. and Faglioni, P. (1978). 'Normative data and screening power of a shortened version of the Token Test'. *Cortex*, 14, 41–9.

Dunn, L. and Dunn, L. (1981). *Peabody Picture Vocabulary Test*. Revised. Circle Pines: American Guidance Service.

Dyken, P. and Krakiecki, N. (1983). 'Neurodegenerative diseases of infancy and childhood'. *The Annals of Neurology*, 13, 351–61.

Egeland, B. and Erickson, M. F. (1987). 'Psychologically unavailable caregiving'. In Brassard, M., Germain, R. and Hair, S. (eds), *Psychological Maltreatment of Children and Youth*. Pergamon General Psychology Series 143. Oxford: Pergamon.

Epstein, G., Sharer, L. R., Oleske, J. M., Connor, E. M., Goudsmit, J., Babdon, L., Robert-Guroff, M. and Koenigsberger, M. R. (1986). 'Neurologic manifestations of human immunodeficiency virus infection in children'. *Paediatrics*, 78, 678–87.

Ewing-Cobbs, L. and Fletcher, J. M. (1987). 'Neuropsychological assessment of head injury in children'. *Journal of Learning Disabilities*, 20, 526–35.

Fagan, J. F. (1988). *Fagan Test of Infant Intelligence*. Cleveland, OH: Infant Test Corporation.

Farwell, J. R., Dodrill, C. B. and Batzel, L. W. (1985). 'Neuropsychological abilities of children with epilepsy'. *Epilepsia*, 26, 395–400.

Finger, S. and Stein, D. G. (1982). *Brain Damage and Recovery*. New York: Academic Press.

Fleishman, E. A. (1964). *The Dynamometer-Basic Fitness Tests: Examiners' Manual*. New York: Prentice-Hall.

Fletcher, J. M. and Copeland, D. R. (1988). 'Neurobehavioural effects of central nervous system prophylactic treatment of cancer in children'. *Journal of Clinical and Experimental Neuropsychology*, 4, 495–538.

Galburda, A. M., Sherman, G., Rosen, G., Aboitiz, F. D. and Geschwind, N. (1985). 'Developmental dyslexia: four consecutive patients with cortical anomalies'. *Annals of Neurology*, 18, 222–44.

Gaussen, T. and Stratton, P. (1985). 'Beyond the infant milestone model: a systems framework for alternative infant assessment procedures'. *Childcare, Health and Development*, 11, 131–50.

Grafman, J. (1988). 'Acalculia'. In F. Boller and J. Grafman (eds), *Handbook of Neuropsychology*, vol. 1. Amsterdam: Elsevier.

Hahn, W. K. (1987). 'Cerebral lateralization of function: from infancy through childhood'. *Psychological Bulletin*, 101, 376–92.

Harding, L. and Beech, J. R. (1991). *Educational Assessment of the Primary School Child*. Windsor: NFER-Nelson.

Hebb, D. O. (1942). 'The effect of early and late brain injury upon test scores, and the nature of normal adult intelligence'. *Proceedings of the American Philosophical Society*, 85, 275–91.

Henderson, S. (1991). 'The assessment of children who are motor impaired'. In L. Harding and J. R. Beech (eds), *Educational Assessment of the Primary School Child*. Windsor: NFER-Nelson.

Henderson, S. E. (1987). 'The assessment of clumsy children: old and new approaches'. *Journal of Child Psychology and Psychiatry*, 28, 511–27.

Henderson, S. E. and Sugden, D. A. (1992). *Movement Assessment Battery for Children*. London: Psychological Corporation.

Hermann, B. and Seidenberg, M. (1989). *Childhood Epilepsies: Neuropsychological, Psychosocial and Intervention Aspects*. Chichester: John Wiley.

Hulme, C. and Lord, R. (1986). 'Clumsy children: a review of recent research'. *Childcare, Health and Development*, 12, 257–69.

Hynd, G. W., Snow, J. and Becker, M. G. (1986). 'Neuropsychological assessment in clinical child psychology'. In B. B. Lahey and A. E. Kazdin (eds), *Advances in Clinical Child Psychology, 9*. New York: Plenum Press.

Johnson, D. A., Britton, J., Johnstone, K. and Rose, F. D. (1993). '8 year follow up of head injured children: preliminary results from C.T. brain scan and cognitive assessment'. Paper presented at the Neuropsychology Conference, Scottish Branch of the British Psychological Society, St Andrews.

Johnson, D. A., Roethig–Johnston, K. and Middleton, J. (1988). 'Development and evaluation of an attention test for head-injured children: 1. Information processing capacity in a normal sample'. *Journal of Child Psychology and Psychiatry*, 29, 199–208.

Laszlo, J. I. and Bairstow, P. J. (1985). *Perceptual-Motor Behaviour: Development, Assessment and Therapy*. Eastbourne: Holt, Rinehart and Winston.

Lesser, R. P., Luders, H., Wyllie, E., Dinner, D. S. and Norris, H. H. (1986). 'Mental deterioration in epilepsy'. *Epilepsia*, 27 (Suppl. 2), S105–S123.

Levin, H. S., Elsenberg, H. M., Widd, M. D. and Kobayashi, K. (1982). 'Memory and intellectual ability after head injury in children and adolescents'. *Neurosurgery*, 11, 668–73.

Light, R., Neumann, E., Lewis, R., Morecki–Oberg, C., Asarnow, R. and Satz, P. (1987). 'An evaluation of a neuropsychologically based re-education project for the head injured child'. *Journal of Head Trauma Rehabilitation*, 2, 11–25.

Livingstone, M. G. and McCabe, R. J. R. (1990). 'Psychosocial consequences of head injury in children and adolescents: implications for rehabilitation'. *Paediatrician*, 17, 255–61.

Lord, R. and Hulme, C. (1987). 'Kinaesthetic sensitivity of normal and clumsy children'. *Developmental Medicine and Child Neurology*, 29, 720–5.

Milner, B. (1975). 'Psychological aspects of focal epilepsy and its neurosurgical management'. *Advances in Neurology*, 8, 299–321.

Neale, M. (1988). *Neale Analysis of Reading Ability*. Windsor: NFER-Nelson.

Osterreith, P. (1944). 'Le test de copie d'une figure complexe'. *Archives of Psychology*, 30, 206–356.

Perrot, S. B., Taylor, H. G. and Montes, J. L. (1991). 'Neuropsychological sequelae, familial stress and environmental adaption following paediatric head injury'. *Developmental Neuropsychology*, 7, 69–86.

Raimondi, A. J. and Hirschauer, J. S. (1984). 'Head injury in the infant and toddler: coma scoring and outcome scale'. *Child's Brain*, 11, 12–35.

Raspin, I. and Allen, D. A. (1983). 'Developmental language disorders: nosological considerations'. In U. Kirk (ed.), *Neuropsychology of Language, Reading and Spelling*. New York: Academic Press.

Read, C. (1986). *Children's Creative Spelling*. London: Routledge and Kegan Paul.

Renfrew, C. F. (1966). *Action Picture Test*. Available from the author at North Place, Old Headington, Oxford.

Renfrew, C. F. (1969). *Word Finding Test*. Available from the author at North Place, Old Headington, Oxford.

Ridgway, J. and Harding, L. (1991). 'The assessment of mathematical skills'. In L. Harding and J. R. Beech (eds), *Educational Assessment of the Primary School Child*. Windsor: NFER-Nelson.

Rourke, B. P., Young, G. C., Strang, J. D. and Russell, D. L. (1986). 'Adult outcomes of central processing deficits in childhood'. In I. Grant and K. M. Adams (eds), *Neuropsychological Assessment of Neuropsychiatric Disorders*. New York: Oxford University Press.

Rutter, M., Tizard, J. and Whitmore, K. (1970). *Education, Health and Behaviour*. London: Longman.

Satz, P. and Bullard-Bates, C. (1981). 'Acquired aphasia in children'. In H. T. Sarno (ed.), *Acquired Aphasia*. New York: Academic Press.

Seidenberg, M. (1989). 'Neuropsychological functioning of children with epilepsy'. In B. Hermann and M. Seidenberg (eds), *Childhood Epilepsies: Neuropsychological, Psychosocial and Intervention Aspects*. Chichester: John Wiley.

Shaffer, D., Bijur, P. and Rutter, M. L. (1980). 'Head injury and later reading disability'. *Journal of the Academy of Child Psychiatry*, 19, 592–610.

Slee, P. T. (1988). *Child Observation Skills*. Beckenham: Croom Helm.

Spreen, O. and Gaddes, W. H. (1969). 'Developmental norms for 15 neuropsychological tests, age 6–15'. *Cortex*, 5, 171–191.

Stanley, F. and Alberman, E. (1984). 'The epidemiology of the cerebral palsies'. Clinics in Developmental Medicine, No. 87, London and Oxford: Spastics International Medical Publications and Blackwell Scientific.

Stott, D. H., Moyes, F. A. and Henderson, S. E. (1984). *Test of Motor Impairment (TOMI)*. Henderson revision. London: Psychological Corporation.

Stuart, M. and Coltheart, M. (1988). 'Does reading develop in a sequence of stages?'. *Cognition*, 30, 139–81.

Swift, A., Dyken, P. and Du Rant, R. (1984). 'Psychological follow-up in childhood dementia: a report of studies in sub-acute sclerosing panencephalitis'. *Journal of Paediatric Psychology*.

Taylor, E. (1986). 'Attention deficit'. In E. Taylor (ed.), *The Overactive Child*. Clinics in Developmental Medicine, No. 97. London and Oxford: Spastics International Medical Publications and Blackwell Scientific.

Taylor, H. G., Michaels, R. H., Mazur, P. M., Bauer, R. E. and Liden, C. B. (1984). 'Intellectual, neuropsychological, and achievement outcomes in children six to eight years after recovery from haemophilus influenzae meningitis'. *Paediatrics*, 74, 198–205.

Temple, C. (1991a) 'Developmental and acquired disorders of childhood'. In S. Segalowtiz and I. Rapin (eds), *Handbook of Neuropsychology*. Amsterdam: Elsevier.

Temple, C. (1991b) 'Procedural dyscalculia and number fact dyscalculia: double dissociation in developmental dyscalculia'. *Cognitive Neuropsychology*, 8(2), 155–76.

Temple, C. M. (1988). 'Red is read but eye is blue: a case study of developmental dyslexia and follow up report'. *Brain and Language*, 34, 13–37.

Temple, C. M. and Marshall, J. (1983). 'A case study of developmental phonological dyslexia'. *British Journal of Psychology*, 74, 517–33.

Tharp, B. R. (1987). 'An overview of paediatric seizure disorders and epileptic syndromes'. *Epilepsia*, 28 (Suppl. 1), S36–S45.

Vincent, E., Green, L., Francis, J. and Powney, J. (1983). *A Review of Reading Tests*. Windsor: NFER-Nelson.

Volpe, J. J. (1987). 'Neuronal proliferation, migration, organisation and myelination'. In M. Markowitz (ed.), *Major Problems in Clinical Paediatrics, 22*. Philadelphia and London: Saunders.

Waber, D. P. and Holmes, J. M. (1986). 'Assessing children's memory productions of the Rey–Osterreith complex figure'. *Journal of Clinical and Experimental Neuropsychology*, 8, 563–80.

Ward, M. (1979). *Mathematics and the 10 Year Old*. Schools Council Working Paper 61. London: Evans/Methuen Educational.

Wiig, E. H. and Secord, W. (1985). *Test of Language Competence, 9–19 Years*. New York: Harcourt Brace Jovanovich.

Wiig, E. H. and Secord, W. (1987). *Test of Language Competence, 4–9 Years*. New York: Harcourt Brace Jovanovich.

Wilson, B. A., Invani-Chalian, R. and Aldrich, F. (1992). 'Children's Rivermead Behavioural Memory Test'. Bury St Edmunds: Thames Valley.

Ysseldyke, J. E. and Mirkin, P. K. (1982). 'The use of assessment information to plan instructional interventions: a review of the research'. In C. Reynolds and T. Gurkin (eds), *The Handbook of School Psychology*. New York: John Wiley.

Yule, W., Lansdown, R. and Urbanowicz, M. (1982). 'Predicting educational achievement in a primary school sample'. *British Journal of Clinical Psychology*, 21, 43–6.

3

ASSESSMENT OF INTELLIGENCE AND COGNITIVE ABILITIES ACROSS THE LIFE SPAN

Clive Skilbeck

THEORETICAL ASPECTS OF ASSESSING INTELLIGENCE

This chapter concentrates upon the neuropsychological value of a cognitive area often termed 'intelligence' or 'intellectual functioning'. The definition usually includes reference to the measurement of IQ and its subtests, and may be used to encompass a much wider range of functions, including concept formation. The discussion which has continued over the years as to the definition and nature of 'intelligence', whether IQ tests measure it adequately, and the relative contribution of genetic and environmental factors in its determination are not central, happily, to neuropsychological usage. Tests of intelligence or IQ are used by clinical neuropsychologists as one (albeit central) component in assessing cognitive functioning. The important aspects for neuropsychologists tend to relate to information provided by tests on specific intellectual functions, rather than to overall intelligence level. As there is not a predictable relationship between overall IQ and amount of acquired brain damage, these tests are used to examine patterns of functional impairment and the relationship of these to type of pathology and extent (general, lateralized, localized) of brain lesion. As will be described below, there are particular relationships between test performance and brain lesions which help us to understand what organizational damage the brain has sustained, what its current functional capacities are, and what its future recovery and performance might be. The brain–behaviour relationships which are examined using tests of intellectual functioning need to take account of potentially confounding factors. For example, mood disturbance can often complicate the interpretation of tests of intellectual functioning (see Caine, 1986, for review). Specific comments on the effects of anxiety, depression and other factors upon intellectual performance will be offered in the next section.

The history of clinical neuropsychology has been based upon three lines

47

of development: psychometric tests, tests clinically validated against organic lesions and experimental tasks. The latter (such as reaction time and other information-processing measures) have not yet been adequately exploited, although there are a number of clinical neuropsychology tests and batteries whose origin and usage is based upon specific validation against proven site, extent and pathology of damage (such as the Halstead–Reitan Test Battery; Reitan and Davison, 1974). The psychometric line of development is strongly represented by IQ tests. For these tests (such as WAIS/WAIS-R) the primary reason for development was not clinical neuropsychological in nature. Rather than being devised to identify and describe acquired brain damage, they were developed to offer instruments with a strong standard-ized and normative background for the measurement of overall intelligence level, or IQ, in the general population. Obviously, given that the brain is the seat of cognitive functions, there are expected correlations between damage to the brain and the scores provided by IQ/intellectual tests, though the theoretical underpinnings of these tests do not draw upon brain structure and organization. In this sense, the brain–behaviour relationships which have been demonstrated using IQ tests are largely empirical.

ASSESSMENT TECHNIQUES: IQ/INTELLIGENCE TESTS

Most tests which have been developed to assess IQ level include a number of separate subtests. The Wechsler Scales provide the best examples of this type of test. Sometimes the whole of the test is geared to generating a simple overall intellectual level (such as the Ravens tests: Raven, 1977).

Wechsler Scales

The Wechsler Adult Intelligence Scale (WAIS; see Matarazzo, 1972) was devised over forty years ago, but it and its more recent replacement (WAIS-Revised; Wechsler, 1981) continue to be the most frequently used English language IQ test. The WAIS-R includes alternation of verbal and perform-ance subtest administration, and there is revision of the content and scoring of some scales. The WAIS-R was thought necessary because of some outdated WAIS items, and the fact that age-scale norms for Similarities and Picture Arrangement relating to older people were too low on the WAIS, allowing 'impaired' performances to be classified artificially high (Lezak, 1983). The WAIS-R has been carefully constructed, using an 1880 standardization sample with stratification according to age, race, education, etc. A number of short forms of the WAIS have been proposed, abbreviation being achieved either by reducing the number of items per scale or by omitting some scales altogether.

References to the WAIS during the 1960s pointed towards a large relative increase in the amount of research relating to brain damage and to samples of people with a mental handicap, or those requiring special education. The number of papers concerned with specific diagnosis also rose, and towards the end of the 1960s rehabilitation reports began to appear. Reviews by neuropsychologists (e.g. Filskov and Leli, 1981; McFie, 1975; Lezak, 1983) confirmed the invaluable contribution of the WAIS to this field. Many studies have highlighted the role of the WAIS not only in identifying the presence of brain damage, but also in providing information on lateralization and localization of lesions. Lezak (1983) viewed the WAIS as an important component in her neuropsychological examination, some subtests making a distinctive contribution to the assessment of specific abilities. As she concluded, 'A basic review of intellectual functions in which a WAIS battery serves as the core instrument is usually sufficient to demonstrate an absence of significant intellectual disability or to provide clues to altered functions.' Given some differences between WAIS and WAIS-R, it has not yet been confirmed that the latter behaves identically to its predecessor. Because of this, some clinical neuropsychologists will continue to use the WAIS in medico-legal work for some time to come, although it is to be expected that factor-analytic studies and those involving samples with patients showing brain damage, lateralized lesions, or localized damage will continue to appear in relation to the WAIS-R, so reinforcing its use.

Amongst others, Lezak (1983) and McFie (1975) have provided detailed reviews of the specific information available from the WAIS for clinical neuropsychology in terms of localized and lateralized brain lesions. These can be summarized, somewhat simplistically (because a patient's WAIS or WAIS-R scores must be interpreted in the light of the full array of test data, qualitative observations of the patient's behaviour during testing, and other clinical data or history), as follows:

1 Summary IQ scores show no direct relationships to neuro-anatomical structures, but Verbal IQ (VIQ) tends to be depressed differentially by left-hemisphere lesions and reduction in Performance IQ (PIQ) (less reliably) can be related to right-hemisphere damage. PIQ loses hemisphere specificity because any brain damage tends to affect the particularly time-dependant performance subtests adversely (for instance, Digit Symbol).

2 Most specific neuropsychological information can be obtained from some of the constituent subtests. The less 'useful' subtests for clinical neuropsychology are Information, Comprehension and Object Assembly; this has led some neuropsychology groups to utilize a short WAIS with these subtests ommitted.

3 A number of formulae have been developed to try and identify patients whose intellectual functions have significantly declined as a result of brain damage. Each formula generally uses the concept of 'hold' and 'don't hold'

tests. 'Hold' tests are defined as those WAIS/WAIS-R subtests whose age-corrected scores are said to resist deterioration (from either increasing age or pathological process). They are generally taken to include Information, Comprehension, Vocabulary, Picture Completion and Object Assembly. An example set of the 'don't hold' tests, favoured by Wechsler, comprises Digit Span, Similarities, Digit Symbol and Block Design. Variations in the formulae which have been proposed are described and reviewed by Lezak (1983). Using purely actuarial approaches to identify the presence of brain damage at best yields a 70–75 per cent success rate, although a hit rate as high as 85–88 per cent has been reported by studies under discrimination of non-psychotic psychiatric patients from organic patients. Although the developed formulae are not fully satisfactory when used alone, in combination with the observations and judgement of an experienced clinical psychologist they can be useful in routine clinical practice.

4 Other analyses of age-scale subtest patterns can yield valuable information on localization of cortical lesions. McFie (1975) offered detailed information in this area, although his opinions about brain-specific subtest relationships were probably too black and white. Although the following should not be assumed without consideration of other clinical test results and observational data, the findings on brain-WAIS/WAIS-R subtest relationships which have been replicated include the following:
(a) Relatively poor mental arithmetic subtest performance may be specifically associated with damage to the left parietal lobe (particularly if other verbal subtest scores remain well preserved), although impaired performances may also reflect left hemisphere dysfunction more generally, or memory dysfunction without localizing features.
(b) A lowered Similarities score can predict left-hemisphere damage, its localizing value being related to the integrity of left temporal lobe functioning.
(c) Like Similarities, Digit Span scores are sensitive to left-hemisphere lesions generally. McFie (1975) has also suggested that these results are particularly vulnerable to anterior left-hemisphere damage, which may arise from the sequencing aspect of the task, rather than from its memory component; rote skills from the Wechsler Memory Scale (see Barbara Wilson, Chapter 9, this volume) may also share this effect, given the sequencing of information involved.
(d) Digit-Symbol performance is extremely sensitive to any cortical lesion, whatever its location, size or pathology.
(e) Block-Design performance is likely to be depressed by right-hemisphere damage, particularly if the parietal lobe is involved.
(f) Picture-Arrangement score, too, tends to be adversely affected by right-hemisphere damage and is particularly sensitive to anterior lesions.

It must be stressed that the above is a crude summary. Identification of the site and nature of particular brain lesions would not usually be undertaken purely on the basis of the relationships suggested: a range of clinical data would normally be utilized. Also, the WAIS/WAIS-R is usually administered to depict the pattern of preserved and impaired intellectual abilities, rather than to specify lesion details.

Journal articles over the last ten years confirm the high interest in the WAIS/WAIS-R. This continues to be the 'frame-of-reference' IQ test when examining cognitive functions, even amongst more experimentally inclined neuropsychologists. For example, in a study of frontal-lobe lesions and their effects upon cognitive estimation and spatial memory performance, Smith and Milner (1985) employed the WAIS to provide background IQ data. Much of the very recent research, of course, has concentrated upon the WAIS-R in attempts to confirm neuropsychological findings expected from it and the WAIS, and in providing the same kind of supporting information to that available for use with the WAIS. Naglieri (1982), for instance, has used data on the standard error of measurement taken from the manual to offer tables on the confidence intervals for the WAIS-R scores in different age groups, and for determining the Verbal–Performance IQ discrepancy required for statistical significance, again by age. Similarly, Matarazzo and Herman (1984) examined test–retest reliability of Verbal–Performance differences on the WAIS-R to provide base-rate data.

Prifitera and Barley (1985) raised questions concerning the substitution of the WAIS-R for the WAIS in test-combination interpretations; these authors noted WAIS FSIQs (Full Scale IQs) to be seven points higher, on average, than the WAIS-R FSIQs. This difference is important when judging the pathology of the memory quotient (MQ) obtained from the Wechsler Memory Scale (WMS; see Barbara Wilson, Chapter 9, this volume): a number of authors have suggested that an MQ of twelve or more points below WAIS FSIQ can be used to define memory impairment. Prifitera and Barley's work showed that the WAIS-R cannot directly replace the WAIS in this formula, because MQs appear inflated due to the WAIS-R yielding lower IQ values. These authors suggest, therefore, that the WMS should probably be renormed for compatibility with WAIS-R. Crawford *et al.* (1990), too, examined the equivalence of the WAIS and WAIS-R. They tested 275 UK subjects in matched samples (sex, age) on either the WAIS or WAIS-R to compare the generated IQ estimates. They noted significantly higher FSIQ, VIQ and PIQ (all $P < .001$) values in the WAIS, consistent with similar USA studies. Happily, the WAIS-R FSIQ (101.1), VIQ (102.0) and PIQ (99.8) estimates were all very close to 100. The study also included National Adult Reading Test (NART) data and showed a good correlation between NART errors and WAIS-R FSIQ (-0.72). Research on the performance stability of the WAIS-R has usually been reassuring. Beck *et al.* (1985) attempted to replicate the factor-analytic structure of WAIS-R in other samples, including those of 200 general medical and 271 psychiatric patients. Across all samples, the coefficient of concordance for the two expected main factors (verbal, performance) was at least 0.97, and for the third factor (freedom from distractability) the range was 0.93–0.97, reflecting the very robust factor structure of the WAIS-R. These findings parallel those from earlier studies on the WAIS (e.g. Larrabee *et al.* 1983). Beck and his co-workers suggested that future research might focus on further cross-validation of the structure with additional (clinical) populations.

There is, of course, an enormous amount of research needed before clinicians can be certain of the WAIS-R–brain relationships to the same degree as that pertaining to the WAIS. Bornstein (1984) demonstrated the expected pattern of IQ findings in relation to unilateral lesions (verbal lower than performance in left-hemisphere damage, and vice versa for right-hemisphere lesions). Introduction of the WAIS-R does not yet seem to have reduced the large amount of neuropsychological research annually appearing on the WAIS. For example, Kane *et al.* (1985) have examined the discriminative accuracy and statistical relationships of the WAIS, Halstead–Reitan Test Battery and Luria–Nebraska Test Battery in detecting brain damage.

The WAIS and WAIS-R are often used to assess intellectual ability in elderly people. Whilst the WAIS-R is probably generally to be preferred to its predecessor for older people (because of the alternation of verbal and performance subtest scores), the WAIS still offers the best reference data for people over 75 years of age. However, data is accumulating rapidly on the WAIS-R, and Snow *et al.* (1990) demonstrated its high one-year test–retest reliability in a sample of normal elderly people, for FSIQ (0.90), VIQ (0.86) and PIQ (0.85), with a median subtest reliability coefficient of 0.71 (highest were Digit Symbol at 0.91, Block Design at 0.84, Information at 0.81 and Picture Arrangement at 0.74). The Verbal–Performance discrepancy reliability, however, was only 0.69. Also popular for use with elderly people is the Revised Kendrick Battery (Kendrick *et al.*, 1979), which consists of the Object Learning Test and the Digit Copying Test. The latter shares some features with the WAIS/WAIS-R Digit Symbol task. It has the advantage of being brief to administer, though, as Beardsall and Brayne (1990) have pointed out, even short tests such as the NART (see below), which involves reading irregular and difficult words, may be stressful to older people. These authors derived a 'half' form (twenty-five items) and regression equations to predict total NART score, validating against an unselected group (n = 122) of elderly people. Predicted total NART score was significantly correlated with actual total score (0.93) for the total group, and for subgroups of demented (0.95) and depressed (0.93) subjects. Wechsler Intelligence Scales for children and adolescents (age range 4–17) are considered by Beardsworth with Harding, Chapter 2, this volume).

Ravens Scales: Progressive Matrices (RPM) and Coloured Matrices (RCM)

These tests both assess visual perception and reasoning (Raven, 1977). Particular strengths of both the adult version (RPM) and the children and elderly format (RCM) are the relatively brief administration time and the facts that no language is required on the part of the patient and only a minimal motor response is needed. Test items consist of multiple-choice administration of pattern matching and analogy reasoning. Percentile norms are available for 6–16 years and 20–65 years (RPM), and 5–11 years and 65 years and older (RCM).

As might be expected, the RPM correlates well with other visuo-spatial tests. It has been shown to be reasonably sensitive to the presence of brain damage, although it does not show good discriminative power for separating right- and left-hemisphere lesions. David and Skilbeck (1984) noted significant correlations between Ravens IQ and communication ability in aphasic stroke patients. Unlike the RPM, the RCM results are differentially impaired by right-hemisphere lesions, presumably because of visuo-constructional difficulties, as posterior lesions show the greatest effect. Lezak (1983) reviewed the RPM, pointing out that poor performances are often associated with constructional difficulties and that patients with lateralized lesions (particularly those affecting the right posterior region) frequently show positional preferences for responses on the ipsilateral side to the lesion due to visual neglect. The language-independent administration characteristics, and the simple motor responses required for completing the RPM and RCM, make them particularly useful to clinical neuropsychologists: for example, Luria sometimes used the RPM in his highly individual examination of patients, and Lezak includes this instrument in her neuropsychological battery. In addition, a number of the other neuropsychological test batteries described by Lezak (1983) include the RCM.

Other measures of intellectual level

The National Adult Reading Test (NART; Nelson, 1982) was developed through research on dementia (Nelson and O'Connell, 1978) and findings which confirm that word-reading ability and IQ are highly correlated (0.75) in normal adults. The NART was designed to provide an estimate of premorbid IQ in patients suspected of showing intellectual deterioration. The test consists of fifty words which a patient has to pronounce aloud, the total error score being used to obtain a predicted IQ. The NART has been standardized on 120 non-brain-damaged patients aged 20–70 years. Findings indicated no significant correlation between NART errors and age, and no social class effects. Clinical validation has included samples of demented (n = 45) and control (n = 98) subjects. Crawford et al. (1989) extended the data collected on the NART, and in generating new WAIS-prediction equations confirmed the relationship between the two instruments. Results to date suggest that the NART is highly resistant to processes which produce intellectual deterioration. Its manual provides tables for converting error score into predicted FSIQ, VIQ and PIQ, and then calculating the percentage of normal subjects who would be expected to obtain any particular predicted–obtained IQ discrepancy. The clinician or researcher is thus able to tell at a glance how unusual a patient's discrepancy score is, and therefore whether any evidence of intellectual deterioration is demonstrated in that patient. Nelson has suggested that the NART might be used in assessing the effects of drugs in psychiatric disturbances upon intellectual functioning, and that it should be very useful in providing a quick estimate of IQ level for subject matching in research studies. The test, therefore, has a high clinical and research utility, and is increasingly popular amongst neuropsychologists.

As indicated at the beginning of this chapter, IQ procedures usually gain their neuropsychological utility by having been included in a number of clinical studies on the specific and/or global affects of brain damage. The large majority of IQ tests were not constructed with neuropsychological functioning in mind, nor were the assessment of discrete cognitive functions. A clear exception to this is offered by the British Ability Scales. The British Ability Scales-Revised (BAS-R; Elliott et al., 1983) offers a rare example of a general intellectual test whose construction was based upon cognitive processes. In addition to yielding IQs (short and full forms), the BAS-R produces scores on:

Speed of Information Processing
Reasoning
Spatial Imagery
Perceptual Matching
Short-term Memory
Retrieval and Application of Knowledge

It covers the age range 2.5–17.5 years of age. Because the BAS-R is said to aid in the diagnosis of children's learning deficits, and in assessing change over time, it may have a place in clinical neuropsychological practice. Of greater potential value to clinical neuropsychology, however, is its 'cognitive' construction: the provision of a general model of intellectual/cognitive functioning incorporating specific abilities is attractive. If the BAS-R is to obtain widespread recognition as a routine instrument, it will be necessary for many more researchers to employ it in relevant clinical studies on neurological patients. A number of less frequently used instruments are available for assessing children (see Beardsworth with Harding, Chapter 2, this volume).

Finally, a mention should be made of the Wide Range Achievement Test (WRAT; Jastak and Jastak, 1965). The WRAT is a true 'wide-range' test, as it covers the age range 5–45 years. It is based on educational attainments in spelling, reading and written arithmetic. Good norms are available, and raw scores can be converted into standard scores, percentiles or school grades. Lezak (1983) praised WRAT's flexibility, and pointed to the neuropsychological value and the variety of its arithmetic problems: information on whether spatial dyscalculia, number alexia, or loss of number concepts as the underlying deficit is obtained. Some components of the WRAT (usually the reading items) may be included in isolation in a clinical neuropsychologist's test battery, and the WRAT is often included with other neuropsychological tests for research purposes (for example Korman *et al.*, 1981, used it with the WAIS and Halstead–Reitan Test Battery in their study of inhalant solvent abusers).

OTHER INTELLECTUAL TESTS

This section briefly introduces instruments which are not classified as IQ tests, and are not covered elsewhere in this book. The general area to which these tests relate may be variously described as concept formation, reasoning or abstracting ability. Often, though not exclusively, impaired performance on these tests is noted in frontal-lobe lesions. The two best-known tests in this area are the Halstead–Reitan Category Test (see Reitan and Davison, 1974), and the Wisconsin Card Sorting Test (WCST: popularized by Milner, 1963). The WCST has been modified (MCST), though not replaced, by Nelson (1976). Reitan and Wolfson (1986) cited the Category Test as one of the four most sensitive measures of the HRTB (Halstead–Reitan Test Battery), and Finlayson *et al.* (1986), responding to criticism concerning its lengthy period of administration, pointed out that most patients can complete the Category Test in 20–50 minutes and that its validity is excellent. Boyle (1988) recently investigated the nature of the Category Test, noting, via factor analysis, that it loads highly in terms of general intelligence. Boyle's results were supported by Zillmer *et al.* (1988), who obtained correlations of the Category Test error score with WAIS VIQ and PIQ of -0.41 and -0.51, respectively, in their sample of 151 neuropsychiatric patients.

A number of studies have confirmed impaired WCST/MCST performance in frontal-lobe dysfunction (e.g. Milner, 1963; Nelson, 1976; Robinson *et al.*, 1980). Both versions of the test involve a patient sorting a pack of response cards under four possible stimulus cards, according to concept (each card contains attributes of shape, colour and number). The examiner has a concept or 'rule' in mind for how the response cards should be sorted and provides the patient with feedback ('right', 'wrong') under conditions of trial-and-error learning. Once the patient has demonstrated that the concept has been learned, via a sequence of six correct responses, then the examiner introduces a new concept. Test scores include the number of concepts learned (maximum six) before the pack of response cards is exhausted, the number of errors produced, and the percentage of errors which are perseverative. The principal modification in producing the MCST involved removing from the pack all response cards which were ambiguous, in that they shared more than one attribute with the stimulus card, and changing the definition of a perseverative response. Also, in the MCST the patient is informed that the concept to be learned has changed, whereas in the WCST version no such warning is given. Although it has some draw-backs, the WCST is still often used. For instance, Robinson et al. (1980) investigated the utility of perseverative error score in discriminating patients with frontal-lobe lesions from normals, and from other patient groups with non-frontal focal or diffuse damage. The WCST performed well, except that it failed to differentiate between frontal-lobe patients and those with diffused damage. The Robinson et al. study demonstrated that the WCST was superior to any single test from the HRNB battery in identifying frontal versus non-frontal lesions. The MCST is probably now more popular amongst neuropsychologists in the UK, due to the improvements it offers over the original. Nelson's (1976) paper showed that the MCST performed satisfactorily, although it would still benefit from further work on the effects of pre-morbid IQ, type of pathological process, and age. With regard to the last of these, until the research of Chelune and Baer (1986), no children's norms were available for the WCST. Their work indicated that by 10 years of age, children's WCST performances are very similar to those obtained from adults.

EXAMPLES OF CLINICAL APPLICATIONS

Head injury

Head injury is common: research quoted in the Field report (1976) indicated that the annual incidence of severe head injury (defined as a post-traumatic amnesia period longer than twenty-four hours) in England and Wales is 150 per million. This means that in the 'average' health district of 200,000 population an incidence of approximately thirty would be expected, six of whom could be left with a major permanent disability precluding return to ordinary work, and two of whom would require permanent nursing care. In terms of prevalence, this size of health district would contain about 112 people showing considerable disability following head injury.

A number of studies have assessed the effects of closed head injury upon IQ, work most often employing the WAIS (e.g. Mandleberg and Brooks, 1975: Levin et al., 1979). Generally, reports suggest that VIQ recovers well, approximately to pre-morbid level, but PIQ shows both greater deficit initially and often a prolonged period of impairment. Some performance functions appear to show permanent deficits, particularly after more severe

56

head injury. Mandleberg and Brooks (1975) conducted serial testing on a group of severely injured patients, their results showing no significant change, in any verbal WAIS scale when the scores of patients at the 4–6 months' follow-up were compared with those at the 13 months' follow-up. However, significant gains (P < .05) were noted for all performance subtests except Picture Completion, and overall performance IQ improvement was significant (P < .01). In group comparisons of patients against the control group (neurotic psychiatric patients), head-injured patients scored significantly lower at the 0–3 months' follow-up for VIQ (P < .01) and PIQ (P < .001), at the 4–6 months' follow-up for VIQ (P < .05) and PIQ (P < .001), and at the 7–12 months' point for PIQ alone. The only subtest to offer significant results for comparison of the two groups at every follow-up was Digit Span, although Digit Symbol and Picture Arrangement yielded significant differences at all except the final one. No significant IQ comparisons were noted at follow-up beyond this point. Given that Picture Completion often acts as a 'hold' test, it is perhaps not surprising it tends not to show significant recovery with time post-trauma. In contrast, the finding that Digit Symbol shows a continuing sensitivity to cognitive recovery after head injury is consistent with its vulnerability to impairment by any brain lesion.

Stuss and Benson (1985) obtained even less impressive findings, failing to note any significant differences between head-injured patients (all of whom were at least five months post-trauma) and matched controls on any WAIS scale. However, it should be noted that Stuss's patients tended to have suffered milder injuries (35 per cent of the sample had a post-traumatic amnesia [PTA] of less than one day). Brooks (1984) pointed out that a number of hypotheses have been advanced to account for the different post-injury course seen in VIQ and PIQ, including suggestions that performance tasks require sustained effort, involve a speed component, or are intrinsically more complex in nature. Attempts have been made to relate the level of intellectual deficit observed to indices of severity of injury. Whilst duration of coma does not help to predict subsequent intellectual performance, increasing length of PTA is associated with greater intellectual impairment, especially for PIQ (Brooks, 1984). In addition, there is some evidence (Cullum and Bigler, 1986) that WAIS PIQ shows significant negative correlations with volumetric ventrical–brain ratio (VBR) and with degree of cortical atrophy. The clearest relationships with VBR measures are provided by Block Design and Digit Symbol, as might be expected given their 'don't hold' status, discussed above.

Overall, IQ tests do not appear particularly sensitive general indicators of cognitive functioning following closed head injury in adults, compared with results obtained from assessing memory and concentration. Given that stability is a valued feature of an IQ test, this suggested lack of sensitivity is not surprising and not necessarily a drawback to the neuropsychological use of IQ tests generally. However, another limitation to their use in the field of head injury is their general lack of parallel forms. Frequently, clinical neuropsychologists will wish to carry out repeated assessments of recovery in head-injury patients in the first twelve months post-trauma. Readministration of identical IQ test items carries the danger of practice affects: for instance, Brooks (1984) reported some evidence of possible practice affects using the Ravens PM with head-injured patients.

Dementias

Dementia is an acquired, persisting, usually progressive deterioration in Cognitive functioning arising from diffuse brain dysfunction. Alzheimer's disease is probably the most frequent cause of progressive dementia (Walton, 1985), usually with an onset after 50 years of age, accounting for approximately 25–50 per cent of dementia cases. Miller (1976) provided a thorough review of the intellectual changes associated with dementia, particularly concentrating on the WAIS and RPM. In general, PIQ deterioration is greater than for VIQ and WAIS 'don't hold' subtests (particularly Digit Symbol and Block Design) have often been quoted as being more sensitive to deterioration arising from general dementia. Savage *et al.* (1973) cautioned against overreliance on Wechsler's deterioration quotient (DQ). These authors found great variability in the DQ, leading to a significant misclassification rate in dementia. A number of studies (e.g. Fuld, 1984; Filley *et al.*, 1987) have noted the 'Fuld profile' on the WAIS-R to be associated with dementia of the Alzheimer type (DAT). The Fuld profile employs age-corrected scale scores, in the following formulae:

A = (Information plus Vocabulary)/2
B = (Similarities plus Digit Span)/2
C = (Block Design plus Digit Symbol)/2
D = (Object Assembly)

These values are then checked for fit against the following expression:

If $A > B > C < D$, and $A > D$, then this suggests a DAT diagnosis.

However, recent evidence (Logsdon *et al.*, 1989) has cast doubt on the power of the Fuld profile to discriminate DAT patients from normal or depressed elderly people. The prognosis for DAT is usually poor, progression reflecting increased severity and range of deficits, until eventually 'hold' tests such as Vocabulary and Information are compromised.

Quite often a request for intellectual assessment has a diagnostic aspect to it; for example, seeking the clinical psychologist's opinion on whether the referred patient is depressed, shows brain damage lateralized to one cerebral hemisphere, or has diffuse damage affecting both hemispheres. Numerous clinical research studies have been carried out in this area, Kluger and

Goldberg (1990) offering a recent meta-analysis and review of thirty-eight studies. Examination of IQ results does not offer diagnostic certainty, though it generally holds that patients with left hemisphere damage (for example, with aetiology of tumour, cerebrovascular disease, epilepsy) will obtain a lower VIQ than PIQ. In contrast, groups of patients with damage limited to the right hemisphere will show a lower PIQ than VIQ. These findings can be very useful in delineating laterality of damage, though when the differential diagnosis involves affective disorder and organic damage the situation is complicated by the fact that groups of patients with mood disturbances usually show a 'right-hemisphere' picture – that is, their PIQs are lower than their VIQs. In addition, patients showing bilateral cortical damage also generally present with a lower PIQ. This latter group obtains a PIQ/VIQ ratio (0.96) which is identical to that noted for the group of affective patients, helping to discrimate both of these groups from patients with right-hemisphere damage only (ratio: 0.88) and those with left-hemi- sphere damage only (ratio: 1.10). Kluger and Goldberg (1990) noted that one possible interpretation of these findings is that affective patients show bilateral, diffuse cortical dysfunction, although the studies examined by these authors pooled a wide spectrum of affective disorder and possibly relevant factors (such as pharmacological status, subtype of mood distur- bance, acuteness of disorder, etc.).

The problem of differential diagnosis is a particularly relevant and difficult area with elderly people. For example, the use of very 'clean' (that is, extremely easy to differentiate) subgroups of 'demented' and 'depressed' patients in the standard samples of the revised Kendrick battery (Kendrick *et al.*, 1979) probably led to inflated expectations regarding its diagnostic performance; with less than clear-cut cases it may misclassify a high percentage of patients (Gibson *et al.*, 1980). As the treatment consequences for elderly people of being diagnosed depressed are very different from those of being diagnosed demented, the issue is important. Woods and Britton (1985) recommended that cognitive tests be used to describe, rather than to diagnose, elderly people.

Age-referents (for example, labelling general deterioration as 'senile de- mentia' when a patient is over 65 years of age) are artificial and largely irrelevant to the test patterns observed. It is worthwhile, however, separating DAT from multi-infarct dementia (MID), given the latter's typical picture of a step-wise progression in the deterioration process. Given its cerebrovas- cular basis, MID (which accounts for approximately 12 per cent of cases of suspected dementia) could have been considered below with strokes. MID, in contrast to DAT, often has an acute rather than an insidious onset, and cognitive deficits may fluctuate on a day-to-day basis. This type of dementia has a high incidence in men, and hypertension is often a pre-morbid factor.

Another group of dementias are those in which the brain degeneration has primarily affected subcortical areas (such as Parkinson's disease,

59

Huntington's disease). Patients with these diseases tend not to show widespread intellectual deficits, but rather to display motor dysfunction, which is apparent on the timed performance subtests of WAIS/WAIS-R. Neuropsychological differential diagnosis procedures can be important because of treatment consequences and the advice that should be offered to relatives and their agencies. Research on differentiating various diseases of elderly people using neuropsychological assessment has accumulated over the years, to provide clinicians with some guidance. A number of these research studies have focused upon Parkinson's disease and Alzheimer's disease; for example, Sullivan *et al.* (1989) noted that patients with Parkinson's disease had difficulty with the WAIS-R Picture Arrangement subtest in the presence of a normal Vocabulary score, whereas Alzheimer's disease patients appeared impaired on both subtests.

It is beyond the remit of this chapter to discuss other dementias in any detail. However, it is worth pointing out that an alcoholic dementia is said to exist, arising from long-term abuse, in which features of visuo-spatial and visuo-motor processing deficit may be prominent. These may be detected on WAIS Digit Symbol and Block Design subtests, in the presence of relatively good preservation of verbal functions. An important dementia to diagnose correctly, because of its reversibility, is that of normal pressure hydrocephalus, which results from obstructed cerebrospinal fluid flow (Bigler, 1988). The WAIS/WAIS-R subtests of mental Arithmetic, Digit Span and timed performance seem best able to detect its associated cognitive changes (Lezak, 1983).

Cerebrovascular disease and stroke

MID has already been mentioned above. The incidence of stroke is about 1.5 per 1,000 population per year. Pre-morbid factors often influence the type and severity of cognitive deficit arising from a stroke. For example, transient ischaemic attacks are common prior to stroke, and these cause cognitive deficits on the WAIS 'don't hold' subtests (e.g. Delaney *et al.* 1980). The research of Dull and her co-workers (Dull *et al.*, 1982) also provided data suggestive of pre-stroke deficits (the WAIS Digit Symbol subtest being particularly sensitive). The pattern of intellectual deficit produced by completed stroke depends upon which cerebral hemisphere is implicated, which vessels are affected (site and extent of damage), and type of stroke (haemorrhagic strokes can be more obliterative of brain tissue); the actual WAIS/WAIS-R profile obtained can be expected broadly to reflect the description offered earlier. Use of the Raven's Coloured Matrices is becoming more popular as a measure of intellectual level in stroke. Its relevant age norms, brief completion time, minimal motor requirements, and lack of need for competence in verbal expression or comprehension make it particularly suitable in cases of hemiplegic and/or communication-disordered stroke. David and Skilbeck (1984) noted that extremely poor performance on the RCM at initial assessment (at approximately two months post-stroke) in their sample of 148 patients was associated with death as outcome.

The Category Test of the Halstead–Reitan Test Battery has sometimes been used to assess concept formation ability in cerebrovascular disease. For example, Goldman *et al.* (1974) noted its sensitivity: in their sample of patients, hypertension was associated with adverse effects on the test. Interestingly, reduction in blood pressure led to fewer errors being made on the test.

Alcohol and drug abuse

The cognitive effects acquired from misuse of alcohol have long been of interest to neuropsychologists, and a number of general reviews are available (e.g. Tarter and Edwards, 1986; Ryan and Butters, 1986). Chronic alcohol abuse yields intellectual deficits particularly associated with frontal-lobe activity (including decreased flexibility in thinking, and loss of ability to maintain 'set'). The large literature review carried out by Parsons and Farr (1981) pointed to impaired performance by alcoholics on the Category Test. Similar findings have been reported for the Wisconsin Card Sorting Test (e.g. Tarter, 1973). On the WAIS/WAIS-R, consistent findings are that time-dependent subtests are most adversely affected (particularly Digit Symbol and Block Design), and this pattern is observed in the presence of relatively well-preserved VIQ. Even when alcoholism has progressed to the point of Korsakoff's psychosis (see Ryan and Butters, 1986), where massive memory deficits are apparent, Digit Span performance tends to remain relatively unimpaired.

In general, intellectual test performance of Korsakoff's patients is very similar to that noted from chronic alcoholic patients, and Korsakoff's patients show no deficit when compared with non-alcoholics on WAIS Information, Vocabulary, Arithmetic, Digit Span, Similarities and Picture Completion (Butters, 1981). However, the situation in alcoholic dementia (the existence of which are still the subject of some controversy; see above), is different, with general intellectual deterioration being seen. Detoxified alcoholics still seem to show persisting deficits in relation to WAIS Block-Design and Digit-Symbol performance. An added complication in assessing the relationships between alcohol misuse and intellectual functioning is the presence or absence of associated hepatic encephalopathy (see review by Tartar *et al.*, 1986). For example, alcoholics with liver cirrhosis have been shown to obtain lower WAIS PIQs than those without cirrhosis (Gilberstadt *et al.*, 1980), there being significant negative correlations of Digit Symbol, Block Design and overall PIQ, with serum albumin levels in cirrhotic patients.

61

In relation to drug abuse, studies generally fail to show intellectual deficits associated with the use of marijuana. Some laboratory studies (review by Miller, 1976) have suggested dose-related Digit Symbol slowing during use and Braff et al. (1981) also observed slowed information-processing capacity during use. The Category Test has been used to demonstrate intellectual deficit in LSD users (e.g. McGlothin et al., 1969; Acord and Barker, 1973), and Cohen and Edwards (1969) also observed such deficit using the RPM. The Category Test and RPM were both used by Hill et al. (1979) when noting that heroin users performed more poorly than both alcoholic abusers and normal controlled subjects.

Epilepsy

Epilepsy can arise from a number of factors which produce brain-tissue excitation. It is not a single disease entity, but rather a collection of symptoms relating to brain damage (though often no underlying physiological defect is identified). As epilepsy can arise from a number of different causes, it may manifest in a variety of ways, rather than presenting a specific pattern of intellectual dysfunction. The different patterns of dysfunction which are observed are characteristic of the particular variety of epilepsy under study. Similarly, the extent of intellectual dysfunction seems dependent upon how generalized seizure activity is, and also increases with the frequency of seizures. With regard to the latter, Seidenberg et al. (1981) found an impairment in WAIS VIQ and PIQ for patients whose frequency of seizure fell during the test–retest interval, whereas in patients whose seizure frequency remained stable or increased, only PIQ improved on retest. Patients with a primary focus in the left hemisphere generally show greater VIQ deficits (irrespective of whether the epileptic disturbance is acute, chronic or progressive), whereas PIQ is more adversely affected by a right hemisphere epileptic focus. The WAIS/WAIS-R subtests most affected by a temporal-lobe epilepsy focus are Digit Span, Arithmetic, Digit Symbol and Block Design. Hermann et al. (1988) found that WCST performance varied according to type of epilepsy. In patients with complex partial seizures (CPS) of the non-dominant temporal lobe, 74 per cent produced perseverative errors, compared with 39 per cent of patients with CPS of the dominant temporal lobe and 17 per cent of patients with primary generalized epilepsy. In an often-quoted WAIS study, Dikmen et al. (1975) observed that early onset epilepsy (prior to 5 years of age) was associated with greater impairment than onset between 10 and 15 years of age. Trimble and Thompson (1986) reviewed the effects of anticonvulsant medication upon cognitive functions. There are insufficient available studies to assess the effects of a range of anticonvulsants, and the evidence regarding serum level and cognitive performance is not yet conclusive. However, results suggest that prolonged usage is associated with adverse effects, and that phenobarbital yields the greatest cognitive impairment, with carbamazepine producing the fewest deficits. The adverse effects of anticonvulsant use seem most often to include concentration, information-processing speed and motor speed. The WAIS/WAIS-R subtests of Digit Span, Arithmetic and Digit Symbol might be expected to reflect these cognitive difficulties best. A number of good general reviews of the effect of epilepsy upon cognitive function have been produced, including that provided by Trimble and Thompson (1986).

Infections and HIV/AIDS

A number of meningitic or encephalitic infections can result in neuropsychological impairment. Of particular interest is herpes simplex encephalitis, which, although rare, can result in quite specific deficits if the patient survives the acute phase. This virus particularly attacks temporal and frontal cerebral tissue, the latter area of damage tending to impair goal-direct behaviour. The severity of the residual intellectual and memory deficits is variable, although the latter are often profound. In an interesting case study, Giles and Morgan (1989) described a retraining programme for a patient with herpes simplex encephalitis. The patient, who had been a university undergraduate, suffered massive intellectual deterioration as a result of his encephalitis (WAIS VIQ: 81, PIQ: 90). Five years after his encephalitis he received a functional training programme, the results of which included improvement in verbal intellectual level (8 points) and performance intellectual level (11 points).

The AIDS virus has received considerable attention in recent years, and evidence has accrued over the last three years to suggest that about two-thirds of patients with AIDS or AIDS-related complex (ARC) show neuropsychological deficits. One relevant study is that carried out by Van Gorp et al. (1989). These authors examined 47 homosexual men, including 20 with the diagnosis of AIDS, 14 with ARC, and 13 control subjects who were seronegative with no pre-morbid history of neurologically relevant disease. As part of their neuropsychological test battery Van Gorp et al. included a shortened WAIS-R (excluding the Information subtest). Their results demonstrated significantly better seronegative group scores for VIQ (P < .001) and PIQ (P < .01) compared with the AIDS patients, although not the ARC group. Within the WAIS-R no significant differences between the groups emerged in relation to Arithmetic, Vocabulary, Object Assembly, Comprehension, or Picture Arrangement, although seronegative patients scored higher on Block Design (P < .002), Digit Symbol (P < .01) and Similarities (P < .01) compared with the AIDS group. The pattern of findings was, therefore, largely one of 'don't hold' subtest sensitivity.

The fast-expanding literature on cognitive changes associated with HIV-positivity or AIDS has led the American National Institute of Mental

Health (NIMH) to suggest an extended (approximately 7–9 hours) neuropsychological test battery, and a brief (1–2 hours) battery for use with these patients (Butters *et al.*, 1990). The extended battery includes WAIS-R subtests in its components on 'indications of pre-morbid intelligence' (Vocabulary, also included here is the National Adult Reading Test), 'attention' (Digit Span), 'visuo-spatial' (Digit Symbol) and 'constructional abilities' (Block Design). The Category Test (see above) forms part of the 'abstraction' component. The NIMH recommended the extended battery for the early detection of the AIDS Dementia Complex and other neurological involvement in HIV-positive, asymptomatic people. Some data is available to suggest that cognitive deterioration associated with HIV positive status offers an early detection route, prior to the emergence of other AIDS signs. This early detection is very important, given that antiviral treatments, currently under development, are likely to be most effective in the earliest stages of the disease.

Neurotoxic problems

A small, though continuing, field in neuropsychology interest is that of toxic problems, and a number of papers in recent years have explored the relationship between toxic substances (usually industrial/occupational) and intellectual performance. For example, Eskelinen *et al.* (1986) selected a subset of WAIS subtests (Similarities, Picture Completion, Block Design, Digit Span) and noted significant impairments in all these when testing workers exposed to organic solvents. The greatest deficit was observed in relation to Digit Span. Workers in the highest 25 per cent of scores relating to urinary cadmium levels performed significantly more poorly than those in the lowest 25 per cent band on a range of cognitive tasks, with the results in relation to WCST just failing to reach a statistically acceptable level (P < .07). This latter finding was obtained again when WCST errors were examined in workers with either high or low urinary cadmium levels, the high-level subjects performing more poorly (Smith *et al.*, 1989). These subjects also showed significantly lower (P < .002) WAIS-R Digit Symbol scores. Hawkins (1990) recently reviewed the neuropsychological contribution to occupational neurotoxicology, including issues of malingering and medico-legal or compensation involvement.

In some life-threatening conditions, it is necessary to administer treatments which of themselves may have toxic side effects. Perhaps the most obvious example is that where chemical CNS (central nervous system) prophylaxis is administered to exclude cancer infiltrating into the CNS, these infiltrates not being detectable by the diagnostic techniques available at present. Fletcher and Copeland (1988) reviewed forty-one studies involving the use of prophylactic CNS chemotherapy in childhood cancers; generally these studies utilized the WISC/WISC-R as part of the neuropsychological battery, although the BAS was included in two reports. Fletcher and Copeland offered a very rigorous review of the available research and the difficulties in interpreting results where the number of potential factors influencing intellectual functioning is high. Overall, the results of these studies are suggestive of intellectual impairment associated with CNS prophylactic chemotherapy, with PIQ more often tending to show deficits.

SUMMARY

This chapter briefly introduces brain–behaviour relationships involving tests of intellectual functioning. The WAIS and WAIS-R are considered in some detail, including reference to the effects of general, lateralized and localized brain lesions upon IQ and intellectual subtests. Correspondence between WAIS-R and WAIS is good, although the latter yields higher FSIQs. Popular neuropsychological tests for assessing children's intellectual abilities include Wechsler's Scales and those developed by Raven. Other intellectual measures sometimes employed in neuropsychology include the National Adult Reading Test, Stanford–Binet, Peabody Picture Vocabulary Test and the Wide Range Achievement Tests. Although the British Ability Scales appear attractive, given their basis in a cognitive processes model, they have not yet been adopted widely in routine clinical practice.

The Halstead-Reitan Category Test and the Wisconsin Card Sorting Test are often employed when a concept formation or reasoning task is required. The Category Test is very sensitive in identifying the presence of acquired brain damage, and the WCST (and its derivative the MCST) performs well in discriminating frontal-lobe lesions from other types of specific damage.

The remainder of the chapter presents a number of clinical applications of intellectual tests, including head injury, dementias, stroke and epilepsy. The specific profiles expected from intellectual tests in these neurological conditions are outlined, concentrating as far as possible upon recent research findings.

REFERENCES

Acord, L. D. and Barker, D. D. (1973). 'Hallucinogenic drugs and cerebral deficit'. *Journal of Nervous and Mental Diseases*, 156, 281–3.

Beardsall, L. and Brayne, C. (1990). 'Estimation of verbal intelligence in an elderly community: a prediction analysis using a shortened NART'. *British Journal of Clinical Psychology*, 29, 83–90.

Beck, N. C., Horwitz, E., Seidenberg, M., Parker, J. and Frank, R. (1985). 'WAIS-R factor structure in psychiatric and general medical patients'. *Journal of Consulting and Clinical Psychology*, 53, 402–5.

Bigler, E. D. (1988). 'The neuropsychology of hydrocephalus'. *Archives of Clinical Neuropsychology*, 3, 81–100.

Bornstein, R. A. (1984). 'Unilateral lesions and WAIS-R: no sex differences'. *Journal of Consulting and Clinical Psychology*, 52, 604–8.

Boyle, G. J. (1988). 'What does the neuropsychological category test measure?' *Archives of Clinical Neuropsychology*, 3, 69–76.

Braff, D. L., Silverton, L., Saccuzzo, D. P. and Janowsky, D. S. (1981). 'Impaired speed of visual information processing in marijuana intoxication'. *American Journal of Psychiatry*, 138, 613–17.

Brooks, D. N. (ed.) (1984). *Closed Head Injury: Psychological, Social and Family Consequences*. Oxford and New York: Oxford University Press.

Butters, N. (1981). 'The Wernicke–Korsakoff syndrome: a review of psychological, neuropathological and aetiological factors'. In M. Galanter (ed.), *Currents in Alcoholism*, vol. 8. New York: Grune and Stratton.

Butters, N., Grant, I., Haxby, J. *et al.* (1990). 'Assessment of Aids-related cognitive changes: recommendations of the NIMH workshop on neuropsychological assessment approaches'. *Journal of Clinical and Experimental Neuropsychology*, 12, 963–78.

Caine, E. D. (1986). 'The neuropsychology of depression: the pseudodementia syndrome'. In I. Grant and K. M. Adams (eds), *Neuropsychological Assessment of Neuropsychiatric Disorders*. Oxford and New York: Oxford University Press.

Chelune, G. J. and Baer, R. A. (1986). 'Developmental norms for the Wisconsin Card Sorting Test'. *Journal of Clinical and Experimental Neuropsychology*, 8, 219–28.

Cohen, S. and Edwards, A. E. (1969). 'LSD and organic brain impairment'. *Drug Dependence*, 2, 1–4.

Crawford, J. R., Allan, K. M., Besson, J. A. O., Cochrane, R. H. B. and Stewart, L. E. (1990). 'A comparison of the WAIS and WAIS-R in matched UK samples'. *British Journal of Clinical Psychology*, 29, 105–10.

Crawford, J. R., Parker, D. M., Stewart, L. E., Besson, V. A. O. and De Lacey, G. (1989). 'Prediction of WAIS IQ with the National Adult Reading Test: cross-validation and extension'. *British Journal of Clinical Psychology*, 28, 267–74.

Cullum, C. M. and Bigler, E. D. (1986). 'Ventricle size, cortical atrophy and the relationship with neuropsychological status in closed head injury: a quantitative analysis'. *Journal of Clinical and Experimental Neuropsychology*, 8, 437–52.

David, R. M. and Skilbeck, C. E. (1984). 'Raven IQ and language recovery following stroke'. *Journal of Clinical Neuropsychology*, 6, 302–8.

Delaney, R. C., Wallace, J. D. and Egelko, S. (1980). 'Transient cerebral ischaemic attacks and neuropsychological deficit'. *Journal of Clinical Neuropsychology*, 2, 107–14.

Dikmen, S., Matthews, C. G. and Harley, J. P. (1975). 'The effect of early versus late onset of major motor epilepsy upon cognitive-intellectual functions'. *Epilepsia*, 16, 73–81.

Dull, R. A., Brown, G., Adams, K. M., Shatz, M. W., Diaz, F. G. and Ausman, J. I. (1982). 'Preoperative neurobehavioural impairment in cerebral revascularisation candidates'. *Journal of Clinical Neuropsychology*, 4, 151–66.

Elliott, C. D., Murray, D. J. and Pearson, L. S. (1983). *The British Ability Scales – Revised*. Windsor: NFER-Nelson.

Eskelinen, L., Luisto, M., Tenkane, L. and Mattel, O. (1986). 'Neuropsychological methods in the differentiation of organic solvent intoxication from certain neurological conditions'. *Journal of Clinical and Experimental Neuropsychology*, 8, 239–56.

Field, J. H. (1976). *Epidemiology of Head Injuries in England and Wales*. London: HMSO.

Filley, C. M., Kobayashi, J. and Heaton, R. K. (1987). 'Wechsler Intelligence Scale profiles, the cholinergic system, and Alzheimer's disease'. *Journal of Clinical and Experimental Neuropsychology*, 9, 180–6.

Filskov, S. B. and Leli, D. A. (1981). 'Assessment of the individual in neuropsychological practice'. In S. B. Filskov and T. J. Boll (eds), *Handbook of Clinical Neuropsychology*. Chichester: John Wiley.

Finlayson, M. A. J., Sullivan, J. F. and Alfano, D. P. (1986). 'Halstead's Category Test: withstanding the test of time'. *Journal of Clinical and Experimental Neuropsychology*, 8, 706–26.

Fletcher, J. M. and Copeland, D. R. (1988). 'Neurobehavioural effects of central nervous system prophylactic treatment of cancer in children'. *Journal of Clinical and Experimental Neuropsychology*, 10, 495–537.

Fuld, P. A. (1984). 'Test profile of cholinergic dysfunction and of Alzheimer's disease'. *Journal of Clinical and Experimental Neuropsychology*, 6, 380–92.

Gibson, A. J., Moyes, I. C. A. and Kendrick, D. C. (1980). 'Cognitive assessment of the elderly long stay patient'. *British Journal of Psychiatry*, 137, 537–57.

Gilberstadt, S., Gilberstadt, H., Zieve, L., Buegal, B., Collier, R. O. and McClain, C. J. (1980). 'Psychomotor performance deficits in cirrhotic patients without overt encephalopathy'. *Archives of Internal Medicine*, 140, 519–21.

Giles, G. M. and Morgan, J. H. (1989). 'Training functional skills following herpes simplex encephalitis: A single-case study'. *Journal of Clinical and Experimental Neuropsychology*, 11, 311–18.

Goldman, H., Kleinman, K. M., Snow, M. Y. *et al.* (1974). 'Correlation of diastolic blood pressure and signs of cognitive dysfunction in essential hypertension'. *Diseases of the Nervous System*, 35, 571–2.

Hawkins, K. A. (1990). 'Occupational neurotoxicology: some neuropsychological issues and challenges'. *Journal of Clinical and Experimental Neuropsychology*, 12, 664–80.

Hermann, B. P., Wyler, A. R. and Richey, E. T. (1988). 'Wisconsin Card Sorting Test performance in patients with complex partial seizures of temporal-lobe origin'. *Journal of Clinical and Experimental Neuropsychology*, 10, 467–76.

Hill, S. Y., Reyes, R. B., Mikhael, M. and Ayre, F. (1979). 'A Comparison of alcoholics and heroin abusers: computerised transaxial tomography and neuropsychological functioning'. *Currents in Alcoholism*, 5, 187–205.

Jastak, J. F. and Jastak, S. R. (1965). *Wide Range Achievements Test Manual*. Chicago: Guidance Associates.

Kane, R. L., Parsons, O. A. and Goldstein, G. (1985). 'Statistical relationships and discriminative accuracy of the Halstead–Reitan, Luria–Nebraska and Wechsler IQ scores in the identification of brain damage'. *Journal of Clinical and Experimental Neuropsychology*, 7, 211–23.

Kendrick, D. C., Gibson, A. N. and Moyes, I. C. A. (1979). 'The Revised Kendrick Battery: clinical studies'. *British Journal of Social and Clinical Psychology*, 18, 329–39.

Kluger, A. and Goldberg, E. (1990). 'IQ patterns in affective disorder, lateralised and diffuse brain damage'. *Journal of Clinical and Experimental Neuropsychology*, 12, 182–94.

Korman, M., Mathews, R. W. and Lovitt, R. (1981). 'Neuropsychological effects of abuse of inhalants'. *Perceptual and Motor Skills*, 53, 547–53.

Larrabee, G. J., Kane, R. L. and Schuck, J. R. (1983). 'Factor analysis of the WAIS and Wechsler Memory Scale: an analysis of the construct validity of the Wechsler Memory Scale'. *Journal of Clinical Neuropsychology*, 5, 159–68.

Levin, H. S., Grossman, R. G., Rose, J. E. and Teasdale, G. (1979). 'Long-term neuropsychological outcome of closed head injury'. *Journal of Neurosurgery*, 50, 412–22.

Lezak, M. D. (1983). *Neuropsychological Assessment*. 2nd edn. Oxford and New York: Oxford University Press.

Logsdon, R. G., Teri, L., Williams, D. E., Vitiello, M. V. and Prinz, P. N. (1989). 'The WAIS-R Profile: a diagnostic tool for Alzheimer's disease?'. *Journal of Clinical and Experimental Neuropsychology*, 6, 892–8.

McFie, J. (1975). *Assessment of Organic Intellectual Impairment*. London: Academic Press.

McGlothin, W. H., Arnold, D. O. and Freedman, D. X. (1969). 'Organicity measurements following repeated LSD ingestion.' *Archives of General Psychiatry*, 21, 704–9.

Mandleberg, I. A. and Brooks, D. N. (1975). 'Cognitive recovery after severe head injury, serial testing on the Wechsler Adult Intelligence Scale'. *Journal of Neurology, Neurosurgery and Psychiatry*, 38, 1121–6.

Matarazzo, G. D. (1972). *Wechsler's Measurement and Appraisal of Adult Intelligence*. 5th edn. Baltimore: Williams and Wilkins.

Matarazzo, G. D. and Herman, D. O. (1984). 'Base rate, data for the WAIS-R: test–retest reliability and VIQ–PIQ differences'. *Journal of Clinical Neuropsychology*, 6, 351–66.

Miller, L. L. (1976). 'Marijuana and human cognition: a review of laboratory investigations'. In S. Cohen and R. C. Stillman (eds), *The Therapeutic Potential of Marijuana*. London: Plenum Press.

Milner, B. (1963). 'Effects of different brain lesions on card sorting'. *Archives of Neurology*, 9, 90–100.

Naglieri, J. A. (1982). 'Two types of table for use with the WAIS-R'. *Journal of Consulting and Clinical Psychology*, 50, 319–21.

Nelson, H. E. (1976). 'A modified Card Sorting Test sensitive to frontal lobe defects'. *Cortex*, 12, 313–24.

Nelson, H. (1982). *The National Adult Reading Test*. Windsor: NFER-Nelson.

Nelson, H. E. and O'Connell, A. (1978). 'Dementia: the estimation of premorbid intelligence levels using the New Adult Reading Test'. *Cortex*, 14, 234–44.

Parsons, O. A. and Farr, S. D. (1981). 'The neuropsychology of alcohol and drug abuse'. In S. B. Filskov and T. J. Boll (eds), *Handbook of Clinical Neuropsychology*. Chichester: John Wiley.

Prifitera, A. and Barley, W. D. (1985). 'Cautions in interpretation of comparisons between the WAIS-R and the WMS'. *Journal of Consulting and Clinical Psychology*, 53, 564–5.

Raven, J. C. (1977). *Manuals for Raven's Progressive Matrices and Coloured Matrices*. London: Lewis.

Reitan, R. M. and Davison, L. A. (eds) (1974). *Clinical Neuropsychology: Current Status and Applications*. Buckingham: Winston-Wiley.

Reitan, R. M. and Wolfson, D. (1986). 'The Halstead–Reitan Neuropsychological Test Battery'. In D. Wedding, A. M. Horton and J. Webster (eds), *The Neuropsychology Handbook*. New York: Springer.

Robinson, A. L., Heaton, R. K., Lehmen, R. A. and Stilson, D. (1980). 'The utility of the WCST in detecting and localising frontal lobe regions'. *Journal of Consulting and Clinical Psychology*, 48, 605–14.

Ryan, C. and Butters, N. (1986). 'The neuropsychology of alcoholism'. In D. Wedding, A. M. Horton and J. Webster (eds), *The Neuropsychology Handbook*. New York: Springer.

Savage, R. D., Britton, P. G., Bolton, N. and Hall, E. H. (1973). *Intellectual Functioning in the Aged*. London: Harper and Row.

Seidenberg, M., O'Leary, D. S., Berent, S. and Boll, T. (1981). 'Changes in seizure frequency and test–retest scores on the Wechsler Adult Intelligence Scale'. *Epilepsia*, 22, 75–83.

Smith, A. and Milner, B. (1985). 'Differential effects of frontal lobe lesions on cognitive estimation and spatial memory'. *Neuropsychologia*, 22, 697–705.

Smith, B. D., Meyers, M. B. and Kline, R. (1989). 'Neuropsychological effects of occupational exposure to cadmium'. *Journal of Clinical and Experimental Neuropsychology*, 11, 933–43.

Snow, W. G., Tierney, M. C., Zorzitto, M. I. *et al.* (1990). 'WAIS-R test–retest reliability in a normal elderly sample'. *Journal of Clinical and Experimental Neuropsychology*, 12(b), 873–86.

Stuss, D. T. and Benson, F. D. (1985). *The Frontal Lobes*. London: Raven Press.

Sullivan, E. V., Sagar, J. D. E., Gabrieli, J. D. E., Corkin, S. and Crowdon, J. H. (1989). 'Different cognitive profiles on standard behavioural tests in Parkinson's disease and Alzheimer's disease'. *Journal of Clinical and Experimental Neuropsychology*, 11, 799–820.

Tarter, R. E. (1973). 'An analysis of cognitive deficits in chronic alcoholics'. *Journal of Nervous and Mental Diseases*, 157, 138–47.

Tarter, R. and Edwards, K. (1986). 'Neuropsychology of alcoholism'. In R. Tarter and D. Van Thiel (eds), *Alcohol and the Brain: Chronic Effects*. London: Plenum Press.

Tarter, R. E., Edwards, K. L. and Van Thiel, D. H. (1986). 'Hepatic encephalopathy'. In G. Goldstein and R. E. Tarter (eds), *Advances in Clinical Neuropsychology*, vol. 3. London: Plenum Press.

Trimble, M. R. and Thompson, P. J. (1986). 'Neuropsychological aspects of epilepsy'. In I. Grant and K. M. Adams (eds), *Neuropsychological Assessment of Neuropsychiatric Disorders*'. Oxford and New York: Oxford University Press.

Van Gorp, W., Miller, E. N., Satz, P. and Visscher, B. (1989). 'Neuropsychological performance in HIV-I immunocompromised patients: a preliminary report'. *Journal of Clinical and Experimental Neuropsychology*, 11, 763–73.

Walton, J. (1985). *Brain's Diseases of the Nervous System*. 9th edn. Oxford and New York: Oxford University Press.

Wechsler, D. (1981). *WAIS-R Manual*. London: Psychological Corporation.

Woods, R. T. and Britton, P. G. (1985). *Clinical Psychology with the Elderly*. London: Croom Helm.

Zillmer, E. A., Fowler, P. C., Newman, A. C. and Archer, R. P. (1988). 'Relationships between the WAIS and neuropsychological measures for neuropsychiatric inpatients'. *Archives of Clinical Neuropsychology*, 3, 33–46.

Part II

4

ASSESSMENT OF DEFICITS IN VISUAL FUNCTION

Alistair G. R. Rennie

The purpose of this chapter is to familiarize the reader with ophthalmic tests which will help with the overall assessment of the patient with neurological deficit. As well as assessment of pure visual function, full clinical examination of the eyes, including assessment of the ocular contents, response of the pupils to light and accommodation, and examination of uniocular and binocular eye movements, is necessary.

The main tests of visual function are assessment of:

1 visual acuity

2 visual fields

3 optokinetic nystagmus and nystagmus present

4 electrophysiology of the eyes

5 colour vision

6 dark adaptation

7 binocularity

VISUAL ACUITY

Visual acuity is a measurement of the resolving power of the eye and is commonly expressed as a fraction. For example, 6/6 is the acuity at 6 metres of what can normally be seen at this distance; 6/36 is the acuity at 6 metres of what can normally be seen at 36 metres (about 16 per cent of normal distance acuity).

The Landolt Ring Test uses a chart with a series of broken rings, where the break can normally be seen at given distances. Similarly, Snellan's Types have been constructed so that individual letters can be discerned at a given distance (Figure 4.1). No knowledge of letters is necessary in the Landolt Ring Test and matching tests such as the E Test and Sheridan Gardiner Test, where the patient compares what he or she sees in the

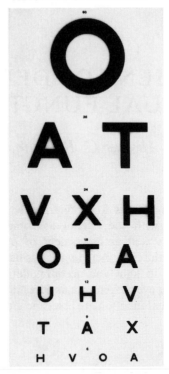

Figure 4.1 Snellan's Test Types

distance with a similar pattern held in his or her hand. Vision poorer than 1/60 is recorded by the ability to count fingers at one metre and, if less than this, by the recognition of hand movements before the eye. The poorest level of vision is perception of light with inaccurate localization of the light (poor projection). Near vision is measured at 25 cm and is expressed in terms of the size of print which can be read. Good illumination is necessary for these tests, and testing both distance and near acuity can give useful information regarding any visual deficit. Good near vision and poor distance vision suggest short sight.

Refraction is the means by which a spectacle error can be assessed. A beam of light is shone into the eye being tested and the effect of the optical system of the eye on the movement of the light reflected from the eye noted. Appropriate lenses are then placed in front of the eye to neutralize the effect of the eye on the beam of light, and adjustments are made to the findings to produce the final spectacle correction. In the absence of any opacification of the media of the eye, the refractive error can be corrected by holding a card with a pinhole in front of the eye and reading the Snellan's chart to give a rough assessment of corrected visual acuity.

Accommodation decreases with age, so that a separate distance and near

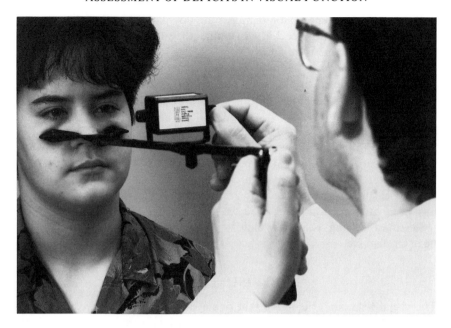

Figure 4.2 The RAF Near Point Rule

spectacle correction may be necessary (presbyopia). It is therefore important for distance and near acuity to be measured with the appropriate spectacle correction. The RAF Near Point Rule (Figure 4.2) can be used to assess accommodation and convergence. In the first instance the distance at which the print blurs on the rule gives the near point of accommodation. A single line can also be presented to the eyes and the distance at which it doubles gives the nearpoint of convergence. Unlike accommodation, convergence is not affected by ageing, but the latter is affected by extraocular muscle imbalance, and both can be affected by neurological disease. Visual acuity is often assessed uniocularly.

Covering one eye can induce *nystagmus* in the uncovered eye (latent nystagmus). This rhythmic involuntary oscillation of the eye will cause poorer uniocular acuity than might be expected from the binocular acuity. Latent nystagmus, particularly common in subjects who have squints, should therefore be looked for and binocular acuity assessed in these cases so that a better idea of visual ability is obtained.

In *amblyopia* (defective vision developed in childhood to avoid blurred vision from a squinting eye) a row of letters is seen less clearly than individual letters (crowding phenomenon). A test of acuity based on individual letters or symbols therefore gives a less accurate assessment of visual ability in amblyopia.

Blind sight is a phenomenon demonstrated by patients with occipital lobe pathology who do not see but insist that they can (Anton's Syndrome). Routine acuity testing is obviously impossible.

In *hysterical blindness* the patient denies seeing, usually for short periods, and may complain of bright lights and colours interfering with his or her vision. When some vision is felt to be present, constricted fields of vision are usually found on testing.

In very young children some idea of visual acuity may be obtained by looking for following movements of the eyes with Catford's equipment, which presents an oscillating dot at 25 cm. The size of the dot can be varied and an attempt has been made to correlate this to an equivalent distance acuity measurement. More recently, assessment of vision in the very young has been attempted using contrasted patterns and the phenomenon of preferential viewing, where the child will choose to observe the pattern that he or she can see.

THE VISUAL FIELD

The visual field is all the space that one eye can see at any given instance. Visual field defects can be demonstrated on a flat screen (campimetry) or on an instrument which is hemispherical or arc-shaped (perimetry). In the first case central visual field is tested and in the latter peripheral visual field, as well as central, can be tested.

Kinetic field testing involves moving test objects, and static field testing involves assessment of the sensitivity of the eye at pre-selected locations. With the Goldman perimeter, kinetic central and peripheral field testing as well as static field testing can be performed (Figure 4.3).

When a portion of the visual field is defective or blind but surrounded by vision that is better than the visual function in the defective area, the affected area is called a *scotoma*. This may be absolute or relative depending on its presence or absence with different strengths of stimuli.

Hemianopia is a field defect where there is contraction of half of the field of vision of either or both eyes. Because of the arrangement of the nerve fibres in the visual pathway, lesions involving the optic chiasma typically cause partial or complete loss of the temporal field of both eyes, that is, bitemporal hemianopia. Lesions further back are likely to involve the nasal field on the same side and the temporal field on the opposite side, resulting in a homonymous hemianopia. Similar homonymous defects are said to be congruous. Perfectly congruous field defects are usually caused by lesions in or near the visual cortex. Incongruous homonymous defects are usually caused by optic tract lesions immediately behind the chiasma. In lesions of the visual cortex the hemianopic defect rarely involves fixation, whereas further forwards splitting of the macula (central fixation) commonly occurs, causing increased visual difficulty (Figure 4.4).

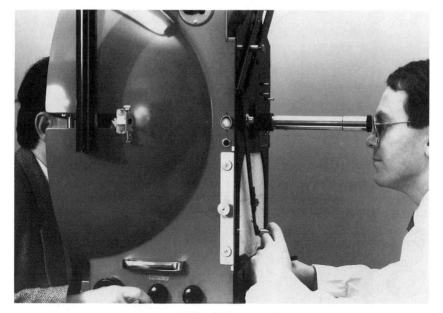

Figure 4.3 The Goldman perimeter

Unilateral neglect typically occurs in parietal lobe lesions. It appears that the body image depends on an intact parietal lobe. Lesions of one side cause neglect of the opposite side of the body and surrounding field of vision so that bilateral simultaneous stimuli are not recognized, but when tested separately, fields of vision are present on both sides.

OPTOKINETIC NYSTAGMUS

Optokinetic nystagmus can be used to demonstrate the presence of vision as, for example, in hysterical blindness. Rotating a striped drum in front of the patient gives rise to biphasic, jerky, rhythmic movements with a slow phase in the direction of movement and a fast phase back to central fixation. In hemianopia due to lesions of the chiasma or optic tracts, optokinetic nystagmus is retained although its amplitude may be diminished. In hemianopia due to lesions further back, the response varies. Lesions in the parietal lobe usually given an asymmetrical optokinetic response with horizontal testing, probably due to interference with the efferent pathway of the optokinetic reflex rather than the hemianopia.

The spontaneous presence of jerky nystagmus may indicate the presence of central nervous system disease. However, congenital nystagmus, which may be X-linked, recessive or dominant in inheritance, is usually a jerky nystagmus and has no sinister associations. Spasmus nutans is characterized

77

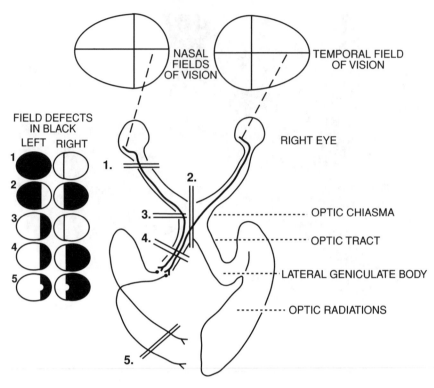

Figure 4.4 Field defects due to damage to the visual pathway:
1 Blindness of the left eye
2 Bitemporal hemianopia
3 Left nasal hemianopia
4 Right homonymous hemianopia (when left nasal and right temporal fields are lost).
5 Right homonymous hemianopia with sparing of the macular vision

by a pendular nystagmus (the speed of this nystagmus is the same in both directions) and develops between four and twelve months of age in association with an abnormal head posture and head nodding. It usually disappears by 3 years of age. Nystagmus due to ocular conditions occurs in congenital cataract, albinism and disease of the retina and optic nerve. If a child loses central vision prior to 2 years of age, he or she usually develops nystagmus. This is typically pendular and horizontal.

ELECTROPHYSIOLOGICAL TESTS OF THE EYES

Electrophysiological tests of the eye can help locate the site of a visual defect.

The electroretinogram

The electroretinogram (ERG) measures changes in the corneo-retinal potential when the retina is illuminated. One electrode is placed on the cornea and the other on the face. The patient's pupils are dilated and the eyes dark-adapted to give maximum response. The normal ERG has three main components: the A Wave, produced by the retinal photoreceptors; the B Wave, produced by the retinal Muller's cells, and the C Wave, produced by the retinal pigment epithelium. Subnormal responses occur when large areas of the retina do not function. Negative responses occur in acute and total retinal circulatory disturbances. Reduced or extinguished response occurs in failure of retinal function, such as in retinitis pigmentosa.

The electro-oculogram

The electro-oculogram (EOG) is also a measurement of the corneo-retinal potential. It is measured with one electrode attached to the skin at the medial canthus and the other at the lateral canthus, and the eye moved from side to side through 30 to 40 degrees. The potential is generated in part by the pigment epithelium and so is reduced in disease of the retinal pigment epithelium. The EOG sometimes shows changes at an earlier stage than the ERG.

The visual evoked response

The visual evoked response (VER) is a refinement of the electro-encephalo-gram. It is the electrical response to repeated flashes of light which can be detected with electrodes in the occipital region. The VER is predominantly a foveal response but also reflects the function of peripheral retina, as well as the central visual pathways. Prolongation of the time from stimulation to electrical activity (latency) and reduced amplitude of VER occur in gross damage of the visual pathways; for example, in demyelinating disease.

OTHER FORMS OF ASSESSMENT

Colour vision testing

This is a test of cone function. Diseases affecting cone function can change colour values. Defects in colour vision can be inherited and are commoner in males than females. When testing for colour vision defects it is important that appropriate spectacles are worn. The Farnsworth Munsell 100 Hue Test involves matching varying hues and scoring the errors made. Simpler tests, such as the City University and Guy's Colour Vision Test for Children, are also of value. The Ishihara pseudo-isochromatic plates do not pick up blue–yellow defects. Normally three cone types are available to assess colour (tricromats). When only two cone types are available the individuals are known as dicromats, and when only one cone type is present vision is restricted to black, white and grey (monocromats).

Dark adaptation testing

This can show defective rod function. The first part of the response is rapid and is due to cone dark adaptation. Thereafter the response is slowed, but by the end of one hour the vision has increased many thousand times due to rod function. This is not a routine clinical test but can be used to support the diagnosis of conditions like retinitis pigmentosa. Various dark adaptometers have been devised to measure this increased sensitivity of the retina on passing from light to dark.

Tests of binocular single vision

These are of value when a sharp image is not formed on the fovea of each eye simultaneously. If this problem persists during the first eight years of life, binocular single vision may never be attained, with its advantages of increased visual acuity, increased field of vision and stereopsis. Simultaneous macular perception, fusion and stereopsis are the three grades of binocular single vision and can be tested on the synoptophore (Figure 4.5).

The Frisby Stereotest is a useful portable test of stereopsis, in which the subject is required to discern a patterned circle lying on the opposite side of plates of varying thickness with a similar pattern covering the rest of the other side.

Latent squint, which is squint which can normally be controlled, can be demonstrated by dissociating the eyes (the cover test). If the control breaks down, a manifest squint results. Other squints are caused by paresis of extraocular muscles. Such disruptions of binocularity are likely to interfere with the visual component of reading if suppression of the vision of the squinting eye does not occur.

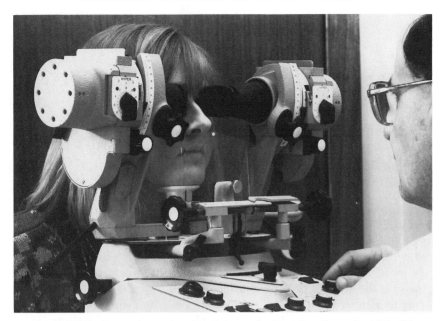

Figure 4.5 The synotophore, showing the two viewing tubes through which slides can be viewed by each eye to test for the grades of binocular single vision present

Divergent squints or even latent divergent squints are particularly likely to interfere with convergence, an important mechanism in reading at near. It is important to look at eye movements for distance and near as well as the eye movements from distance to near, as some tracking defects can be corrected with good effect. Another test which can be done with the synotophore is the Dunlop Test, which assesses ocular dominance. Some dyslexic children lack a dominant eye and after the age of 8 years can derive benefit from occlusion of one eye over a short period of time to give them a dominant eye. This can produce apparent improvement in reading ability.

FURTHER READING

Cogan, D. G. (1966). *Neurology of the Visual System*. Chicago: Thomas.
Duke-Elder, S. (1971). *System of Ophthalmology. Vol. XII, Neuro-Ophthalmology*. London: Henry Kimpton.
Stein, J. and Fowler S. (1985). 'Effect of monocular occlusion on visumotor perception and reading in dyslexic children'. *Lancet*, 13 July, 69.

5

ASSESSMENT OF SENSORI-MOTOR IMPAIRMENTS

David M. Anderson and Elizabeth Fairgrieve

Sensori-motor impairment can be the consequence of disease, insult or injury. Effects on functional daily living can be disabling in varying ways, some transient and others more permanent. Therapists frequently have to judge these effects in planning therapeutic programmes and have therefore developed assessment strategies. Many consist of structured observations based on the findings of early neurologists and psychologists, the purpose being to identify the degree of dysfunction on daily living, to plan therapy and to measure change. Planning remediation involves consideration of the aetiology of dysfunction and consequent possibilities for recovery versus teaching adaptive strategies. More recently, specific standardized assessments have emerged, a number of them devised by therapists.

Structured observation may be a convenient tool for assessment of adult dysfunction, but with children it poses more problems. Sensori-motor efficiency and skill develop from the dependence of the infant through school years to the functional competence of adult life, and decline in old age. Impairment may be a subtle but more disabling adjunct to physical handicap, or be equally disabling without or with only mild motor dysfunction. It can result in a hidden handicap.

This chapter concentrates on the effects of sensori-motor impairment resulting from dysfunction, disease or injury within the central nervous system. The processing of sensori-motor function within the central nervous system is not fully known. Much has been developed on the basis of possible hypotheses and has led to the development of several assessment tools (Ayres, 1979; Laszlo and Bairstow, 1985). Publication has stimulated debate and the proposed theoretical frameworks have been questioned. Nevertheless, there is a recognition that assessment in this sphere is complex.

Dysfunction may be the consequence of perceptual as well as sensori-motor impairments; hence several standardized assessment batteries have recognized the interplay between perceptual and somatosensory processing on function. Emphasis is also placed on evaluation of the patient's mental competence, state of alertness and behavioural reactions. Observations may be recorded on check-lists included with standardized tests, or drafted into a structured format to ensure comprehensive information.

Assessments described in this chapter are those used by physiotherapists or occupational therapists in clinical work. Throughout the text 'therapist' is used without differentiation. Within the multi-disciplinary team, physiotherapists traditionally focus on posture and mobility and occupational therapists on hand function and perceptual and self-care skills. Both are involved with the functional effects of disability. Overlapping aspects in multi-disciplinary assessment can be helpful in ensuring a holistic view of the patient's needs is maintained. Kielhofner's (1985) model of human occupation is useful here as it emphasizes the importance of linking assessment and therapeutic intervention with a patient's lifestyle and ambitions.

Throughout the text, reference is made to a range of standardized test batteries and individual tests used by therapists. Selection of appropriate assessment tools is influenced by diagnosis, available assessment tools, cost and the examiner's skills. Henderson's (1987) classification of tests used in the assessment of 'clumsy' children fell into three categories – descriptive, diagnostic and neurodevelopmental – and provided insight into the advantages and limitations of each type which merits consideration for all age groups. Tobin and Henderson (1991) have drawn attention to other multifaceted aspects of assessment which are focused on throughout this chapter. To assist selection, two publications, King-Thomas and Hacker (1987) and Whittle and Wood (1992), give a survey of assessments available for therapists working with children.

Structured observation and clinical tests continue to form a significant part of therapy assessments. The validity and reliability of assessments and their interpretation have been questioned, since results reflect subjective professional opinion and are dependent on knowledge, expertise and post-qualification experience. Structured assessment formats linked with administration and scoring guidelines are being developed. Some have been published. Reliability can be assisted by opportunity to assess normal subjects. Parallel assessment of patients and interdisciplinary assessment also support reliability when results reach common conclusions.

MUSCLE TONE AND SPASTICITY

Definition and use of the term 'muscle tone' can be influenced by the sphere of interest from which it is viewed. It may be thought of in terms of its purpose and defined as that state of resting muscle which is necessary to preserve posture or which is maintained to be prepared for quick action (Sherrington, 1906). Clinicians describe muscle tone as that sensation of resistance encountered by the examiner's hand when passively extending a muscle, with the subject attempting to relax.

Dysfunction within the central nervous system may result in disturbance of muscle tone. Various terms are used to describe disturbances of muscle tone, such as 'hypotonia', 'hypertonia', 'dyskinesia' and 'bradykinesia'. For this chapter the focus is on hypotonia and spastic hypertonia. Clinically they are comparatively easy to recognize, but they prove difficult to describe and quantify accurately. Both hypotonia and spastic hypertonia result in impaired movement, the effects on patients differing in the severity and balance of the various components of the syndromes. Changes in tone over a period of time can be part of the pathology.

Hypotonia is characterized by impaired voluntary movement, limited co-contraction of muscles affecting joint stability, increased range of motion and fatiguability. Tendon reflexes may be reduced but the presence of brisk reflexes can be diagnostically significant. Estimation of presence or lack of muscle power can also be significant. Differentiation between the pattern of symptoms within hypotonia can aid diagnosis; dysfunction can arise from different parts of the motor system.

Spasticity has been defined as 'a condition resulting from hyper-excitability of the stretch reflex'. It is characterized by impaired voluntary movement, weakness, fatiguability and abnormal cutaneous reflexes (Katz and Zev Rymer, 1989). The impaired movement results from weak and poorly co-ordinated contraction of the agonist muscles combined with inappropriate contraction of the antagonists. There is stiffness or resistance to passive movement due to an exaggeration of the stretch reflex, which has been confirmed electromyographically. The effects of exaggerated stretch reflexes are encountered most strongly in anti-gravity muscles, namely the adductors of the arms and legs, the flexors of the arms and the extensors of the legs.

Modes of assessment

Observation of the way in which patients move and passive movement of the patients' trunk and limbs have been the traditional means of assessment. This gives imprecise information, and is subjective and dependent on clinical expertise. The effect of passive movement at joints is complex; for instance, where there is resistance the extremity will attempt to preserve its state of rest, caused by either the inherent physical characteristics of connective and muscle tissue, or the involuntary reaction of the tissues in response to an external stimulus. Nevertheless, observation combined with passive movement remains the most common method of assessment.

Observation focuses on posture, quality of movement and strategies adopted by the patient to overcome dysfunction. Information gained from handling the patient can be through palpating muscles, determining range of motion and ability to move through the range and sustain co-contraction.

A variety of clinical scales, electrophysiological studies and pendulum models have been used to quantify spastic hypertonia. The Ashworth Scale

(Ashworth, 1964: see Box 5.1) is a subjective method of evaluating spasticity and can be applied to the whole body. The pendulum model and sphygmomanometer technique are applied to lower limbs only.

Box 5.1

The Ashworth Scale

1 No increase in muscle tone.
2 Slight increase in tone when affected part(s) moved in flexion or extension.
3 More marked increase in tone but affected part(s) easily flexed.
4 Considerable increase in tone: passive movement difficult.
5 Affected part(s) rigid in flexion or extension.

Recently reintroduced and computerized, the Wartenberg Pendulum Test (1951) is a simple but precise test to evaluate spasticity. The present form can be applied to individuals from early teens onwards (Brown *et al.*, 1993). The patient sits on a bench with legs hanging freely from the knee. An electronic goniometer is attached to the knee joint. This measures knee angle and allows subsequent analysis by a microcomputer. The relaxed leg is lifted to horizontal and released to swing freely. Reflex contraction of the quadriceps muscle modifies the swing pattern of the leg. Validity is dependent on the patient being relaxed and neither assisting nor resisting pendular movement of the leg.

From neonate to early teenage years the degree of hypertonicity can be quantified by using a standard sphygmomanometer (Young *et al.*, 1978). Used in Dundee since 1977, its validity was tested in 1988 on normal schoolchildren between $4\frac{1}{2}$ and $7\frac{1}{2}$ years.

The relaxed child lies supine with the head in mid-line. The paediatric cuff of a standard mercury sphygmomanometer is inflated to give a reading of 10 mm/Hg. The inflated cuff is placed along the long axis of the child's foot and held in place by the examiner, knee extension being maintained by his or her free hand. The child's foot is gently dorsi-flexed to the plantigrade position. Readings are taken from the scale during the first two or three excursions of the foot.

These methods of assessing muscle tone can alert therapists to changes in pathology and the effects of drugs or therapy. The effects of growth spurts on muscle tone particularly in cerebral palsied children can be readily monitored and will influence, for example, orthotic prescription (Meadows *et al.*, 1980) and other physiotherapeutic interventions.

SOMATOSENSORY PERCEPTION

Skilled movement is dependent on sensory feedback. Without an intact and integrated somatosensory system, dysfunction can result in neglect of specific body parts or unco-ordinated movement. Processing information from the body senses via mechanoreceptors is largely unconscious. Awareness of the automatic adjustments made by sensory feedback comes to a conscious level when the unfamiliar or unexpected occurs; for example, preparing to lift a weighty parcel only to find it lighter than anticipated. Quick adjustment is necessary. Memory from previous experience influences preparation to lift; rapid feedback and feed-forward impulses from body senses promote adjustment effort.

Somatosenses are divided into three groups: tactile, proprioceptive and vestibular. Touch alone has direct contact with the enviroment and, though included with special senses, combines with proprioception for discriminative function. At birth, sensory pathways are present but not totally functional. Developing efficiency of sensory-system processing is dependent on interplay between continued development of central nervous system processes and sensori-motor experience. Arising from this interplay are learned skills which become automatic as they no longer require conscious awareness.

Disturbance of sensori-motor function is determined by the type and distribution of trauma, disease or dysfunction. Consequences may result in sensory loss, sensory disturbance or the inability to attach meaning to sensory stimuli. Examples of the different functional effects include unilateral neglect, one consequence of cerebral damage; sensory disturbance, as in multiple sclerosis; or delayed maturation in children with sensori-motor dysfunction.

Several researchers have proposed inadequate somatosensory processing as contributing to motor-learning difficulties in children. Laszlo and Bairstow (1985) focus on kinaesthesia, while Ayres (1979, 1988) considers tactile, proprioceptive and vestibular systems important. Ayres' hypothesis also suggests that children may have hypo- or hyper-responsive systems. However, such causal relationships should be viewed with caution. Hypotheses may appear logical, but further research is needed before such relationships are universally confirmed. Awareness of current theoretical frameworks may assist analysis provided caution is exercised when reporting results.

Modes of assessment

To examine somatosensory function, vision must be occluded and care taken to exclude other sensory cues. Comparison of interpretation of sensory stimuli between unaffected and affected parts is essential. Presentation of trial items to unaffected or least affected parts first can assist understanding of the test process. Thereafter more random presentation can be used but ensuring stimuli are evenly distributed.

Clinical tests of somatosensory perception have been devised by neurolo-

Box 5.2

The assessment of somatosensory perception: range of clinical tests

System	Test	Measures
Tactile (screen to obscure vision)	Localization of tactile stimuli	Accuracy of indicating where touched by one or two stimuli
	Finger agnosia	Identification of finger(s) touched
	Graphesthesia	Tactile perception of shape drawn on dorsum of hand
	Stereognosis	Tactile/proprioceptive discrimination of form placed in hand
Proprioceptive (eyes closed or limbs obscured by screen)	Joint position sense	Ability to maintain limb position without vision and to match position with contralateral limb
	Kinaesthesia	Ability to replicate the direction and excursion of movement between target points
Vestibular	Static balance	Ability to maintain upright position against gravity when eyes closed
	Dynamic balance	Postural reactions to sudden displacement of position in space

gists and psychologists. Some have been adapted and standardized within test batteries to be appropriate for children or adults (e.g. Sensory Integration and Praxis Tests, Miller Assessment for Preschoolers, Luria–Nebraska Neuropsychological Battery, Contributions to Neuropsychological Assessment). Of these examples, only Miller Assessment for Preschoolers is available for use by therapists in the UK. Therefore structured assessment formats have been devised to test discriminative somatosensory functions, identified in Box 5.2. Dunn (1981), amongst others, has identified relevant normative data for one specific age range in children.

Due to interdependence of function within the central nervous system, results give broad indications of dysfunction. This is particularly true of the relationship between vestibular and proprioceptive systems with postural equilibrium. Tests isolating the vestibular system include measures of the duration of post-rotatory nystagmus. While possible clinically, more accurate measures require laboratory test situations (Polatajko, 1985).

However, recent work by Wilson *et al.* (1992) has addressed issues of validity and reliability when assessing postural and motor skills. Their study suggests six items that could constitute a reliable screening tool for children between 5 years and 9 years 11 months.

Clinical tests for pain, temperature and crude touch are not included in this chapter. While having less significance to sensori-motor dysfunction, loss or disturbance of these senses can have a bearing on safety in functional living.

MOTOR IMPAIRMENT

Assessments of motor impairment focus on determining the functional effects of disability; the outcome of disturbances of muscle tone, somatosensory processing and/or perceptual-motor problems. They are mainly task-oriented, results being measured by the pattern of ability/inability scores, but also include clinical tests measured through handling and moving the patient. Standardized and structured assessments present test items which reflect specific skills linked with broader motor performance. For example, tying shoelaces requires the ability to sit and to reach one's feet, bilateral manual dexterity, and the concept of tying a bow. Schedules of daily living skills (Klein and Bell, 1982; Whitehouse, 1983) may identify which mobility, self-care, domestic or work-related abilities are lost or impaired. More detailed assessment of basic (core) motor performance skills can assist in defining the degree and range of skills affected.

To complement scores obtained from assessment procedures, observation of the quality of motor patterns and effect of effort on performance is advisable. Formal assessment is normally completed within a set time allocation. Skilled observation of the quality of movement and behavioural response may suggest impairment even when test tasks score within normal limits. Additional information on performance in everyday situations is vital to obtaining a comprehensive profile of the balance of abilities, impairment and endurance.

The use of behavioural check-lists or guidelines can be useful, as can participation in therapeutic workshop activities. Whatever the situation, structured observation formats can assist the examiner, the patient, carers and others in highlighting significant factors affecting performance.

From information given in a referral and history, therapists can determine the possible type(s) of functional impairment, which assists in determining priorities for assessment. Specific assessment formats have been devised for specific diagnostic groups or theoretical frameworks. Impairment may be a consequence of physical handicap or a 'hidden' handicap, when the functional consequences can affect gross and/or fine motor skills and be a

Box 5.3

Summary of core skills of motor assessment undertaken in assessment

Posture and mobility	Hand function	Associated factors
Presence of primitive and postural reflexes	Hand preference	Uncertain hand preference
Effect of muscle tone on function: noting presence and influence of tremor and/or associated postural reactions		Awareness of laterality (right/left discrimination)
Range of movement	Functional reach (range of movement plus ability to move between and within positions)	Avoidance of crossing mid-line of body
Detection of contractures/ deformities	Patterns of grasp/release: unilateral and bilateral	Inadequate integration of both sides of body
Ability to move between positions	Manual dexterity	
Gait/independent mobility	Use of tools	

Plus overall effect on everyday living skills within person's lifestyle and ambition.

source of frustration and embarrassment to the patient. Apraxia, described later in this chapter, is one example, as is dysgraphia, described by Marshall, Chapter 8, this volume. 'Hidden' handicap can also complicate the effects of physical handicap and frustrate a patient's participation and progress in rehabilitation.

Modes of assessment

Aspects of motor performance and impairment included in assessment are outlined in Box 5.3. Structured observation of the patient's motor reactions to being moved and handled, plus performance of tasks, are the main focus. Additional information and/or observation of daily living skills can be included.

For a number of assessment procedures, precise measurements are feasible. A goniometer can measure range of movement and a stopwatch can time tests of manual dexterity. Further evaluation of walking can be achieved by referral for gait analysis. Within the scope of clinical tests on Box 5.3, analysis of results depends on the skill, knowledge and expertise of the therapist. Normative data assists determining performance age levels in children. Erhardt's Developmental Assessment of Prehension (1982) identifies patterns of hand function in infancy and early childhood.

Standardized test batteries have been designed to analyse the skills/impairments of children with motor-learning difficulties or developmental co-ordination disorders ('hidden' handicaps). Scoring and interpretation reflect the range of normal limits for different age bands. Included in these are tests based on sensory integration theory (Sensory Integration and Praxis Tests), those geared to preschool children (the Miller Assessment for Preschoolers, First Steps) and other more broadly based tests (Movement Assessment Battery for Children, the Bruininks–Oseretsky Test of Motor Proficiency). Individual tests of visuo-motor competence can aid further information.

The Chessington Occupational Therapy Neurological Assessment Battery, standardized for people between 16 and 65 years, combines assessment of visual perception, constructional ability, sensori-motor ability and ability to follow instructions. Other standardized measures focus on specific skills (e.g. Test of Hand Function: Jebson and Taylor, 1969). The Assessment of Motor and Process Skills, at present being standardized on a cross-cultural basis, tackles issues mentioned earlier in this chapter. It combines motor scales and process scales to determine why a patient cannot perform functional daily living tasks. It can be used across the span of youth to old age and with a wide range of diagnoses. Items of relevant motor function form part of assessment batteries not available for therapists' use; hence the continued reliance on structured observation.

APRAXIA

The person suffering from dyspraxia/apraxia has significant problems in functional living. Praxis has been defined as the ability to manipulate or deal intelligently with objects and the environment. In the published text of a lecture comparing dyspraxia/apraxia in children and adults, Ayres (1985) has defined praxis as a uniquely human skill enabling interaction with the physical world and representing a crucial link between brain and behaviour. Drawing on the work of other authors, emphasis is placed on careful differentiation between dysfunctions associated with direct insult to sensory or motor cortex and their pathways; from problems of interpreting language, or from inattention to verbal instruction. Current thinking suggests that praxis has more bihemispheric cortical representation, but that the left hemisphere remains dominant for praxic skill in right-handed persons.

Nevertheless praxis is dependent on the integration of afferent sensori-impulses with motor responses, modified by sensory feedback and experience. Both cortical and subcortical structures are thought to participate in the integration process leading to efficient function.

Complete absence of praxic skill is rare. Dyspraxia (disorder of praxis) represents a more accurate description. With adults the term 'apraxia' is usually used, and it is most frequently the consequence of trauma to the cerebral hemispheres (cerebral-vascular accident, head injury, tumour). Damage is imposed on a mature central nervous system. In children aetiology may be unclear. Because praxic skill develops from infancy onwards, dysfunction in children may limit attainment of potential as the central nervous system continues to mature after birth. The terms 'developmental dyspraxia' (Ayres, 1979) and more recently 'somato dyspraxia' (Fisher et al., 1991) describe the syndrome in children where the aetiology is non-specific.

Problems associated with dyspraxia can present in different forms. In describing manifestations in the adult stroke patient, Siev and Frieshtat (1976) described five types. These manifestations continue to be recognized in adult-onset dyspraxia, whatever the aetiology (Grieve, 1993). Ayres (1985) identified six areas for assessment in children and these have led to identification of different categories of dyspraxia (Ayres, 1988; Fisher et al., 1991). However, a universal consensus of opinion on the types of dyspraxia seen in children does not exist at present.

It has been suggested that praxic skill has three components. Consideration of which process is affected may provide clues towards diagnosis and remediation.

1 *Ideation* – formation of an idea for action

2 *Planning* – selecting and organizing appropriate action (motor planning)

3 *Execution* – performance of action (adaptive response)

The motor-planning process is most significant to the diagnosis of dyspraxia.

Modes of assessment

A number of standardized tests include items which could indicate existence of dyspraxia. Siev and Frieshtat (1976) have brought together a range of tests, some standardized, which may be used to assess for presence of apraxia in adults (Box 5.4).

In a similar way, aspects of praxis can be investigated in children (Box 5.5), but use of normative data is essential for comparison of attainment with chronological age. The work of Vulpe (1994) details stages in development in different skill areas with greater precision than many developmental schedules.

Standardized assessment procedures have been designed to evaluate the

Box 5.4

The assessment of adult-onset apraxia

Constructional	Dressing	Motor	Ideo-motor	Ideational
Copying design: house, clock, flower from card – geometric designs Matchstick designs: – copying designs using 2–9 matches Block bridges: – copying sequence of 3, 7 and 9 block bridges	Observation of task related to: – orientation of garments to body – awareness of garment inside out – organization of body movement to garment – problems with fastenings: manipulation and alignment	Observation of performance: – inability to carry out task on command may be able to do simple tasks automatically NB Patient understands task	Observation and interview: – inability to carry out task on command NB Patient understands task and could describe it. Sometimes can achieve spontaneously	Observation and interview: – inability to carry out activities because does not understand concept of act
Benton's 3D Constructional Praxis test: – copying constructions, blocks various shapes and sizes *Bender Gestalt Test: – drawing design from 9 stimulus cards			Difficult to differentiate: assessment tasks similar Goodglass Test for Apraxia – tasks presented at three levels: on command, imitation, with real objects *Ayres Imitation of Postures (C) Solet Test for Apraxia	

* Standardized tests (restricted use)
(C) Children 4–9 years
Source: Adapted from Siev and Frieshtat, 1976

Box 5.5

The assessment of dyspraxia in children

Type of praxis	Measures	Options available
Constructional praxis	Visuo-spatial skills Motor planning	Block designs Construction toys
Design copying	*Visuo-motor skills Graphic praxis	Shape copying Design copying: dot to dot
Postural praxis	Imitation of postures: motor planning	Copying actions Games – Simon Says, Statues
Bilateral motor co-ordination	*Ability of both arms and feet to move together Motor-planning + bilateral integration	Catch and throw Jump, skip Copying bilateral activity slow and fast
Praxis on verbal command	*Motor planning + auditory language processing	Observation of performance – copying easier than following instruction
Motor accuracy	*Visuo-motor control Motor planning	Drawing: tracing Dot to dot
Sequential praxis	*Repetition of hand and finger movements	Copying hand and finger games such as Pat-a-cake, Itsy-Bitsy Spider
Oral praxis	Motor planning: oral positions and movement sequences	Funny faces Pretend games, such as drinking via straw, licking lollipop

* Care needed in interpretation: more than one process involved

presence of dyspraxia in children. Some seek comprehensive assessment within test batteries while others tap individual aspects.

Whatever mode of assessment is selected, it is important to remember that assessment tasks can also indicate different functions. The 'purity' of test items is doubtful, and therefore observation of approach and performance to the task is as significant as noting success or failure. Structure of an assessment to detect dyspraxia should include a range of tasks (Boxes 5.4 and 5.5) and comprise part of a total assessment package for sensori-motor function which includes active consideration of functional effects in daily living as stated by the individual and carers.

SUMMARY

The content of this chapter has endeavoured to represent broad perspectives influencing assessment of sensori-motor function, introducing clinical and standardized options for assessment. While therapists continue to rely on structured observation and clinical tests as their main tools, standardized assessment methods are emerging, but to date they are not comprehensive across the life span or appropriate for all neurological dysfunctions. Of those available, only a selected but increasing number are identified for use by therapists.

Individual researchers have contributed to the development of current standardized assessment procedures. Underlying theoretical frameworks are not universally accepted; much remains hypothesis and open to debate.

Therapists have tended to indulge in rationalization as a substitute for precise measurement. Such precision is not always feasible. Sometimes the best that can be achieved is accurate observation and clinical tests. Greater structure within these is emerging. Validity and reliability using non-standardized methods can be recognized when results correspond with those of assessments done by colleagues. Frequently there is overlap. Professional judgement made independently with results corresponding suggests a degree of reliability, often the most consistent result where objective measurement is not available.

REFERENCES

Ashworth, B. (1964). 'Preliminary trial of Carisprodol in multiple sclerosis'. *Practitioner*, 192, 540–2.

Ayres, A. J. (1979). *Sensory Integration and the Child*. Los Angeles: Western Psychological Services.

Ayres, A. J. (1985). *Developmental Dyspraxia and Adult Onset Apraxia*. Torrance, CA: Sensory Integration International.

Ayres, A. J. (1988). *Sensory Integration and Praxis Tests*. Los Angeles: Western Psychological Services.

Benton, A. L. and Fogel, M. L. (1962). 'Three dimensional constructional praxis: a clinical test'. *Archives of Neurology*, 7, 347–54.

Benton, A., Hamsher, K. de S., Varney, N. and Spreen, O. (1978). *Contributions to Neuropsychological Assessment*. Windsor: NFER-Nelson.

Brown, R. A., Holdsworth, L., Leslie, G. C., Mutch, W. J. and Part, N. J. (1993). 'The effects of time after stroke and selected therapeutic techniques on quadriceps muscle tone in stroke patients'. *Physiotherapy Theory and Practice*, 9(3), 131–42.

Bruininks, R. (1978). *Bruininks–Oseretsky Test of Motor Proficiency*. Windsor: NFER-Nelson.

Dunn, W. (1981). *A Guide to Testing Clinical Observations in Kindergarteners*. Rockville, MD: American Occupational Therapy Association.

Erhardt, R. P. (1982). *Developmental Hand Dysfunction*. Tucson, AZ: Therapy Skill Builders.

Fisher, A. G. (1993). 'Assessment of motor and process skills'. Unpublished research, edition 6.2. Colorado State University, Occupational Therapy Department, Fort Collins, CO.

Fisher, A. G., Murray, E. A. and Bundy, A. C. (1991). *Sensory Integration, Theory and Praxis*. Philadelphia, PA: F. A. Davis.

Golden, C., Hammeke, F. and Purisch, A. (1987). *Luria–Nebraska Neuropsychological Batteries*. Windsor: NFER-Nelson.

Grieve, J. (1993). *Neuropsychology for Occupational Therapists*. Oxford: Blackwell Scientific.

Henderson, S. E. (1987). 'The assessment of "clumsy" children: old and new approaches'. *Journal of Child Psychology and Psychiatry*, 28(4), 511–27.

Henderson, S. E. and Sugden, D. A. (1992). *Movement Assessment Battery for Children*. London: Psychological Corporation.

Jebson, R. H. and Taylor, N. (1969). 'An objective and standardised test of hand function'. *Archives of Physical Medicine and Rehabilitation*, 50, 311.

Katz, R. T. and Zev Rymer, W. (1989). 'Spastic hypertonia: mechanism and measurement', *Archives of Physical Medicine and Rehabilitation*, 70, 144–55.

Kielhofner, G. (1985). *Model of Human Occupation*. Baltimore, MD: Williams and Wilkins.

King-Thomas, L. and Hacker, B. J. (1987). *A Therapist's Guide to Paediatric Assessment*. Boston, MA: Little, Brown.

Klein, R. M. and Bell, B. (1982). 'Self-care skills: behavioural measurement with Klein–Bell ADL Scale'. *Archives of Physical Medicine and Rehabilitation*, 63, 335–8.

Laszlo, J. and Bairstow, P. (1985). *Perceptual-motor Behaviour: Developmental Assessment and Therapy*. Eastbourne: Holt Rinehart and Winston.

Meadows, C. B., Anderson, D. M., Duncan, L. M. and Sturrock, M. B. T. (1980). *The Use of Polypropylene Ankle–Foot Orthoses in the Management of the Young Cerebral Palsied Child*. Dundee: Tayside Rehabilitation Engineering Services, Tayside Health Board.

Miller, L. J. (1988). *Miller Assessment for Pre-Schoolers*. London: Psychological Corporation.

Miller, L. J. (1993). *First Steps Screening Test for Evaluating Pre-Schoolers*. London: Psychological Corporation.

Polatajko, H. J. (1985). 'A critical look at vestibular function in the learning disabled child'. *Developmental Medicine and Child Neurology*, 27, 283–92.

Sherrington, C. S. (1906). *Integrative Action of the Nervous System*. London: Constable.

Siev, E. and Frieshtat, B. (1976). *Perceptual Dysfunction in the Adult Stroke Patient*. Thorofare, NJ: Charles B. Slack.

Tobin, W. and Henderson, S. E. (1991). 'The assessment of motor impairment in children'. In L. Harding and J. R. Beech (eds), *Assessment of Primary School Children*. Windsor: NFER-Nelson.

Tyerman, R., Tyerman, A., Price, H., Hadfield, C. *et al.* (1986). *Chessington Occupational Therapy Neurological Assessment Battery*. Nottingham: Nottingham Rehab. Ltd.

Vulpe, S. G. (1994). *Vulpe Assessment Battery Revised*. East Aurora, NY: Slosson Educational.

Wartenberg, R. (1951). 'Pendulousness of the legs as a diagnostic test'. *Neurology*, 1, 18–24.

Whitehouse, J. (1983). *Mossford Assessment Chart for Physically Handicapped*. Windsor: NFER-Nelson.

Whittle, A. and Wood, P. (1992). *The Occupational Therapist's Guide to Paediatric Tests*. Nottingham: Whittle-Wood.

Wilson, B., Pollock, N., Kaplan, B. J., Law, M. and Faris, P. (1992). 'Rehability and construct validity of the clinical observations of motor and postural skills'. *American Journal of Occupational Therapy*, 46 (9).

Young, J. A., Bell, J. R. and Anderson, D. M. (1978). 'Clinical experience in the use of baclofen in children with spastic cerebral palsy: a preliminary report'. In *Baclofen: Spasticity and Cerebral Pathology*. No. 68. Cambridge: Cambridge Medical Publications.

6

ASSESSMENT OF VISUAL PERCEPTUAL IMPAIRMENT

Andrew W. Young

Studies of neuropsychological deficits have demonstrated striking dissociations between impairments which affect different visual perceptual abilities (Ellis and Young, 1988). For example, brain-injured patients may lose the ability to recognize many visual objects, yet show a relatively normal appreciation of their spatial locations, or vice versa. These dissociable deficits are widely interpreted as consistent with evidence from physiological studies of a degree of functional specialization of the different regions of cerebral cortex involved in vision (Cowey, 1985, 1994).

The existence of functional specialization and dissociable deficits leads to an approach that is in some ways the opposite to that employed in tests which deliberately sample as wide a range of abilities as possible and pool these into a composite score. There is usually little point in doing this for vision. For example, if we knew that vision involved the perception of colour, movement, location and form as separate abilities, it would be unhelpful to say that someone who has lost only the perception of colour has 75 per cent effective vision. The statement combines qualitatively different aspects of vision in an arbitrary way, and says nothing informative about the *circumstances* under which this impairment might prove problematic. Much more useful would be a profile which emphasizes the person's 100 per cent effective vision of movement, location and form, and 0 per cent effective colour vision.

In practice, though, this is not so easily achieved. This is partly because we still do not know with certainty what the different functional components of the visual system are, and partly because even for those components for which there is some confidence it is difficult to arrive at tests that are primarily dependent on that component only.

It is quite common in the research literature to find that a distinction is drawn between impairments which affect basic visual abilities, such as visual field defects or loss of contrast sensitivity at different spatial frequencies, and impairments of higher-order abilities involved in the recognition of seen objects, perception of space, and so on (Farah and Ratcliff, 1994). The reason for making this very approximate distinction is that impairments

97

of basic and higher-order visual abilities can be dissociated from each other (De Haan et al., 1995; Ettlinger, 1956). For example, patients with contrast sensitivity impairments may remain able to recognize faces, whilst patients with face recognition impairments need not show impairments of contrast sensitivity (Newcombe *et al.*, 1989).

Here, we will concentrate on what are usually considered to be higher-order impairments, since impairments of basic visual abilities are dealt with by Rennie, Chapter 4, this volume. However, the dissociations between basic and higher-order visual impairments found in some cases should not be taken to mean that investigation of basic visual functions is unnecessary when higher-order impairment is suspected. It is always prudent to consider the possibility that problems in tasks requiring higher-order abilities may actually reflect severe sensory loss (Warrington, 1987).

Although we will consider visual recognition impairments in some detail, this will not extend to problems in reading, which are discussed by Marshall, Chapter 8, this volume. Problems in the perception of movement (Zihl *et al.*, 1983) are not discussed at all, because they require technical facilities unlikely at present to be available to most clinical psychologists.

I have grouped material into topics concerned with objects, faces, colour and space, which correspond to problem areas that patients may raise on initial presentation. These spontaneous complaints invariably require further investigation, because there are various possible causes for each. A review of neuropsychological knowledge in each area can be found in Ellis and Young (1988, Chs 2–4). Assessment usually proceeds by exclusion, with careful elimination of each potential cause until only one remains. Unfortunately, only a few standardized tests are commercially available. I have tried to draw attention to standard materials or tests when these do exist, but have often had to rely on directing attention to examples of current good practice. This is unfortunate, because, whilst clinical procedures are adequate for some purposes, especially in cases where deficits are flagrant and only a qualitative description is required, they can be inadequate or misleading when quantification of more subtle impairments is needed.

OBJECTS

Inability to identify seen objects by name is a good example of an impairment which can have a number of potential causes, ranging from very poor vision to problems in name retrieval. A thorough discussion of the different possibilities can be found in Ratcliff and Newcombe (1982).

Sets of objects of varying difficulty as far as name retrieval is concerned are given in Oldfield and Wingfield (1965), the Graded Naming Test (McKenna and Warrington, 1980), and the Birmingham Object Recognition Battery (BORB: Riddoch and Humphreys, 1993). These are useful when a naming (rather than a recognition) problem is suspected, since name retrieval problems (in which the patient knows what the object is, but cannot remember its name) are readily picked up by such tests, whereas recognition problems (in which the object is not recognized correctly) lead to a quite different pattern. The BORB also contains sets from visual categories whose members tend to have high (animate) or low (inanimate) inter-item similarity.

A widely used source of materials for investigation of recognition impairments has been the set of pictures published by Snodgrass and Vanderwart (1980), which includes norms for name agreement, image agreement, familiarity and visual complexity. These norms allow the construction of sets of pictures which differ on the property of interest whilst remaining matched on other factors. For example, Young and Ellis (1989) give matched lists of pictures of living and non-living objects, and objects which are often or seldom picked up. Such matched sets are useful because there is evidence that some categories of stimuli may be affected much more than others for some patients (Warrington, 1985; Warrington and Shallice, 1984). Further sets of materials can be found in the BORB (Riddoch and Humphreys, 1993).

Investigations of object recognition impairments are still dominated by the concept of agnosia, introduced by Lissauer in 1890 (see Shallice and Jackson, 1988). In visual agnosia, the loss of ability to recognize objects cannot be attributed to sensory loss or to general intellectual impairment. To arrive at the conclusion that a visual agnosia underlies a patient's object recognition difficulties it is thus necessary to establish that basic visual abilities are sufficient for recognition to be possible (Warrington, 1985, 1987). Tests intended to determine whether gross visual problems contribute to impaired object recognition are contained in the Visual Object and Space Perception Battery (VOSP: Warrington and James, 1991) and the BORB (Riddoch and Humphreys, 1993). In addition, for a visual agnosia, objects which are not recognized from vision should be identifiable from definitions of their functions. When there are problems in identifying objects from definitions, more likely causes are semantic memory impairment (Warrington and Shallice, 1984) or problems in name retrieval.

The clinical features of visual agnosias are well summarized by Rubens (1979). Lissauer had thought of the problem as occurring at the highest levels of visual perception, but he drew a distinction between apperceptive agnosia, in which there was thought to be higher-order perceptual impairment, and associative agnosia, in which higher-order perception was considered to be intact but disconnected from appropriate semantic information ('associations'). A key feature of apperceptive agnosia was held to be that the patient could not copy drawings of objects he or she was unable to recognize (because of the perceptual impairment), whereas in associative agnosia copying was intact (Shallice and Jackson, 1988).

More modern studies have tended to agree with Lissauer's conclusion that there are different types of agnosia, but find the apperceptive versus associative categorization too limited (Ratcliff and Newcombe, 1982; Riddoch and Humphreys, 1987a). In particular, it is clear that the ability to make accurate copies of unrecognized objects is not in itself sufficient to demonstrate completely intact perception, since some patients seem able to deploy successfully a 'line-by-line' copying strategy (Ratcliff and Newcombe, 1982). The most promising approach is to relate patients' deficits to an explicit functional model of object recognition (Humphreys and Riddoch, 1987; Ratcliff and Newcombe, 1982).

A technical problem which often arises in the investigation of visual recognition impairments involves how to arrive at a relatively pure estimate of the patient's ability to perceive shape. No perfect solution has emerged, but the technique devised by Efron (1968) is quite often used. This involves a series of oblong shapes of identical area, which vary in the ratio of length to width of each oblong. The patient is shown two of the oblongs, one of which is always a square (height:width ratio = 1), and asked to decide whether the two stimuli are identical or different. In this way, the discriminability of the stimuli can be measured as the degree of difference between them (change in height:width ratio) is altered.

A condition which is easily mistaken for a visual agnosia is optic aphasia (Beauvois, 1982; Riddoch and Humphreys, 1987b). In optic aphasia, patients cannot name or otherwise verbally identify seen objects, but they *can* demonstrate that they have successfully recognized them by miming their uses. Agnosic patients are unable to do this. Hence in optic aphasia there is evidence of preserved ability to recognize the visual pattern corresponding to a familiar object, even though it cannot be named. One way of assessing this is to look at whether patients can tell pictures of real or familiar objects from pictures of unfamiliar or invented objects, and a test forms part of the BORB (Riddoch and Humphreys, 1993).

Although they have attracted a lot of attention because of their scientific importance, it must be borne in mind that visual agnosias are quite rare. Much more common problems involve difficulty in recognizing stimuli which are overlapping, degraded (De Renzi and Spinnler, 1966), or photographed from unusual views (Humphreys and Riddoch, 1984; Warrington and Taylor, 1978). Warrington and Taylor's (1978) work showed a dissociation between impairments affecting the perceptual classification of objects by form (impaired after right cerebral hemisphere injury) or function (impaired after left cerebral injury), which could turn out to have a number of clinical uses. Materials for investigating problems with overlapping figures or unusual views are contained in the BORB (Riddoch and Humphreys, 1993).

FACES

Most patients with object recognition problems experience equivalent difficulties in recognizing people's faces. But there are also patients who complain more specifically of problems in face recognition. This was first convincingly established as a discrete clinical condition by Bodamer, in 1947 (Ellis and Florence, 1990), and given the name prosopagnosia.

Reviews of the clinical features of prosopagnosia can be found in Meadows (1974a) and Hécaen (1981). In some cases, even the most familiar faces are not recognized overtly; friends, family, and the patient's own face when seen in a mirror. As with visual object agnosia, it is necessary to demonstrate that the patient can see sufficiently well that recognition should be possible, and that familiar people can still be recognized from non-facial cues (such as voices or names). It is particularly important not to confuse face recognition problems due to semantic memory impairments (Hanley et al., 1989) or name retrieval difficulties (Flude et al., 1989; Semenza and Zettin, 1988, 1989) with prosopagnosia; they can be deceptively similar on initial presentation. With both semantic memory and name retrieval problems, however, recognition has been found to be equally impaired to face, voice or name inputs, in contrast to the relatively intact recognition from names or voices found in prosopagnosia.

Although problems in the recognition of familiar faces are the usual source of spontaneous complaint in prosopagnosia, in most cases the deficit is not restricted to faces. Everyday objects can often be recognized without difficulty, but the patients usually experience problems in recognizing individual members of other classes of stimuli with visually similar exemplars. However, this pattern of impaired recognition of all visually homogeneous categories is not universal in cases of prosopagnosia; some patients have problems that do seem specific to faces (De Renzi, 1986; De Renzi et al., 1991; McNeil and Warrington, 1993). Damasio et al. (1982) and De Renzi (1986) provide examples of suitable materials for testing this possibility.

It is now clear that there are different underlying causes of prosopagnosia and, again, relating these to an explicit functional model can be useful (see Ellis and Young, 1988, Ch. 4; Young, 1992). Traditionally, clinicians have distinguished a perceptual form, in which the highest levels of face perception are compromised, and a mnestic form, which seems to centre on problems in face memory (De Renzi, 1986; Hécaen, 1981). This distinction has been strengthened by findings of 'covert' recognition of familiar faces in the mnestic cases (Bauer, 1984; De Haan et al., 1987; Young, 1994). In such cases, there is evidence of preserved recognition of familiar faces which are not recognized overtly.

Bauer (1984) used the 'guilty knowledge' test to demonstrate covert recognition in prosopagnosia, and this is a realistic possibility when equipment is available to record and analyse GSRs (galvanic skin responses). A much simpler procedure is to compare the patient's ability to learn true or untrue names to faces he or she does not recognize overtly (De Haan *et al.*, 1987). Because this involves some learning of untrue information, it is particularly important to ensure that properly informed consent is given.

Findings of covert recognition in prosopagnosia emphasize the parallel between the mnestic form of prosopagnosia and phenomena of 'implicit memory' in amnesia (Schacter, 1987; Young and de Haan, 1990). This illustrates well the point that face recognition impairments lie on the boundary between what might conventionally be considered to involve 'perception' or 'memory'. In prosopagnosia, the face memory impairment has both a retrograde component (faces familiar before the patient's illness are not recognized) and an anterograde component (faces encountered since the illness are not recognized). However, there are also problems of face memory which can take a more purely anterograde form (Hanley *et al.*, 1990, 1991), in which the patient complains that he or she 'cannot learn new faces', but previously familiar faces present no problems. A good pointer to this possibility can be a poor score on the faces section of Warrington's (1984) Recognition Memory Test, and especially a marked face (versus word) discrepancy score.

One of the striking features of prosopagnosia is just how much face-processing ability may be preserved. Even though they cannot recognize familiar faces overtly, prosopagnosic patients may remain able to identify facial expressions or to match photographs of unfamiliar faces as showing same or different people (Bruyer *et al.*, 1983). Impairments of expression processing or unfamiliar face matching can be found after brain injury, but they are to some extent dissociable from prosopagnosia (Bruce and Young, 1986; Young *et al.*, 1993).

Convenient materials for investigating impairments in understanding facial expressions are the series of pictures of happy, angry, sad, surprised, afraid, disgusted and neutral faces published by Ekman and Friesen (1976), which contain norms for the rates at which the emotion portrayed in each picture can be recognized. These can be arranged into tasks which can tap different levels of expression processing; for example, matching of photographs as same or different expressions versus expression labelling (Bowers and Heilman, 1984).

Unfamiliar face matching is examined in the widely used Benton Test of Facial Recognition (Benton *et al.*, 1983). This was initially developed as a test intended to be sensitive to mild forms of prosopagnosia (Benton, 1980), and it caused some surprise when prosopagnosic patients were found to be able to do it (though Newcombe (1979) points out that the possibility of idiosyncratic strategies should always be borne in mind). However, the test has proved clinically useful, because problems in unfamiliar face matching are much more common than prosopagnosia. A similar test of unfamiliar face matching has been used in several studies carried out by Hécaen and his colleagues (Tzavaras *et al.*, 1970).

COLOUR

Impairments of colour vision found after brain injury are quite different to the more well-known types of colour blindness due to deficiencies in the retina. It is more usual to find that all colours are more or less equally affected, rather than particular opponent pairs, which reduces the usefulness of standard tests of colour blindness like the Ishihara plates. The usual spontaneous complaint with impaired colour perception after cerebral injury (achromatopsia) is that colours look washed out, or even that everything is like a black-and-white picture. In some cases the problem is restricted to part of the visual field (Damasio *et al.*, 1980). The most widely used test is the Farnsworth–Munsell 100-Hue Test (Farnsworth, 1957), which requires subtly graded colour chips to be sorted into a correct order. This includes appreciable cognitive demands, so care needs to be taken in interpreting poor scores. More sophisticated techniques for assessing colour vision require facilities not widely available in the psychology clinic (Heywood *et al.*, 1991, 1994).

Meadows (1974b) has reviewed the clinical features of colour-processing impairments. In addition to achromatopsia, there are also impairments affecting colour knowledge (sometimes called colour agnosia) and colour naming. Patients with impaired colour knowledge may have intact perception of colour and yet be unable to answer from memory questions such as 'What colour is a banana?', or choose incorrect crayons if asked to colour object drawings (Kinsbourne and Warrington, 1964). Patients with colour-naming problems *can* state the usual colours of bananas, fire engines, etc., but are unable to put names to patches of colour or the colours of objects (such as clothes) when there is no previously learnt knowledge to rely on (Geschwind and Fusillo, 1966).

SPACE

One of the principal goals of visual perception is to inform us about the location and positioning of objects and surfaces. It is most unusual to find that brain-injured patients experience the visual world as 'flat' (Holmes, 1919), because such a rich variety of monocular and binocular depth information is available, but other problems in the perception of space have been noted. A particularly interesting feature of these space perception impairments is that they can dissociate from visual recognition impairments, showing the independence of neural mechanisms used to determine *what* an object is and *where* it is located (Newcombe *et al.*, 1987).

Holmes's analysis of the clinical aspects of impairments of visual location is unsurpassed (Holmes, 1919). The key features are that whilst location by vision is severely compromised, so that the patient is unable to reach and grasp seen objects, location by sound or touch presents no problem (that is, it is not a motor impairment). Although seen objects cannot be located accurately in terms of direction or distance, even to the point where the patient may not be able to state which of two objects is closer or further away (that is, the problem can involve relative as well as absolute location), recognition of the objects themselves can be unaffected (the patient knows that he or she is looking at a matchbox, but does not know *where* it is).

Visual location problems as severe as those described by Holmes are unusual, but a straightforward technique for measuring more mild (and more common) location problems using a standard perimeter has been developed by Ratcliff and Davies-Jones (1972). This method is suitable as well for examining location disorders which are restricted to a single visual hemifield, and these too are relatively commonly found. Also useful is the procedure devised by Corsi to measure spatial short-term memory span, in which the patient is asked to point to a series of randomly positioned cubes in the same order as the examiner (De Renzi *et al.*, 1977; De Renzi and Nichelli, 1975). This is sensitive to visual location difficulties (which lead to impaired performance even for the first items in a series) as well as problems involving spatial short-term memory.

As happens with recognition impairments, visuo-perceptual spatial problems quickly shade into problems which seem to involve spatial memory, or even spatial thought (see Ellis and Young, 1988, Ch. 3). Patients may show problems in learning new routes, leaving them disoriented in new environments, or may have problems finding their way around places that were previously very familiar to them (topographical disorientation). In the latter case, it is necessary to determine whether the topographical disorientation reflects a genuinely spatial problem (inability to recall the spatial layout of a familiar place), or a visual recognition problem (inability to recognize familiar buildings) which prevents the application of intact spatial knowledge.

The VOSP battery (Warrington and James, 1991) includes a useful set of spatial tests involving counting a set of dots, discriminating the relative positions of a single spot in each of two squares, locating where the position of a spot corresponds to in a different square, and counting the numbers of cubes (including hidden cubes) in drawings of three-dimensional figures.

A quite different problem is unilateral neglect. Patients with unilateral neglect seem to ignore stimuli that fall to one side of space. For example, they may fail to cross out targets placed on one side of a page (Albert, 1973), fail to read one side of a page of text, or leave the food on one side of a plate. In some cases, even one side of a mental image is affected (Bisiach and Luzzatti, 1978). Heilman (1979) discusses the clinical aspects in more detail. The problem is more common after right cerebral hemisphere injury, when it affects the left side of space, but it can also occur to the right side of space after left cerebral hemisphere injury.

There is considerable debate concerning whether neglect should be considered an attentional disorder (as its name implies) or a problem in the mental representation of one side of space (see Ellis and Young, 1988, Ch. 3). This need not concern us here, other than the observation that its close relation to visual extinction is one of the points in favour of the attentional theory. In visual extinction, patients can identify a single stimulus in any part of the visual field, but when stimuli are presented simultaneously in the left and right visual fields they fail to report the stimulus which fell in the visual field opposite to the cerebral lesion (Heilman, 1979).

The crossing-out procedure is a simple and effective test of unilateral spatial neglect (Albert, 1973), and the Behavioural Inattention Test allows a degree of quantification (Wilson *et al.*, 1987). Matters may become more complicated, though, if evidence of dissociable components of neglect continues to be found (Humphreys and Riddoch, 1994; Young *et al.*, 1990b), and when we have a clearer idea of the implications of findings of covert processing of the neglected side (Berti and Rizzolatti, 1992; Marshall and Halligan, 1988; McGlinchey-Berroth *et al.*, 1993).

The importance of covert processing of spatial stimuli is also emphasized in the dissociation of action and conscious perception found in the elegant work of Milner, Goodale and their colleagues (Goodale and Milner, 1992; Goodale *et al.*, 1991; Milner *et al.*, 1991). They have made a very thorough investigation of a single case, DF, with severely impaired shape perception. When DF was asked to make judgements about the orientation or size of an object, she performed very poorly. Yet when DF was asked to put her hand into a slot she immediately oriented it correctly, and she shaped her fingers appropriately for the size of an object she was about to pick up (Goodale and Milner, 1992; Goodale *et al.*, 1991). In general, DF could make accurate responses in tasks which involved a well-practised, everyday movement that can be run off without conscious control (putting your hand into something, or picking something up), whereas she made inaccurate responses in tasks which need continual conscious intervention.

CONCLUSIONS

Knowledge of higher-order visual impairments has increased rapidly during the last twenty years. Much of this increase has concerned the ways in which different impairments can fractionate from each other in comparatively rare cases. Although it is possible to assemble appropriate materials to explore such fractionation in the clinic, few are as yet commercially available. In this review, I have tried to indicate where details of suitable materials can be found, and drawn attention to useful reviews and examples of current 'state-of-the-art' practice in the published literature. I have spent some time on what are often uncommon cases of highly selective and severe impairments, because these represent the background extremes against which cases involving more mild or heterogeneous impairment must be viewed.

Of course, the most appropriate techniques for assessing visual perceptual impairment will depend on the underlying purpose of the assessment. The requirements of assessments intended for the patient and relatives, nursing staff, legal cases, scientific research, and routine evaluation and screening are all quite different. Moreover, they differ not just in the level of detail required, but in the nature of the most suitable approach. For screening purposes, for example, where one simply wants to establish that visual perceptual abilities are not grossly affected, it is often convenient to invert the logic of tests needed for most other purposes and deliberately choose one which is dependent on as many abilities as possible. Satisfactory performance then allows the inference that all of the constituent abilities are present.

One of the features of neuropsychological impairments is that they often form recognizable clusters of associated deficits. For example, prosopagnosia is often found to co-occur with achromatopsia, topographical disorientation, and an upper-left-quadrant visual field defect (Meadows, 1974a), whereas colour-naming problems usually arise in the context of inability to read, and right hemianopia (Geschwind and Fusillo, 1966). These co-occurrences can be very useful clinically. They can quickly suggest what the underlying problem might be, and which aspects of a case need to be explored particularly carefully. They can also be very helpful if a hysterical origin, or even outright fabrication, is suspected (since few people know that prosopagnosia is often found to co-occur with achromatopsia, topographical disorientation, and an upper-left-quadrant visual field defect, etc.). However, they are *not* infallible, which is why I have not emphasized them here. Cases do occur in which the usual patterns of co-occurrence are not found. Readers wanting to know more can consult the various reviews.

Finally, a cautionary note. Many of the techniques I have described are, for very good reasons, grounded in findings which have accumulated from careful investigations of problems presented by patients in clinical settings. In most cases, detailed examination of such patients has served to confirm that they do indeed suffer the problems they report, though more focused or theoretically grounded descriptions are usually achieved. It is thus tempting to place a lot of weight on patients' spontaneous complaints. However, the true position is very much as for the patterns of symptom co-occurrence; whilst spontaneous complaints can be a useful guide, they can also mislead. In cases where covert processing has been demonstrated, for example, the nature of the underlying problem is actually quite different to the way in which patients will typically present it (Young and de Haan, 1990). Even more seriously, there are also conditions (anosognosias) in which patients are *unaware of their own impairments*. In such cases, a problem which shows up as quite severe on formal tests will not be accepted, or may even be denied. This lack of insight seems to reflect impaired monitoring of the ability in question and, importantly, it can be *specific to particular disabilities* (Bisiach *et al.*, 1986; Young *et al.*, 1990a). The moral is that absence of spontaneous complaint does not equate with absence of impairment.

REFERENCES

Albert, M. L. (1973). 'A simple test of visual neglect'. *Neurology*, 23, 658–64.

Bauer, R. M. (1984). 'Autonomic recognition of names and faces in prosopagnosia: a neuropsychological application of the guilty knowledge test'. *Neuropsychologia*, 22, 457–69.

Beauvois, M.-F. (1982). 'Optic aphasia: a process of interaction between vision and language'. *Philosophical Transactions of the Royal Society*, B298, 35–47.

Benton, A. L. (1980). 'The neuropsychology of facial recognition'. *American Psychologist*, 35, 176–86.

Benton, A. L., Hamsher, K. de S., Varney, N. and Spreen, O. (1983). *Contributions to Neuropsychological Assessment: A Clinical Manual*. Oxford: Oxford University Press.

Berti, A. and Rizzolatti, G. (1992). 'Visual processing without awareness: evidence from unilateral neglect'. *Journal of Cognitive Neuroscience*, 4, 345–51.

Bisiach, E. and Luzzatti, C. (1978). 'Unilateral neglect of representational space'. *Cortex*, 14, 129–33.

Bisiach, E., Vallar, G., Perani, D., Papagno, C. and Berti, A. (1986). 'Unawareness of disease following lesions of the right hemisphere: anosognosia for hemiplegia and anosognosia for hemianopia'. *Neuropsychologia*, 24, 471–82.

Bowers, D. and Heilman, K. M. (1984). 'Dissociation between the processing of affective and nonaffective faces: a case study'. *Journal of Clinical Neuropsychology*, 6, 367–79.

Bruce, V. and Young, A. (1986). 'Understanding face recognition'. *British Journal of Psychology*, 77, 305–27.

Bruyer, R., Laterre, C., Seron, X., Feyereisen, P., Strypstein, E., Pierrard, E. and Rectem, D. (1983). 'A case of prosopagnosia with some preserved covert remembrance of familiar faces'. *Brain and Cognition*, 2, 257–84.

Cowey, A. (1985). 'Aspects of cortical organization related to selective attention and selective impairments of visual perception: a tutorial review'. In M. I. Posner and O. S. M. Marin (eds), *Attention and Performance*, XI. Hillsdale, NJ: Lawrence Erlbaum.

Cowey, A. (1994). 'Cortical visual areas and the neurobiology of higher visual processes'. In M. J. Farah and G. Ratcliff (eds), *The Neuropsychology of High-level Vision: Collected Tutorial Essays*. Hillsdale, NJ: Lawrence Erlbaum.

Damasio, A. R., Damasio, H. and Van Hoesen, G. W. (1982). 'Prosopagnosia: anatomic basis and behavioral mechanisms'. *Neurology*, 32, 331–41.

Damasio, A., Yamada, T., Damasio, H., Corbett, J. and McKee, J. (1980). 'Central achromatopsia: behavioral, anatomic, and physiologic aspects'. *Neurology*, 30, 1064–71.

De Haan, E. H. F., Young, A. and Newcombe, F. (1987). 'Face recognition without awareness'. *Cognitive Neuropsychology*, 4, 385–415.

De Haan, E. H. F., Heywood, C. A., Young, A. W., Edelstyn, N. and Newcombe,

ANDREW W. YOUNG

F. (1995). 'Ettlinger revisited: the relationship between agnosia and sensory impairment'. *Journal of Neurology, Neurosurgery, and Psychiatry*, 58, 350–6.

De Renzi, E. (1986). 'Current issues in prosopagnosia'. In H. D. Ellis, M. A. Jeeves, F. Newcombe and A. Young (eds), *Aspects of Face Processing*. Dordrecht: Martinus Nijhoff.

De Renzi, E. and Nichelli, P. (1975). 'Verbal and non-verbal short-term memory impairment following hemispheric damage'. *Cortex*, 11, 341–54.

De Renzi, E. and Spinnler, H. (1966). 'Visual recognition in patients with unilateral cerebral disease'. *Journal of Nervous and Mental Disease*, 142, 515–25.

De Renzi, E., Faglioni, P. and Previdi, P. (1977). 'Spatial memory and hemispheric locus of lesion'. *Cortex*, 13, 424–33.

De Renzi, E., Faglioni, P., Grossi, D. and Nichelli, P. (1991). 'Apperceptive and associative forms of prosopagnosia'. *Cortex*, 27, 213–21.

Efron, R. (1968). 'What is perception?'. In R. S. Cohen and M. W. Wartofsky (eds), *Boston Studies in the Philosophy of Science*, 4. Dordrecht: Reidel.

Ekman, P. and Friesen, W. V. (1976). *Pictures of Facial Affect*. Palo Alto, CA: Consulting Psychologists Press.

Ellis, A. W. and Young, A. W. (1988). *Human Cognitive Neuropsychology*. London: Lawrence Erlbaum.

Ellis, H. D. and Florence, M. (1990). 'Bodamer's (1947) paper on prosopagnosia'. *Cognitive Neuropsychology*, 7, 81–105.

Ettlinger, G. (1956). 'Sensory deficits in visual agnosia'. *Journal of Neurology, Neurosurgery, and Psychiatry*, 19, 297–307.

Farah, M. J. and Ratcliff, G. (eds) (1994). *The Neuropsychology of High-level Vision: Collected Tutorial Essays*. Hillsdale, NJ: Lawrence Erlbaum.

Farnsworth, D. (1957). *The Farnsworth–Munsell 100-Hue Test for the Examination of Color Discrimination*. Baltimore, MD: Munsell Color.

Flude, B. M., Ellis, A. W. and Kay, J. (1989). 'Face processing and name retrieval in an anomic aphasic: names are stored separately from semantic information about familiar people'. *Brain and Cognition*, 11, 60–72.

Geschwind, N. and Fusillo, M. (1966). 'Color-naming defects in association with alexia'. *Archives of Neurology*, 15, 137–46.

Goodale, M. A. and Milner, A. D. (1992). 'Separate visual pathways for perception and action'. *Trends in Neurosciences*, 15, 20–5.

Goodale, M. A., Milner, A. D., Jakobson, L. S. and Carey, D. P. (1991). 'A neurological dissociation between perceiving objects and grasping them'. *Nature*, 349, 154–6.

Hanley, J. R., Pearson, N. and Young, A. W. (1990). 'Impaired memory for new visual forms'. *Brain*, 113, 1131–48.

Hanley, J. R., Young, A. W. and Pearson, N. (1989). 'Defective recognition of familiar people'. *Cognitive Neuropsychology*, 6, 179–210.

Hanley, J. R., Young, A. W. and Pearson, N. (1991). 'Impairment of the visuo-spatial sketch pad'. *Quarterly Journal of Experimental Psychology*, 43A, 101–25.

Hécaen, H. (1981). 'The neuropsychology of face recognition'. In G. Davies, H. Ellis and J. Shepherd (eds), *Perceiving and Remembering Faces*. London: Academic Press.

Heilman, K. M. (1979). 'Neglect and related disorders'. In K. M. Heilman and E. Valenstein (eds), *Clinical Neuropsychology*. New York: Oxford University Press.

Heywood, C. A., Cowey, A. and Newcombe, F. (1991). 'Chromatic discrimination in a cortically colour blind observer'. *European Journal of Neuroscience*, 3, 802–12.

108

Heywood, C. A., Cowey, A. and Newcombe, F. (1994). 'On the role of parvocellular (P) and magnocellular (M) pathways in cerebral achromatopsia'. *Brain*, 117, 245–54.

Holmes, G. (1919). 'Disturbances of visual space perception'. *British Medical Journal*, 2, 230–3.

Humphreys, G. W. and Riddoch, M. J. (1984). 'Routes to object constancy: implications from neurological impairments of object constancy'. *Quarterly Journal of Experimental Psychology*, 36A, 385–415.

Humphreys, G. W. and Riddoch, M. J. (1987). 'The fractionation of visual agnosia'. In G. W. Humphreys and M. J. Riddoch (eds), *Visual Object Processing: A Cognitive Neuropsychological Approach*. London: Lawrence Erlbaum.

Humphreys, G. W. and Riddoch, M. J. (1994). 'Attention to within-object and between-object spatial representations: multiple sites for visual selection'. *Cognitive Neuropsychology*, 11, 207–41.

Kinsbourne, M. and Warrington, E. K. (1964). 'Observations on colour agnosia'. *Journal of Neurology, Neurosurgery, and Psychiatry*, 27, 296–9.

McGlinchey-Berroth, R., Milberg, W. P., Verfaellie, M., Alexander, M. and Kilduff, P. T. (1993). 'Semantic processing in the neglected visual field: evidence from a lexical decision task'. *Cognitive Neuropsychology*, 10, 79–108.

McKenna, P. and Warrington, E. K. (1980). 'Testing for nominal dysphasia'. *Journal of Neurology, Neurosurgery, and Psychiatry*, 43, 781–8.

McNeil, J. E. and Warrington, E. K. (1993). 'Prosopagnosia: a face specific disorder'. *Quarterly Journal of Experimental Psychology*, 46A, 1–10.

Marshall, J. C. and Halligan, P. W. (1988). 'Blindsight and insight in visuo-spatial neglect'. *Nature*, 336, 766–7.

Meadows, J. C. (1974a). 'The anatomical basis of prosopagnosia'. *Journal of Neurology, Neurosurgery, and Psychiatry*, 37, 489–501.

Meadows, J. C. (1974b). 'Disturbed perception of colours associated with localized cerebral lesions'. *Brain*, 97, 615–32.

Milner, A. D., Perrett, D. I., Johnston, R. S., Benson, P. J., Jordan, T. R., Heeley, D. W., Bettucci, D., Mortara, F., Mutani, R., Terazzi, E. and Davidson, D. L. W. (1991). 'Perception and action in "visual form agnosia"'. *Brain*, 114, 405–28.

Newcombe, F. (1979). 'The processing of visual information in prosopagnosia and acquired dyslexia: functional versus physiological interpretation'. In D. J. Oborne, M. M. Gruneberg and J. R. Eiser (eds), *Research in Psychology and Medicine*, vol. 1. London: Academic Press.

Newcombe, F., De Haan, E. H. F., Ross, J. and Young, A. W. (1989). 'Face processing, laterality, and contrast sensitivity'. *Neuropsychologia*, 27, 523–38.

Newcombe, F., Ratcliff, G. and Damasio, H. (1987). 'Dissociable visual and spatial impairments following right posterior cerebral lesions: clinical, neuropsychological and anatomical evidence'. *Neuropsychologia*, 25, 149–61.

Oldfield, R. C. and Wingfield, A. (1965). 'Response latencies in naming objects'. *Quarterly Journal of Experimental Psychology*, 17, 273–81.

Ratcliff, G. and Davies-Jones, G. A. B. (1972). 'Defective visual localization in focal brain wounds'. *Brain*, 95, 49–60.

Ratcliff, G. and Newcombe, F. (1982). 'Object recognition: some deductions from the clinical evidence'. In A. W. Ellis (ed.), *Normality and Pathology in Cognitive Functions*. London: Academic Press.

Riddoch, M. J. and Humphreys, G. W. (1987a). 'A case of integrative visual agnosia'. *Brain*, 110, 1431–62.

Riddoch, M. J. and Humphreys, G. W. (1987b). 'Visual object processing in optic aphasia: a case of semantic access agnosia'. *Cognitive Neuropsychology*, 4, 131–85.

Riddoch, M. J. and Humphreys, G. W. (1993). *BORB: Birmingham Object Recognition Battery*. Hove: Lawrence Erlbaum.

Rubens, A. B. (1979). 'Agnosia'. In K. M. Heilman and E. Valenstein (eds), *Clinical Neuropsychology*. New York: Oxford University Press.

Schacter, D. L. (1987). 'Implicit memory: history and current status'. *Journal of Experimental Psychology: Learning, Memory, and Cognition*, 13, 501–18.

Semenza, C. and Zettin, M. (1988). 'Generating proper names: a case of selective inability'. *Cognitive Neuropsychology*, 5, 711–21.

Semenza, C. and Zettin, M. (1989). 'Evidence from aphasia for the role of proper names as pure referring expressions'. *Nature*, 342, 678–9.

Shallice, T. and Jackson, M. (1988). 'Lissauer on agnosia'. *Cognitive Neuropsychology*, 5, 153–92.

Snodgrass, J. G. and Vanderwart, M. (1980). 'A standardized set of 260 pictures: norms for name agreement, image agreement, familiarity, and visual complexity'. *Journal of Experimental Psychology: Human Learning and Memory*, 6, 174–215.

Tzavaras, A., Hécaen, H. and Le Bras, H. (1970). 'Le problème de la spécificité du déficit de la reconnaissance du visage humain lors des lésions hémisphériques unilatérales'. *Neuropsychologia*, 8, 403–16.

Warrington, E. K. (1984). *Recognition Memory Test*. Windsor: NFER-Nelson.

Warrington, E. K. (1985). 'Agnosia: the impairment of object recognition.' In J. A. M. Frederiks (ed.), *Handbook of Clinical Neurology. 1: Clinical Neuropsychology*. Amsterdam: Elsevier.

Warrington, E. K. (1987). 'Visual deficits associated with occipital lobe lesions in man'. In C. Chagass, R. Gattass and C. Gross (eds), *Pontificiae Academiae Scientarium Scripta Varia*, 54, 247–61.

Warrington, E. K. and James, M. (1991). *VOSP: The Visual Object and Space Perception Battery*. Bury St Edmunds: Thames Valley.

Warrington, E. K. and Shallice, T. (1984). 'Category specific semantic impairments'. *Brain*, 107, 829–54.

Warrington, E. K. and Taylor, A. M. (1978). 'Two categorical stages of object recognition'. *Perception*, 7, 695–705.

Wilson, B., Cockburn, J. and Halligan, P. (1987). *Behavioural Inattention Test*. Bury St Edmunds: Thames Valley.

Young, A. W. (1992). 'Face recognition impairments'. *Philosophical Transactions of the Royal Society, London*, B335, 47–54.

Young, A. W. (1994). 'Covert recognition'. In M. J. Farah and G. Ratcliff (eds), *The Neuropsychology of High-level Vision: Collected Tutorial Essays*. Hillsdale, NJ: Lawrence Erlbaum.

Young, A. W. and De Haan, E. H. F. (1990). 'Impairments of visual awareness'. *Mind and Language*, 5, 29–48.

Young, A. W. and Ellis, H. D. (1989). 'Childhood prosopagnosia'. *Brain and Cognition*, 9, 16–47.

Young, A. W., De Haan, E. H. F. and Newcombe, F. (1990a). 'Unawareness of impaired face recognition'. *Brain and Cognition*, 14, 1–18.

Young, A. W., De Haan, E. H. F., Newcombe, F. and Hay, D. C. (1990b). 'Facial neglect'. *Neuropsychologia*, 28, 391–415.

Young, A. W., Newcombe, F., De Haan, E. H. F., Small, M. and Hay, D. C. (1993). 'Face perception after brain injury: selective impairments affecting identity and expression'. *Brain*, 116, 941–59.

Zihl, J., Von Cramon, D. and Mai, N. (1983). 'Selective disturbance of movement vision after bilateral brain damage'. *Brain*, 106, 313–40.

7

ASSESSMENT OF IMPAIRED LANGUAGE

Christine Skinner

The need for socialization is the core of human existence, and the desire to communicate with others is at the heart of that socialization. Language is the basic form of this communication and is what Chomsky (1972) calls the human essence. The uniqueness of language lies not in the mode of its expression or comprehension but in its ability to transmit symbolic meaning. Language enables the individual to describe and clarify his or her thoughts for himself or herself and others. Human experience and interaction are welded to language, and according to Goodman (1971) the ability to share experience through language, both verbal and written, is a means of homeostasis which enables people to maintain an equilibrium in which they can survive. Goodman (1971) associates language as well with maturity, which he defines as an ability to relate warmly to and with others in their goals, aspirations and hopes. Definitions of maturity seem to involve the ability to use language effectively.

Aphasia is an impairment of language. When an individual has lost language as a result of stroke, head injury or other neurological disorder, not only is he or she devastated but the whole fabric of his or her life and that of his or her family will be severely affected. Aphasia cannot be cured, but appropriate intervention enables many individuals to be able to comprehend and produce language more effectively by heightening each person's language potential maximally within his or her environment.

In order to achieve appropriate and successful intervention, assessment of the language disorder must be an in-depth analysis of all available data.

HISTORICAL APPROACHES TO THE ASSESSMENT OF APHASIA

A number of definitions of aphasia have appeared in the literature over the years, the concepts of which significantly affect the emphasis chosen for assessment analysis. For example, Hughlings Jackson's concept of aphasia is intrinsically linked to his notion of propositional language (Head, 1915). This is an intellectual, volitional, rational language which involves the use of linguistic symbols for the communication of highly specific and highly appropriate ideas and relationships. Within the context of this definition, assessment involves an analysis of patient ability to use spontaneous language in order to propositionalize or communicate specific ideas.

Goldstein (1948) observed that use of abstract language implies an ability to react to things in a conceptual manner. This is used to comprehend relationships between objects and events in the world. In Goldstein's view, individuals with aphasia demonstrate concreteness rather than an abstract attitude. They respond passively to reality and are bound to the immediate experience of objects and events. If one cannot abstract from a situation, one cannot symbolize or embed symbols in a number of specific relationships. The aphasic is unable to use divergent semantic behaviour in order to produce a variety of concepts and to consider things which are only possibilities rather than actualities. Goldstein and his associates (Goldstein and Scheerer 1941) developed a number of assessments designed to analyse the patient's ability to comprehend and produce language which becomes increasingly more abstract and propositional or divergent.

Definitions of aphasia which relate language behaviours to a single common denominator, and which view the language mechanism as a unitary process, support the solidarity of the expressive and receptive as well as the semantic and syntactic components of language. These definitions suggest that damage to such a mechanism results in a general language impairment in which there is equivalent or symmetrical damage in all aspects of language. Shuell *et al.* (1964) produced one of the most popular in-depth, uni-dimensional definitions, defining aphasia as a general language impairment crossing all language modalities: speaking, listening, reading and writing. According to this definition, aphasia is not modality specific; rather it is the inability to retrieve words and rules of an acquired language for communication. Shuell's concept of the cause of this general language breakdown reflects a broad and dynamic view of the language process and appears to encompass far more than a language mechanism which can only generate highly learned input–output responses.

The assessment implications of this definition involve an analysis of patient ability to comprehend and produce language within all four modalities – an analysis of ability to retrieve words and rules of the acquired language and use functional, spontaneous, connected units in order to communicate. Shuell's test, the Minnesota Test for the Differential Diagnosis of Aphasia (MTDDA: Shuell, 1973) is based on this model.

CLASSIFICATION OF APHASIC SYNDROMES

Some authorities in the area of adult aphasia have conceptualized aphasia as a symptom dichotomy based on whether output is fluent or non-fluent. Frequently these definitions are associated with cerebral localization of damage, and categorization of type of aphasia is based on the terms used in classical neurology.

The major subdivision among the aphasic syndromes is based on the character of the speech output. When the anterior portion of the anatomical speech area is involved, the flow of speech is more or less impaired at the levels of speech initiation, finding and sequencing of articulatory movements, and production of grammatical sequences. The resulting speech is referred to as 'non-fluent' (Goodglass and Kaplan, 1983).

Non-fluent aphasia

Broca's aphasia

This is the common 'anterior' or non-fluent aphasia, resulting from a lesion involving the third frontal convolution of the left hemisphere. Its essential characteristics are awkward articulation, restricted vocabulary, restriction of grammar to the simplest, most overlearned forms, and relative preservation of auditory comprehension. Written language follows the pattern of speech, in that writing is usually at least as severely impaired as speech while reading, for meaning, is only mildly affected (Box 7.1).

Box 7.1

A case history of a Broca's aphasic

Nine months prior to examination JT, a 21-year-old right-handed male, was wounded by a mortar shell fragment which penetrated the fronto-parietal region, resulting in a severe right hemiplegia and a severe Broca's aphasia. During the initial interview he was co-operative but demonstrated frustration over his inability to speak fluently. His speech was limited to one-word answers, almost all nouns, and the interview required much questioning and guesswork on the part of the examiner. A sample of the conversation follows:

'What did you do before you were wounded?'
'Forces.'
'You were in the Army?'
'Special forces' (unclear articulation).
'What did you do?'
'Boom.'
'I don't understand.'

'splosions.'
'Do you work alone?'
'Me . . . on guy.'
'Were you alone when you were injured?'
'Recon . . . scout.'
'Why do you come here?'
'Speech.'
'Tell me what is happening in this picture.'
'Cookie jar . . . falling over . . . ov . . . ov . . . ovflow.'
Source: Goodglass and Kaplan, 1983, with permission from the publishers.

The contrasting or 'fluent' forms of aphasia are marked by facility in articulation and many long runs of words in a variety of grammatical constructions, in conjunction with word-finding difficulty for substantives and picturable action words. The fluent aphasias are usually the result of lesions posterior to the rolandic fissure, sparing Broca's area. There is considerable variation in the detailed symptomatology of fluent aphasia due, at least in part, to the site of the injury. The significant, variable components are the amount and type of paraphasia, auditory receptive loss, word-finding difficulties and impaired repetition.

Fluent aphasias

Wernicke's Aphasia

This is the most common of the fluent aphasias and usually depends on a lesion in the posterior portion of the first temporal gyrus of the left hemisphere. The cortical features of this syndrome are impaired auditory comprehension and fluently articulated but paraphasic speech. Paraphasia may include both sound transpositions (literal) such as 'eat cup' for 'tea cup' and word substitutions (verbal) such as 'chair' for 'table'. In addition, word-finding difficulty is an almost constant feature of this disorder, while reading and writing are usually severely impaired as well (Box 7.2).

Anomia

The syndromes of Wernicke's aphasia and anomia do not have a sharp boundary, although the classic forms of each of these 'fluent' aphasias are unmistakably distinct. Some patients, who appear initially as full-blown Wernicke aphasics, evolve into typical anomics in the course of their recovery. The major feature of anomic aphasia is the prominence of word-finding difficulty in the context of fluent, grammatically well-formed speech. It differs from Wernicke's aphasia in the absence of literal and verbal paraphasias and in the relative intactness of auditory comprehension. The

114

Box 7.2

A case history of a Wernicke's aphasic

CM, a 56-year-old medical practitioner, suffered a cerebrovascular accident diagnosed as a thrombosis in the distribution of the left middle cerebral artery. On assessment, eight months post-onset, he had full use of all four limbs with normal sensation. There was a right homonymous hemianopia. Performance on the 'Cookie Theft' picture description was as follows:

Well, this is . . . mother is away here working her work our o'here to get her better, but when shes looking, the 2 boys looking in the other part. One their small tile into her time here. She's working another time because she's getting too. So the 2 boys work together and one is sneakin aroound here making his . . . work and his further funnas his time he had. [and so on]

Source: Goodglass and Kaplan, 1983, with permission from the publishers.

---

classical anomic aphasic speaks freely, but with a dramatic emptiness of substantive words in his or her speech. Circumlocutions may be common, such as 'I had a thing done up where your hair is.' (See Box 7.3.)

Box 7.3

A case history of an anomic aphasic

KR, a 54-year-old right-handed man, suffered the sudden onset of a right hemiplegia and speech difficulty resulting from complete occlusion of the left middle cerebral artery. Three months post-onset he presented with a residual weakness of the right arm, and performance on the 'Cookie Theft' picture description was as follows:

This is a boy and that's a boy an that's . . . thing! An this is going off pretty soon. This is a . . . place that this is mostly in. An this is a girl . . . an that something that they're running an they've got the water foing down here.

Source: Goodglass and Kaplan, 1983, with permission from the publishers.

Conduction aphasia

This is the name applied to the syndrome in which repetition is disproportionately severely impaired in relation to the level of fluency in spontaneous speech and the near-normal level of the auditory comprehension. While it is considered to be one of the 'fluent' aphasias, this fluency may be restricted to brief bursts of speech. In these instances, the patients are unlike Broca's aphasics in that they usually produce well-articulated sequences of first-language phonemes with normal intonation, and initiate a variety of syntactic patterns. The outstanding speech difficulty is in the proper choice and sequencing of phonemes, so that literal paraphasia constantly interferes with production, especially in the repetition tasks (Box 7.4).

Box 7.4

A case history of a conduction aphasic

LX, a 20-year-old male graduate, suffered a 0.22 calibre bullet wound in an accident. The bullet entered the left lower mid-parietal region, crossed the mid-line and came to rest in the right parietal lobe. Bilateral craniotomy was carried out to remove the bullet. Two months post-trauma he had residual right-sided weakness, and his performance on the 'Cookie Theft' picture description was as follows:

Well this um . . . somebody's . . . ah mahther is takin the . . . washin the day she's and the water . . . the water is falling . . . is flowing all over the place and the kids sneakin out in back behind her, takin the cookies in the . . . out of the top in the . . . what do you call this?' (examiner: 'Shelf?') 'Yes . . . and theres a . . . then the girl . . . not the girl . . . the boy who's getting the cookies is on this as . . . strool and startin to fall off. That about all I see.

Source: Goodglass and Kaplan, 1983, with permission from the publishers.

Transcortical sensory aphasia

This rare syndrome is characterized by the remarkable preservation of repetition in the context of the features of a severe Wernicke's aphasia. The typical patient with this disorder does not initiate speech on his or her own. When addressed he or she replies with well-articulated but irrelevant paraphasia, which may include both actual words and neologisms. He or she is totally unable to name to confrontation but usually offers grossly irrelevant responses when asked. These patients often echo the examiner's words instead of replying. There is, in addition to this excellent ability to repeat, an unusual preservation of memorized materials, such as the Lord's Prayer or nursery rhymes. Written language appears completely destroyed for both reading and writing.

Transcortical motor aphasia

This is marked by an absence of spontaneous speech, with some recovery of the ability to make brief replies to questions and fairly good confrontation naming ability. The patient has difficulty in initiating and organizing his or her response, but once initiated, it is usually well articulated. Auditory comprehension is relatively well preserved, as are reading comprehension and oral reading. Repetition is remarkable in that it is prompt, well articulated, grammatically intact and free of the initiation difficulty which marks the rest of the patient's verbal output.

The Boston Diagnostic Aphasia Examination (BDAE: Goodglass and Kaplan, 1983), the Western Aphasia Battery (WAB: Kertesz, 1982) and the Language Modalities Test for Aphasia (Wepman and Jones, 1961) all reflect such classification systems.

ALTERNATIVE APPROACHES TO THE ASSESSMENT OF LANGUAGE FUNCTION

Wepman (1976) suggested that aphasia may be a thought-process disorder, in which impairment of semantic expression is the result of an impairment of thought processes which serve as a catalyst for verbal expression. Within a thought-process definition, assessment involves determining whether the individual can follow a train of thought in his or her spontaneous language, and then subsequently determining whether he or she can elaborate or expand upon topics or ideas.

Luria's (1970, 1976) model of aphasia presents a different and more dynamic characterization of the way language is represented in the brain. It proposes that language has its foundation in the complex interaction of systems which have responsibility not simply for language but also for other cognitive functions. Luria's model is essentially a process model, in the sense that circumscribed areas of cortex are not seen as responsible for the execution of entire functions as they are on a classical model, but cognitive functioning is seen as being processed through modular subcomponents.

The notions of information processing, modularity and subcomponents of cognition are prominent features of the contemporary approach to aphasia, that of cognitive neuropsychology. The information-processing model is the core framework of the cognitive neuropsychology approach for the interpretation of deficits in brain-damaged individuals. This kind of approach views the brain as a special-purpose computer and assumes that components of cognition – for instance, language processing, facial perception and memory – are organized and represented in the brain in a modular fashion (Fodor, 1983).

Cognitive neuropsychology is now well established, but its development has been controversial. Few would disagree with the statement that language utilizes physiological systems and mechanisms for production and comprehension, but the focus of the argument is to what extent language processing is an independent enterprise. Critics submit (Schweiger and Brown, 1988) that the logical computer metaphor, although a useful device allowing

117

clarity of description, cannot be built into an explanatory theory for human cognition because the human brain and brain processing depend upon biological and evolutionary development, and may operate like computers in only the most superficial of ways.

Despite the view that cognitive neuropsychology does not have a satisfactory model which can cope with the complexity of human language, the work carried out by Ellis and Young (1988) demonstrates that it has an important and significant contribution to make to the study of aphasia. This involves a single-case-study approach to research and assessment, resulting in a detailed investigation of impairments through psycholinguistically controlled tests, which give an explanation of underlying patterns of deficit in terms of information processing. An example of such an assessment is the Psycholinguistic Assessments of Language Processing in Aphasia (PALPA: Kay *et al.*, 1992).

PALPA

This consists of sixty assessments designed to help to diagnose language-processing difficulties in individuals with acquired brain damage. According to the authors, PALPA applies a psycholinguistic approach to the interpretation of processes concerned with the recognition, comprehension and production of spoken and written words and sentences. The approach is based on the assumption that the language system is organized in separate modules of processing, and that these can be impaired selectively by brain damage. Kay *et al.* claim that PALPA aims to provide information about the integrity of these modules, and to find those in which the aphasic person seems to be functioning below normal and those which appear to be continuing to function normally or near normally. It is not suggested that PALPA should be administered to an individual in its entirety; rather, the assessments should be tailored to those that are appropriate to the hypothesis under investigation. This should provide a firm grounding for an understanding of a particular processing disorder, on which any treatment programme can be based.

It should now be apparent that there is a range of explanations for the mechanisms underlying aphasic symptomatology. An examination of the variety of views on the nature of aphasia indicates that there has been an evolution from classical models to processing models, from the 'static' to dynamic, from 'types' to individuals, and from the simple to the complex. The characteristics of aphasia that constitute our database for investigation and intervention have not changed, but we know a great deal more about them. What we now have to find is the most efficient and comprehensive way of collecting this data in order to plan the most effective method of intervention and remediation.

ASSESSMENT BASED ON CHAPEY'S APPROACH

In her chapter on assessment in *Language Intervention Strategies in Adult Aphasia* (Chapey, 1986), Chapey cites Muma's (1978) definition of language as consisting of three highly interrelated and integrated components: cognitive, linguistic and communicative. It is this view, which she develops in discussing assessment of aphasia, that provides the framework for this chapter.

Within this context, aphasia is defined by Chapey as an acquired impairment in language and the cognitive processes which underlie language, caused by organic damage to certain areas of the brain. It is characterized by a reduction in and dysfunction of language content or meaning, language form or structure, and language use or function. The cognitive processes underlying language – recognition, comprehension, memory and thinking – may also be impaired. Aphasia is, therefore, manifested in listening, speaking, reading and writing, although not necessarily to the same degree.

It is important to mention differential diagnosis here. Aphasia does not include such single-modality impairments as an acquired isolated impairment in visual processing (agnosia) or an impairment in voluntary motor positioning and sequencing in the absence of paralysis (apraxia). This is a motor-speech disorder in which there is a disruption of central motor planning, causing articulatory and phonemic errors which are variable and inconsistent and which may contravene the phonotactic rules of the language. When a motor-speech deficit is due to an impairment in muscular control, due to subcortical, central and/or peripheral nervous-system damage, it is labelled 'dysarthria' and, in this instance, articulatory errors are consistent and associated with phonatory, respiratory and swallowing dysfunction also.

Darley (1978) identifies these as transmissive types of problems, in which the patient performs significantly worse in one modality than in another. Aphasia, on the other hand, is a general reduction of language regardless of which modality is used.

Because aphasia, agnosia, apraxia and dysarthria can occur in one individual, assessment involves determining which, if any, of these disorders exist and subsequently defining the nature and extent of the particular impairment.

Assessment is defined by Chapey as an organized, goal-directed evaluation of aspects of all of the three interrelated and integrated components of language cited above. Such an evaluation is carried out in order to determine the client's abilities and impairments and the degree to which these can be modified. A thorough, specific and detailed assessment is essential if one is to see patterns of behaviour, describe the complexity of the client's language behaviour, and identify a hierarchy of therapeutic goals which are appropriate to that individual. Specifically, there should be a strong connection

119

between one's definition of language, one's description of the client's language, and the goals that are established for intervention.

Three processes are involved in assessment – data collection, hypothesis formation and hypothesis testing – and it is proposed to conclude this chapter by looking at the variety of ways in which data can be collected.

Data collection is the process of obtaining information which is linked directly or indirectly to the language abilities and impairments of the individual. This information can be obtained through reported observations or direct observations. Reported observations can take the form of an interview or written correspondence, including such structured gatherers of information as questionnaires. This kind of data can be collected from professional colleagues as well as the family and other carers closely involved with the aphasic client. Studies (Wilcox, 1983; Whitbourne, 1976) have shown that data collected through reported observations is often significantly different from that collected by the clinician. Linguistic perform-ance can differ between the contexts of clinical examination and natural settings. Natural settings are rich in familiar contextual cues, which interact with the linguistic input to aid comprehension and to supplement verbal expression. The aphasic individual at home or in familiar social settings may often be able to converse with someone who shares knowledge with him or her on a range of subjects, and the listener can use this knowledge to interpret incomplete aphasic utterances.

Assessment by direct observation of the client by the clinician can occur over several sessions in order to maximize patient ability to respond and to minimize fatigue, stress and failure. It allows the examiner to elicit language in several different contexts, such as unstructured, moderately structured and highly structured spontaneous-language environments.

In unstructured observation, the clinician describes the individual's cogni-tive, linguistic and communicative behaviours in a natural setting where there is a minimum of control or interference. Chapey (1986) suggests that the setting should be familiar to the client and provide an opportunity for the individual to interact verbally with others. Holland (1982) has produced a guideline of observational categories which have been found helpful to those clinicians attempting to observe patients as they go about their daily routines. In this way it may be possible to assess how well an individual is adjusting to his or her residual linguistic capacity, rather than how much progress is being made in relearning linguistic skills.

In moderately structured spontaneous-language observation, the clinician takes an active role in structuring observation by using pre-determined questions or tasks to elicit specific aspects of spontaneous language in context. There are several published profiles for obtaining such information about functional communication or language use. The best known is Sarno's (1969) Functional Communication Profile, which is a check-list of preserved functions. Holland's (1980) Communicative Assessment for Daily

Living demands involvement in role play and comprehension of complex instructions. In compiling the Edinburgh Functional Communication Profile (EFCP: Skinner *et al.*, 1984), the authors felt that neither of the previous methods of data collection accurately investigates natural communication.

The EFCP was, therefore, devised in order to overcome some of the perceived limitations of these assessments, most notably by utilizing a theoretical framework drawn from the field of pragmatics and by maintaining a distinction between measurement and observation. These concerns to apply insights gained from the study of pragmatics to the field of assessment of communication disorder have been reflected in all areas of speech pathology literature (Prinz, 1980; Gallagher and Prutting, 1983; Davis and Wilcox, 1985; McTear, 1985a, 1985b; Prutting and Kirshner, 1987; Penn, 1988).

The revised Edinburgh Functional Communication Profile (Wirz *et al.*, 1990) is designed to structure the observation and analysis of an individual's communicative functioning. The profile focuses upon two parameters in particular: first, the ability to engage in, and sustain, interaction, and second, the modalities, verbal and non-verbal, used to achieve this performance. The EFCP provides two profiles of the client's ability to interact: the International Analysis and the Communicative Performance Analysis. Both profiles are based on the theoretical notion of the 'Speech Act' as described by Searle (1969).

ACQUIRED LANGUAGE DISORDERS IN CHILDREN

Acquired language disorders represent less than 10 per cent of all speech and language problems in childhood. Two groups can be identified. One, traumatic, consists of children with clearly defined focal cerebral damage, such as infarction and closed head injury. The second, convulsive, has been used for those who, without a clear damaging event, acquired their language problem in association with epilepsy (Brooks, 1984).

Studies reported by Lees and Neville (1990) seem to indicate that the majority of children show good recovery of language function, most occurring within three months post-onset, with continuing progress during the first year. However, Lees and Neville point out that examination of qualitative data shows that a large number of these children continue to experience high-level cognitive difficulties in the speed of auditory verbal processing and lexical recall. This is reflected in reported continuing difficulties in school, which need to be established more objectively when trying to meet educational requirements.

Evidence reported in Brooks (1984) suggests that the extent of recovery from brain injury in childhood may have been overestimated. This is probably related to the long-held notion that brain lesions in childhood are less specific than in adult life, because of greater brain plasticity. Recent work by Paquier and Van Dongen (1993) would appear to confirm the notion of early onset of hemispheric specialization for language. Results from their study, like those of Lees and Neville (1990), indicate that as well as persistent language deficits, poor academic performance has been observed in school-aged children even after clinical recovery of language abilities.

Whilst there has been an increase in the number of studies containing detailed clinical reports of the language profiles of children with acquired aphasia, Lees (1993) reports that there has been no consistent use of classification systems for these disorders. The most commonly used system remains that developed by Goodglass and Kaplan (1983), which Lees's study demonstrates is no more effective in categorizing childhood aphasia than it is for aphasia in adults.

There are few appropriate assessments for acquired language disorders in children. Lees suggests that those normally used in assessing adults with aphasia are not suitable for young children and recommends instead those published assessments for developmental child language disorders (see also Beech *et al.*, 1993).

CONCLUSIONS

Strengths and weaknesses are inherent in any approach to assessment. Standardized tests provide a reliable and often quick measure of language that make interpretations and generalizations more comfortable. On the other hand, descriptive and contextual measures lead us to more valid implications and give us insight into how aphasic clients function outside the clinic. Above all, the measures that are selected should be suited to the management needs of each individual: this is far better than attempting to force the client to fit into the mould of an available or favourite test. Specialized tests, selected in concert with a clear impression of unique and individual needs, can allow better assessment and ultimately better management. As Darley (1982) said: 'The limits of what might work in language evaluation are set only by the limits on one's imagination and creativity.'

REFERENCES

Beech, J. R. and Harding, L. with Hilton–Jones, D. (eds) (1993). *Assessment in Speech and Language Therapy*. London and New York: Routledge.

Brooks, N. (ed.) (1984). *Closed Head Injury: Psychological, Social and Family Consequences*. Oxford: Oxford University Press.

Chapey, R. (1986). 'The assessment of language disorders in adults'. In R. Chapey (ed.), *Language Intervention Strategies in Adult Aphasia*. Baltimore, MD: Williams and Wilkins.

Chomsky, N. (1972) *Language and Mind*. New York: Harcourt, Brace and World.

Craig, H. (1983). 'Applications of pragmatic language models for intervention'. In T. M. Gallagher and C. A. Prutting (eds), *Pragmatic Assessment and Intervention Issues in Language*. San Diego, CA: College Hill Press.

Darley, F. (1978). 'Differential diagnosis of acquired motor speech disorders'. In F. Darley and D. Spriestersbach (eds), *Diagnostic Methods in Speech Pathology*. New York: Harper and Row.

Darley, F. (1982). *Aphasia*. Philadelphia, PA: W. and B. Saunders.

Davis, G. A. and Wilcox, M. J. (1985). *Adult Aphasia Rehabilitation: Applied Pragmatics*. Windsor: NFER–Nelson.

Ellis, A. and Young, A. (1988). *Human Cognitive Neuropsychology*. Hove and London: Lawrence Erlbaum.

Fodor, J. (1983). *The Modularity of the Mind*. Cambridge, MA: MIT Press.

Gallagher, T. M. and Prutting, C. A. (eds) (1983). *Pragmatic Assessment and Intervention Issues in Language*. San Diego, CA: College Hill Press.

Goldstein, K. (1948). *Language and Language Disturbances*. New York: Grune and Stratton.

Goldstein, K. and Scheerer, M. (1941). 'Abstract and concrete behaviour in experimental study with special tests'. *Psychological Monographs*, 53, 2.

Goodglass, H. and Kaplan, E. (1983). *The Assessment of Aphasia and Related Disorders*. 2nd edn. Philadelphia, PA: Lea and Febiger.

Goodman, P. (1971). *Speaking and Language: Defense of Poetry*. New York: Random House.

Head, H. (1915). 'Hughlings Jackson on aphasia and kindred disorders'. *Brain*, 38, 1–27.

Holland, A. (1980). *Communication Activities in Daily Living*. Baltimore, MD: University Park Press.

Holland, A. (1982). 'Observing functional communication of aphasic adults'. *Journal of Speech and Hearing Disorders*, 47, 50–6.

Kay, J., Lesser, R. and Coltheart, M. (1992). *Psycholinguistic Assessments of Language Processing in Aphasia*. London: Lawrence Erlbaum.

Kertesz, A. (1982). *Western Aphasia Battery*. New York: Harcourt Brace Jovanovich.

Lees, J. A. (1993). 'Differentiating language disorder subtypes in acquired childhood aphasia'. *Aphasiology*, 7, 481–8.

Lees, J. A. and Neville, B. G. R. (1990). 'Acquired aphasia in children: case studies of five children'. *Aphasiology*, 4, 463–78.

Luria, A. (1970). *Traumatic Aphasia* (trans. D. Bowden). The Hague: Mouton.

Luria, A. (1976). *Basic Problems of Neurolinguistics* (trans. B. Haig). The Hague: Mouton.

McTear, M. (1985a). 'Pragmatic disorders: a question of direction'. *British Journal of Disorders of Communication*, 20, 119–27.

McTear, M. (1985b). 'Pragmatic disorders: a case study of conversational disability'. *British Journal of Disorders of Communication*, 20, 129–42.

Muma, J. (1978). *Language Handbook: Concepts, Assessment and Intervention*. Englewoods Cliffs, NJ: Prentice Hall.

Paquier, P. and Van Dongen, H. R. (1993). 'Current trends in acquired childhood aphasia: an introduction'. *Aphasiology*, 7, 421–40.

Penn, C. (1988). 'The profiling of syntax and pragmatics in aphasia'. *Clinical Linguistics*, 2, 179–207.

Prinz, P. (1980). 'A note on requesting strategies in adult aphasics'. *Journal of Communication Disorders*, 13, 65–73.

Prutting, C. A. and Kirshner, D. M. (1983). 'Applied pragmatics'. In T. M. Gallagher and C. A. Prutting (eds), *Pragmatic Assessment and Intervention Issues.* San Diego, CA: College Hill Press.

Prutting, C. A. and Kirshner, D. M. (1987). 'A clinical appraisal of the pragmatic aspects of language'. *Journal of Speech and Hearing Disorders*, 52, 105–19.

Sarno, M. T. (1969). *The Functional Communication Profile.* New York: Institute of Rehabilitation Medicine, University Medical Centre.

Schweiger, E. and Brown, J. (1988). 'Minds, models and modules: reflections on'. In M. Coltheart, G. Sartori and R. Job (eds), 'The cognitive neuropsychology of language'. *Aphasiology*, 2, 531–43.

Searle, J. (1969). *Speech Acts: An Essay in the Philosophy of Language.* Cambridge: Cambridge University Press.

Shuell, H. (1973). *Differential Diagnosis of Aphasia with the Minnesota Test.* Revised J. Sefer. Minneapolis, MN: Minnesota University Press.

Shuell, H., Jenkins, J. J. and Jimenez-Pabon, E. (1964). *Aphasia in Adults.* New York: Hoeber Medical Division/Harper and Row.

Skinner, C. M., Wirz, S. L., Thompson, I. M. and Davidson, J. (1984). *The Edinburgh Functional Communication Profile.* Bicester: Winslow Press.

Wepman, J. (1976). 'Aphasia: language without thought or thought without language'. *ASHA*, 18, 131–6.

Wepman, J. and Jones, L. (1961). *Studies in Aphasia: An Approach to Testing: The Language Modalities Test for Aphasia.* Chicago: Education Industry Service.

Whitbourne, S. K. (1976). 'Test anxiety in elderly and young adults'. *International Journal of Ageing and Human Development*, 7, 201–10.

Wilcox, M. J. (1983). 'Aphasia: pragmatic considerations'. In K. Butler and R. Bollinger (eds), *Aphasia: Selected Contemporary Considerations.* Gaithersburg, MD: Aspen Systems.

Wirz, S. L., Skinner, C. M. and Dean, E. C. (1990). *The Revised Edinburgh Functional Communication Profile.* Tucson, AZ: American Skill Builders.

8

ASSESSMENT OF IMPAIRMENT IN WRITTEN LANGUAGE

John C. Marshall

INTRODUCTION

The basic clinical typology of acquired disorders of reading and writing is now reasonably well established. Likewise, testing for the presence of these primary forms is a reasonably straightforward matter; a good preliminary diagnosis can usually be established 'at the bedside', with minimum 'apparatus' and expenditure of time. These remarks do not imply that all problems have been solved. New discoveries will undoubtedly continue to be made: a case in point is a recent report of acquired dysgraphia with selective impairment on writing vowels (Cubelli, 1991). Similarly, arguments continue over the theoretical interpretation of the patterns of disorder observed (Humphreys and Evett, 1985), the controversy now fuelled by the rapid development of connectionist models of reading (Hinton and Shallice, 1991).

In most instances of acquired reading and writing disorder, the impairment will be neither pure nor global. In cases of left-hemisphere damage, dyslexia/dysgraphia will usually (but not inevitably) co-occur with more widespread aphasic disorder; after right-hemisphere injury, 'neglect dyslexia' will frequently be seen in the context of more generalized visuo-spatial neglect. Unless these associated disorders are so severe as to make the testing of reading and writing almost impossible, they can usually be ignored when a diagnosis of the specific nature of the dyslexic/dysgraphic impairment is required. Ultimately, the full cognitive picture must be assessed, and due account taken of neurological etiology, but initially reading and writing should be investigated as modules in their own right.

Global disorders of reading and writing, where the patient can make no attempt at all to perform the standard tasks, can be seen, but are extremely rare. Outside the very acute phase of stroke, or the terminal phases of a dementing illness, global alexia/agraphia is close to unknown; the patient will always try to read and write something on demand. However, if the reading disorder is particularly severe, it is worth checking (after visual acuity has been assessed!) whether the patient can recognize alphabetic material as such. That is, can he or she distinguish letters and words in the correct orientation from their inverted counterparts? Can he or she distinguish between English letters (words) and material written in Cyrillic or Chinese? Finally, cross-case matching (and transcription) should be assessed; can the patient match up letters (and words) in lower case with their counterparts in upper case?

For the vast majority of cases who can read (and write) some words correctly but not others, the examiner will require a fairly large corpus of material that can be presented for writing to dictation and for reading aloud. For the most part, words presented singly will suffice; the reading and writing of text will be mentioned later when pertinent.

Stimulus materials

The stimuli for a basic examination will include:

1 individual letters (upper and lower case) for naming (and sounding-out)

2 (a) words of different lengths (measured by both number of letters and number of syllables)

(b) words with regular (for example, *hand*) and irregular or 'exceptional' spellings (for example *gnaw*)

(c) words from different parts of speech (such as nouns, adjectives, verbs, function words)

(d) words of varied frequency of occurrence (for example, *table* versus *marble*)

(e) words of varied 'abstractness' or 'imageability' (for example, *grape* versus *truth*)

(f) words of varied morphological complexity (for example, *retire* versus *refold*, or *decide* versus *decision*, or *walk* versus *walked*).

3 pronounceable non-words of varied length (such as *nup* versus *nupatine*).

For word stimuli, the trick, in so far as it is possible, is to have words matched on all relevant dimensions save one. Useful lists (and references thereto) can be found in Coltheart *et al.* (1980/1987), Patterson *et al.* (1985) and Kay *et al.* (1990). Stimuli of all the above types should be presented for reading aloud and a full record taken of all omissions and errors; in milder cases, a record of reading latencies may be useful.

We also need to know whether written words are understood. Often this can be ascertained by simply asking the patient what the stimulus means. But this should always be supplemented by further formal testing. For words with visualizable denotations, word–picture matching can be employed, with pictures of varied semantic relatedness to the stimulus word. For more abstract words, tests of synonym judgement are available; given a pair of words (such as *pity – compassion* versus *pity – falsehood*), the patient is required to indicate whether or not the two words are closely related in meaning (Kay *et al.*, 1990). A lexical decision test is also useful, especially for severely impaired patients. Here the patient is simply required to say in response to single stimuli whether they are (*man*) or are not (*mun*) real words.

Although detailed research investigations will obviously require a greater range of stimuli and tasks (e.g. Howard and Franklin, 1988), an examination conducted on the above lines is usually sufficient to form an initial clinical diagnosis (and to begin planning behavioural remediation). The seven major varieties of acquired dyslexia that can be so elicited are briefly described in the following section.

TYPOLOGY OF THE ACQUIRED DYSLEXIAS

Letter-by-letter reading

Many dyslexic patients have grossly inadequate access to the overall visual shape of a word. Some are then forced back upon the strategy of interpreting words one letter at a time. They may accordingly *name* these letters sequentially, either out loud or *sotto voce*, and then 'read' the word by 'naming' the letter string so produced (for example, *long* → 'L, O, N, G . . . long'). Individual letter naming may be fairly intact, but in some patients even this is impaired and will give rise to such errors as *rind* → 'R, I, N, G . . . ring'. For obvious reasons, reading is very slow in these patients, and even when no *overt* letter names are vocalized, reading time is proportional to length in letters. If the stimulus word is long(ish), patients may read the first few letters and then 'guess'. This will sometimes produce the correct answer (for example, *elephant* → '(E) (L) (E) (P) . . . elephant', and sometimes not (for example, *rivet* → '(R) (I) (V) (E) . . . river'). The strategy is perfectly normal, in that we can all reconstitute a word from the spoken sequence of its letter names; it is only abnormal in that it is a grossly inefficient way of reading. Classical accounts of letter-by-letter reading are given in Warrington and Shallice (1980) and Patterson and Kay (1982). It can be seen that, in 'pure' form, no variables other than accuracy of individual letter naming, stimulus length in letters, and auditory-verbal short-term memory should influence the error pattern. In most patients, the semantic interpretation assigned to the stimulus will be the meaning of the letter string produced. There are, however, cases in which some semantic information is available from the stimulus despite overt letter-by-letter reading (Shallice and Saffran, 1986; Coslett and Saffran, 1989).

Surface dyslexia

In other cases where access to 'whole word forms' is impaired, the patient reads by a 'phonic' strategy; essentially, the word is 'sounded out' by the

127

more (or most) frequent grapheme-phoneme correspondence rules of English orthography. Words with a regular pronunciation (such as *mint*) will often be read correctly while irregular words will be regularized (for example, *pint* is read with the short *i* characteristic of *dint, hint, lint, mint, tint*, etc.). Silent letters (such as the *s* of *island*, or the *g* of *gnaw*) will be overtly pronounced; ambiguous letters (such as *g*) may take the wrong variant (for example, *gin* read with the *g* of *gull*). Reading aloud is usually slow and laborious, with sequential overt attempts at sounding out the word, but it can be fast, fluent, and wrong (Bub *et al.*, 1985).

The meaning assigned is usually that of the response, not the stimulus (but cf. Kremin, 1985). That is, if the patient reads *shoe* to rhyme with *hoe* (the regular pronunciation), he or she will interpret the stimulus as meaning 'show'. If the regularization produces a non-word (*broad* read to rhyme with *road*), the stimulus will usually be taken as a non-word. Some homophones may be read aloud correctly, but the patient will not know which meaning is the correct one (for example, *pair* → 'Pair . . . it could be two of a kind, apples and . . . or what you do with your finger nails').

Non-words, which can only have regular pronunciations, may be read as accurately as real, regular words. If the pronunciation of a non-word is homophonic with that of a real word (such as *rume*), the stimulus will be interpreted as that word (that is, *room*).

Classic case descriptions can be found in Marshall and Newcombe (1973) and Baxter and Warrington (1987). Variants within the condition are discussed in Patterson *et al.* (1985). 'Phonic' reading is a normal strategy in that everyone must employ the method with non-words (or unknown words). But we, unlike the surface dyslexic, can also recognize that a *pain* is not a *pane*.

Visual dyslexia

The vast majority of patients with an acquired dyslexia, whatever the classification thereof, will make some (perhaps many) errors of visual word analysis. That is, letters and words of similar configuration will be confused (for example, *oar* → 'car'; *saucer* → 'sausage'; *village* → 'mileage', *stake* → 'state'; *perform* → 'perfume'). Such errors can occur in patients with intact single-letter recognition and may occur even when the patient can name correctly all the component letters of the stimulus word. In some patients, however, practically all the errors are of this type, and no stimulus variables other than intrinsic visual confusability and word frequency affect performance; there is no positional pattern to the mistakes. The patient genuinely believes what or he or she thinks he or she has seen, and hence assigns the meaning of the (false) response to the stimulus.

It is accordingly useful to have a term – 'visual dyslexia' – for patients who only (for all practical purposes) make this kind of error on words, and who frequently 'lexicalize' non-words (for example, reading *hib* as 'hip' or *ogen* as 'open'). To borrow an expression from Ellis (1984), there seems to be 'slippage' within the visual whole-word recognition system (see also Howard (1987) for discussion of 'global' aspects of visual recognition in reading). Cases are described and analysed in Marshall and Newcombe (1977) and Newcombe and Marshall (1981). Text reading can be extremely slow in these patients; reading is a laborious and tiring enterprise, especially when the context provides little help in overcoming the core problems of visual analysis.

Phonological dyslexia

Some patients who have relatively well-preserved reading of real words may show a disproportionately severe (although not usually total) inability to read non-words. The 'phonic' route that is overemployed in surface dyslexia is here relatively unavailable. There are usually some visual errors (see above) and non-words may be lexicalized to a close word-neighbour (for example *rild* → 'rind'; *wene* → 'when'). In addition, errors of inflectional (*walked* → 'walk') or derivational (*depart* → 'departure') morphology are often seen, along with a disproportionately severe difficulty in reading function words (*the* → 'then'; *with* → 'which'). Errors with morphology and function words can be very frequent in reading text even when they are fairly rare on single-word reading. In some patients, the length and abstractness (or 'imageability') of individual words makes little difference to accuracy, and there is no effect of orthographic regularity. There are no (or very few) overt semantic errors (such as *sick* → 'ill'). Comprehension of the written word, as assessed by lexical decision, synonym matching and word–picture matching is often (but not inevitably) mildly impaired.

Classical case reports and analyses can be found in Beauvois and Dérouesné (1979), Patterson (1982) and Sartori *et al.* (1984). There may be a continuum of impairment (Glosser and Friedman, 1990) between phonological dyslexia and deep dyslexia (see below). Selective disorder of the phonic route can be seen in the primary degenerative dementias (Diesfeldt, 1991), although stroke is the more common aetiology. In cases with the latter aetiology, deep dyslexia may resolve into phonological dyslexia.

Reading without semantics

Relatively good reading aloud for regular and irregular words (and some non-words) can be found in some patients with a severe impairment of visuo-verbal comprehension. Words with irregular (exceptional) pronunciation (such as *leopard*) are correctly read without any apparent understanding of their meaning, as assessed by a wide variety of overt measures. This 'barking at print', to borrow an expression from teachers of reading, seems to imply the existence of 'direct' associations between whole-word visual forms and whole-word phonological units; the condition is accordingly sometimes called 'direct dyslexia'.

This type of reading impairment is probably most frequent in cases of progressive degenerative disorder ('dementia') with diffuse (often bilateral) cortical atrophy. It has, however, also been observed after relatively focal damage in stroke. Classic case reports include Schwartz *et al.* (1980), Shallice *et al.* (1983), Funnell (1983), Sartori *et al.* (1987) and Lytton and Brust (1989).

Deep dyslexia

The most striking feature and defining sign of deep dyslexia is the presence of significant numbers of semantic paralexias on reading aloud; for example: *lion* → 'tiger'; *bitter* → 'pints'; *train* → 'aeroplane'; *India* → 'Egypt'; *weigh* → 'anchor'. Visual errors and errors of morphological analysis are also frequent. Orthographic regularity has no effect on performance, but there is a hierarchy of difficulty of parts of speech: concrete ('imageable') nouns are read better than adjectives, verbs and abstract nouns. Function words may be almost impossible to read, with some within-class substitutions (*a* → 'this'). Reading of non-words is essentially abolished; the patient will make either no response or an occasional lexicalization (*lep* → 'lip').

There is controversy over whether the patients realize that their semantic errors are wrong, and hence over whether they do or do not comprehend the stimulus word entirely correctly despite the overt error in reading aloud. It would seem that all possibilities can be found across cases; there are patients with comparatively good stimulus comprehension, patients who usually 'believe' that their false responses are correct, and patients in whom performance varies from trial to trial.

Classic cases are described in Marshall and Newcombe (1966), Coltheart *et al.* (1980/1987) and Laine *et al.* (1990). It is possible that, in some cases at least, the symptom complex of deep dyslexia reflects the residual reading capacity of the right hemisphere after it has been released from the inhibitory influence of the left (Coltheart, 1983; Patterson *et al.*, 1989; Schweiger *et al.*, 1989; Bayes, 1990). Text reading usually shows exactly the same pattern of omissions and paralexias as individual word reading (for example, *He put the chicken in the oven* → '. . . bird . . . stove').

Neglect dyslexia

In the vast majority of patients (either right- or left-handed), the previously described dyslexic impairments are seen after left-hemisphere damage. Neglect dyslexia, by contrast, is usually found as part of a more general syndrome of left visuo-spatial neglect after right-hemisphere injury. Patients fail to 'attend' to left (contralesional) space; diagnosis is based on performance on line bisection (rightwards bias of transections), cancellation tasks (stimuli on the left of the stimulus page fail to be crossed out), and drawing and copying (significant features on the left are omitted). Most patients with left neglect have severe reading problems. On reading text, they will miss out whole columns on the left, or only read the right half of individual lines; they may then be puzzled as to why the newspapers no longer make any sense.

When reading individual words, the patients may make large numbers of omissions (*glove* → 'love'; *yellow* → 'low') or, even more frequently, substitutions (*cabin* → 'robin'; *yellow* → 'pillow') on the left. Substitutions usually preserve the letter length of the original stimulus and are typically real words.

Classic case reports include Kinsbourne and Warrington (1962) and Ellis *et al.* (1987). Cases of severe right neglect, including right-neglect dyslexia, are rare but do unequivocally exist (Caramazza and Hillis, 1990; Warrington, 1991). The latter cases can be distinguished from visual dyslexia by the significant positional bias of the errors (*lip* → 'lit'; *wash* → 'waste'; *short* → 'shore'). The nature of the spatial reference frame within which the neglect dyslexia is manifest can be discovered by presenting words in different orientations (for example, written vertically or in reverse letter order).

VARIETIES OF ACQUIRED DYSGRAPHIA

Testing for the acquired dysgraphias follows the principles outlined above. In visual dysgraphia (Newcombe and Marshall, 1973), errors on writing to dictation are predominantly visual confusions ('pig' → *big*; 'rob' → *rub*; 'mow' → *mon*). In surface dysgraphia (Hatfield and Patterson, 1983; Newcombe and Marshall, 1985), words are written 'phonically' ('shoe' → *shu*; 'liquid' → *likwid*; 'yacht' → *yot*). In phonological dysgraphia (Shallice, 1981), non-words cannot be written and errors on words are often morphologically based ('loveliness' → *lovely*; 'truth' → *true*; 'defect' → *defection*). In deep dysgraphia (Marshall and Newcombe, 1966; Bub and Kertesz, 1982), semantic errors are common ('star' → *moon*; 'give' → *take*; 'cousin' → *sister*) and non-words cannot be written to dictation. In neglect dysgraphia for oral spelling (Baxter and Warrington, 1983), errors are concentrated at the beginning of words. When writing, patients with left neglect squash the text over into the right-hand side of the page.

Other aspects of the acquired dysgraphias, including the praxic components, are discussed in Ellis (1982), Margolin (1984), Roeltgen (1985) and McCarthy and Warrington (1990). The last of these references also provides an excellent account of oral spelling problems.

In the individual patient, the qualitative form of the acquired dyslexia is usually (but not invariably) paralleled by the form of the acquired dysgraphia (Marshall, 1987). Surface dysgraphia can, for example, occur in the context of phonological dyslexia, or surface dyslexia in the context of deep dysgraphia. Likewise dyslexia without dysgraphia, or dysgraphia without dyslexia, although rare, do occur.

REFERENCES

Baxter, D. M. and Warrington, E. K. (1983). 'Neglect dysgraphia'. *Journal of Neurology, Neurosurgery, and Psychiatry*, 46, 1073–8.

Baxter, D. M. and Warrington, E. K. (1987) 'Transcoding sound to spelling: single or multiple sound unit correspondences'. *Cortex*, 23, 11–28.

Bayes, K. (1990). 'Language and reading in the right hemisphere: highways or byways of the brain?' *Journal of Cognitive Neuroscience*, 2, 159–79.

Beauvois, M.-F. and Dérouesné, J. (1979). 'Phonological alexia: three dissociations'. *Journal of Neurology, Neurosurgery, and Psychiatry*, 42, 1115–24.

Bub, D. and Kertesz, A. (1982). 'Deep agraphia'. *Brain and Language*, 17, 146–65.

Bub, D., Cancelliere, A. and Kertesz, A. (1985). 'Whole word and analytic translation of spelling-to-sound in a non-semantic reader'. In K. E. Patterson, J. C. Marshall and M. Coltheart (eds), *Surface Dyslexia: Neuropsychological and Cognitive Studies of Phonological Reading*. London: Lawrence Erlbaum.

Caramazza, A. and Hillis, A. E. (1990). 'Levels of representation, co-ordinate frames, and unilateral neglect'. *Cognitive Neuropsychology*, 7, 391–445.

Coltheart, M. (1983). 'The right hemisphere and disorders of reading'. In A. W. Young (ed.), *Functions of the Right Cerebral Hemisphere*. London: Academic Press.

Coltheart, M., Patterson, K. E. and Marshall, J. C. (eds) (1980/1987). *Deep Dyslexia*. London: Routledge.

Coslett, H. B. and Saffran, E. M. (1989). 'Evidence for preserved reading in "pure" alexia'. *Brain*, 112, 327–59.

Cubelli, R. (1991). 'A selective deficit for writing vowels in acquired dysgraphia'. *Nature*, 353, 258–60.

Diesfeldt, H. F. A. (1991). 'Impaired phonological reading in primary degenerative dementia'. *Brain*, 114, 1631–46.

Ellis, A. W. (1982). 'Spelling and writing (and reading and speaking)'. In A. W. Ellis (ed.), *Normality and Pathology in Cognitive Functions*. New York: Academic Press.

Ellis, A. W. (1984): *Reading, Writing and Dyslexia: A Cognitive Analysis*. London: Lawrence Erlbaum.

Ellis, A. W., Flude, B. M. and Young, A. W. (1987). '"Neglect dyslexia" and the early visual processing of letters in words'. *Cognitive Neuropsychology*, 4, 439–64.

Funnell, E. (1983). 'Phonological processing in reading: new evidence from acquired dyslexia'. *British Journal of Psychology*, 74, 159–80.

Glosser, G. and Friedman, R. B. (1990). 'The continuum of deep/phonological alexia'. *Cortex*, 26, 343–59.

Hatfield, F. M. and Patterson, K. E. (1983). 'Phonological spelling'. *Quarterly Journal of Experimental Psychology*, 35A, 451–68.

Hinton, G. and Shallice, T. (1991). 'Lesioning an attractor network: investigations of acquired dyslexia'. *Psychological Review*, 98, 74–95.

Howard, D. (1987). 'Reading without letters?' In M. Coltheart, G. Sartori and

R. Job (eds), *The Cognitive Neuropsychology of Language*. London: Lawrence Erlbaum.

Howard, D. and Franklin, S. (1988). *Missing the Meaning? A Cognitive Neuropsychological Study of the Processing of Words by an Aphasic Patient*. Cambridge, MA: MIT Press.

Humphreys, G. W. and Evett, L. J. (1985). 'Are there independent lexical and nonlexical routes in word processing? An evaluation of the dual-route theory of reading'. *The Behavioral and Brain Sciences*, 8, 689–740.

Kay, J., Lesser, R. and Coltheart, M. (1990). *PALPA: Psycholinguistic Assessments of Language Processing in Aphasia*. London: Lawrence Erlbaum.

Kinsbourne, M. and Warrington, E. K. (1962). 'A variety of reading disability associated with right hemisphere lesions'. *Journal of Neurology, Neurosurgery, and Psychiatry*, 25, 339–44.

Kremin, H. (1985). 'Routes and strategies in surface dyslexia and dysgraphia'. In K. E. Patterson, J. C. Marshall and M. Coltheart (eds), *Surface Dyslexia: Neuropsychological and Cognitive Studies of Phonological Reading*. London: Lawrence Erlbaum.

Laine, M., Niemi, P., Niemi, J. and Koivuselkä-Sallinen, P. (1990). 'Semantic errors in a deep dyslexic'. *Brain and Language*, 38, 207–14.

Lytton, W. W. and Brust, J. C. M. (1989). 'Direct dyslexia. Preserved oral reading of real words in Wernicke's aphasia'. *Brain*, 112, 583–94.

McCarthy, R. A. and Warrington, E. K. (1990). *Cognitive Neuropsychology: A Clinical Introduction*. New York: Academic Press.

Margolin, D. (1984). 'The neuropsychology of writing and spelling: semantic, phonological, motor and perceptual processes'. *Quarterly Journal of Experimental Psychology*, 36A, 459–89.

Marshall, J. C. (1987). 'Routes and representations in the processing of written language'. In E. Keller and M. Gopnik (eds), *Motor and Sensory Processes of Language*. London: Lawrence Erlbaum.

Marshall, J. C. and Newcombe, F. (1966). 'Syntactic and semantic errors in paralexia'. *Neuropsychologia*, 4, 169–76.

Marshall, J. C. and Newcombe, F. (1973). 'Patterns of paralexia: a psycho-linguistic approach'. *Journal of Psycholinguistic Research*, 2, 175–99.

Marshall, J. C. and Newcombe, F. (1977). 'Variability and constraint in acquired dyslexia'. In H. Whitaker and H. A. Whitaker (eds), *Studies in Neurolinguistics*, vol. 3. New York: Academic Press.

Newcombe, F. and Marshall, J. C. (1973). 'Stages in recovery from dyslexia following a left cerebral abscess'. *Cortex*, 9, 329–32.

Newcombe, F. and Marshall, J. C. (1981). 'On psycholinguistic classifications of the acquired dyslexias'. *Bulletin of the Orton Society*, 31, 29–46.

Newcombe, F. and Marshall, J. C. (1985). 'Sound-by-sound reading and writing'. In M. Coltheart, K. E. Patterson and J. C. Marshall (eds), *Surface Dyslexia: Neuropsychological and Cognitive Studies of Phonological Reading*. London: Lawrence Erlbaum.

Patterson, K. E. (1982). 'The relation between reading and phonological coding: further neuropsychological observations'. In A. W. Ellis (ed.), *Normality and Pathology in Cognitive Functions*. London: Academic Press.

Patterson, K. E. and Kay, J. (1982). 'Letter-by-letter reading: psychological descriptions of a neurological syndrome'. *Quarterly Journal of Experimental Psychology*, 34A, 411–41.

Patterson, K. E., Marshall, J. C. and Coltheart, M. (eds) (1985). *Surface Dyslexia: Neuropsychological and Cognitive Studies of Phonological Reading*. London: Lawrence Erlbaum.

133

Patterson, K. E., Vargha-Khadem, F. and Polkey, C. E. (1989). 'Reading with one hemisphere'. *Brain*, 112, 39–63.

Roeltgen, D. (1985). 'Agraphia'. In K. M. Heilman and E. Valenstein (eds), *Clinical Neuropsychology*. New York: Oxford University Press.

Sartori, G., Barry, C. and Job, R. (1984). 'Phonological dyslexia: a review'. In R. N. Malatesha and H. A. Whitaker (eds), *Dyslexia: A Global Issue*. The Hague: Nijhoff.

Sartori, G., Masterson, J. and Job, R. (1987). 'Direct-route reading and the locus of lexical decision'. In M. Coltheart, G. Sartori and R. Job (eds), *The Cognitive Neuropsychology of Language*. London: Lawrence Erlbaum.

Schwartz, M. F., Saffran, E. M. and Marin, O. S. M. (1980). 'Fractionating the reading process in dementia: evidence for word-specific print-to-sound associations'. In M. Coltheart, K. E. Patterson and J. C. Marshall (eds), *Deep Dyslexia*. London: Routledge.

Schweiger, A., Zaidel, E., Field, T. and Dobkin, B. (1989). 'Right hemisphere contribution to lexical access in an aphasic with deep dyslexia'. *Brain and Language*, 37, 73–89.

Shallice, T. (1981). 'Phonological agraphia and the lexical route in writing'. *Brain*, 104, 413–29.

Shallice, T. and Saffran, E. M. (1986). 'Lexical processing in the absence of explicit word identification: evidence from a letter-by-letter reader'. *Cognitive Neuropsychology*, 3, 429–58.

Shallice, T., Warrington, E. K. and McCarthy, R. A. (1983). 'Reading without semantics'. *Quarterly Journal of Experimental Psychology*, 35A, 111–38.

Warrington, E. K. (1991). 'Right neglect dyslexia: a single case study'. *Cognitive Neuropsychology*, 8, 193–212.

Warrington, E. K. and Shallice, T. (1980). 'Word-form dyslexia'. *Brain*, 103, 99–112.

9

ASSESSMENT OF MEMORY

Barbara Wilson

HUMAN MEMORY

The working memory model of Baddeley and Hitch (1974) is one of a number of models which propose that human memory can be divided into three broad categories or systems known as sensory memory, short-term memory (STM) and long-term memory (LTM). These systems differ according to the length of time they hold or store memory.

According to the model, sensory memory stores information for less than a quarter of a second. Patients with visual sensory memory deficits will present with perceptual problems, and those with auditory sensory memory deficits will present with comprehension problems.

STM stores information for a few seconds, uses acoustic or articulatory coding, and is relatively unaffected by the rate at which information is presented. Although a few brain-injured patients present with STM deficits, such occurrences are rare unless the STM is secondary to a language impairment such as conduction aphasia. Unfortunately, confusion persists amongst lay people, and even amongst those health-service staff who are not trained psychologists, concerning the nature or, more accurately, the duration of short-term memory. It is thus possible to find people referring to short-term memory as lasting anything from a few minutes to a few months. In order to avoid this confusion it is perhaps useful for psychologists to substitute the term 'immediate memory' when discussing short-term memory with non-psychologists.

LTM is a durable system which holds information for periods of time varying from minutes to decades. Because most brain-injured patients with memory impairments will have LTM deficits, many existing memory tests attempt to explore or measure its various aspects. LTM uses semantic coding, is influenced by the rate at which information is presented, and can be further subdivided into visual and verbal memory. These, in turn, can be further subdivided into recall and recognition memory. Alternative subdivisions of LTM are semantic and episodic or procedural and declarative memory. Baddeley (1990a) provides an excellent discussion of the human memory model as outlined briefly above.

CHARACTERISTICS OF ORGANIC MEMORY IMPAIRMENT

Some memory-impaired people will have the amnesic syndrome. Amnesia means literally 'an absence of (or lack of) memory'. In practice, however, amnesia refers to failure in some part(s) of the memory system. The human amnesic syndrome is characterized by: (1) difficulty in learning and remembering new information; (2) normal STM when this is measured by digit span or the recency effect in free recall; and (3) normal or near-normal functioning of other cognitive abilities. Patients with the amnesic syndrome typically also have a period of retrograde amnesia (RA): that is, loss of memory for a period of time before the onset of the amnesia. This RA may range from minutes to decades and is occasionally absent altogether (Wilson, 1991).

Although people with the amnesic syndrome exist, they are seen much less frequently than other memory-impaired people who have additional cognitive problems in areas such as attention, reasoning, word finding or perception, or who have a general slowing down of intellectual activity. However, whether one is assessing a person with a pure amnesia or with mixed cognitive problems, certain features can be expected. First, the immediate span is likely to be normal or near normal. Second, memory problems become apparent once there has been a delay or distraction. Third, memories from a long time before injury to the brain are likely to be recalled more easily than those from a short time before. Fourth, people usually remember how to do things they were well practised in, such as driving, swimming or playing the piano. There will of course be variations to the pattern as described here, and these will depend, to some extent, on the nature and severity of other cognitive problems.

PURPOSES OF ASSESSMENT OF MEMORY

There are numerous reasons for assessing memory. Sometimes it is necessary to test out a theoretical model, or contribute to research into processes involved in memory disorders. Mayes (1986), for example, discusses the different concerns of researchers and clinicians. It is recognized that the former are more concerned with the desire to specify underlying processes and storage mechanisms involved in memory disorders. Clinicians are likely to be more concerned with answering questions such as the following:

1 Does this person have an organic memory deficit?

2 Is the memory problem global or restricted to certain kinds of material?

3 Is the memory problem secondary to language or attentional deficits?

4 How does this person compare with others of the same age?

Tests which can be described as objective and standardized can answer these and other questions with a fair degree of reliability. They cannot answer certain other questions such as:

1 How do memory problems affect the subject's everyday life?

2 How do the patient and family cope with difficulties arising from memory impairment?

3 Which difficulties cause greatest distress?

4 What kinds of treatment should be offered?

Behavioural assessments are more appropriately applied to the latter group of questions. Behavioural assessment involves analysis of the relationship between the patient's behaviour, its antecedents and its consequences. Such assessment is carried out to identify problems for treatment and to evaluate the effectiveness of treatment. This topic is described in some detail by Wilson (1987) and Wilson et al. (1989a).

This chapter is concerned with the former, that is, standardized tests, which are based on standardization and aim to be objective in principle, method and interpretation. Their value is limited in certain respects: they do not provide much in the way of guidance when it comes to planning a treatment or rehabilitation programme; and they cannot supply psychologists or other therapists with information that will help to select goals, plan or evaluate treatment. However, standardized psychological assessment is essential for planners of treatment who require knowledge of a subject's cognitive strengths and weaknesses in order to ensure the feasibility of therapeutic strategies.

Erikson et al. (1980) discuss the requirements of a memory test. They suggest that the major justification of such a test lies in its ability to contribute to the understanding and remediation of a memory problem. They go on to say that items in the test should be analogues to real-life behavioural demands, and validated in terms of everyday behaviour. However, I would suggest that there are a number of existing standardized tests which, despite not having everyday analogues, are able to be predictive as to whether organic impairment is likely. Sunderland et al. (1984), for example, showed that recall of a prose passage was a good predictor of brain injury but a poor predictor of problems individual subjects might expect to face in their daily lives.

WHAT ASPECTS OF MEMORY SHOULD BE ASSESSED?

Not every person referred for memory assessment requires testing in great detail. Several screening batteries exist which are perfectly adequate for specified purposes. If our concern is with the elimination of organic memory impairment, for example, then the Wechsler Memory Scale-Revised

(WMS-R: Wechsler, 1987), or the Adult Memory and Information Processing Battery (Coughlan and Hollows, 1984, 1985) would be sufficient. The WMS-R grew out of the original Wechsler Memory Scale (WMS: Wechsler, 1945) which was designed to be a 'rapid, simple and practical memory examination' (p. 3) to detect organic memory impairment. Erickson and Scott (1977) suggested, however, that the WMS did not do this satisfactorily. The revised version is an improvement which includes additional subtests, tests of delayed recall and scoring methods to obtain five memory indices. The last named are: general memory, visual memory, verbal memory, delayed memory, and attention and concentration. One big disadvantage of the WMS-R is its lack of an alternative version, so that subjects tested on all the above items cannot be tested soon after to see whether changes have taken place in these various abilities, as it would be unclear whether higher scores are due to a practice effect.

The Adult Memory and Information Processing Battery (AMIPB) was designed to help clinicians detect and evaluate memory impairment; that is, to determine whether scores on the subtests are in the abnormal range.

The Rivermead Behavioural Memory Test (RBMT: Wilson et al., 1985, 1989) is an appropriate screening battery for the tester who wishes to find out whether a subject might be experiencing memory problems in everyday life. This test was specifically designed (1) to predict which people will experience everyday memory problems, and (2) to predict change over time. There are four parallel versions to enable the tester to examine a particular person on a number of consecutive occasions, thus obtaining measures of changes over time that have not been distorted by practice effects. It was originally designed for adults aged 16–65 years; norms for older people appeared in 1989 (Cockburn and Smith), norms for adolescents aged 11–14 years in 1990 (Wilson et al.), and a modified version for 5–10-year-old children in 1991 (Wilson et al.). A pilot study using the children's version of the RBMT with adults with Down's syndrome has recently been completed (Wilson and Ivani-Chalian, 1995).

One final screening test worth mentioning is the Test for Longitudinal Measurement of Mild to Moderate Deficits (Randt et al., 1980). This also has four parallel versions and includes measures of incidental learning and 24-hour delayed recall.

When it is confirmed that a subject has memory deficits, a tester may need to proceed with a finer-grained assessment to build up a more detailed picture of which parts of the memory system are affected and which are intact. This picture of strengths and weaknesses is particularly desirable if one is planning to implement a treatment programme. Box 9.1 provides a list of possible aspects of memory functioning to assess in these cases.

Box 9.1

Testing aspects of memory functioning

1 Short-term memory	(a) verbal
	(b) visual
2 Long-term episodic memory	(a) verbal – recall
	– recognition
	(b) visual – recall
	– recognition
3 New (episodic) learning	(a) verbal
	(b) visual
4 Procedural or implicit learning	(a) motor
	(b) verbal
	(c) visual
5 Remote memory	(a) autobiographical
	(b) (retrograde amnesia)
6 Prospective memory	(a) remembering to do things at a given time
	(b) remember to do things within a certain interval
	(c) remember to do things after a certain time interval
7 Orientation	(a) for time
	(b) for place
	(c) for person
8 Semantic memory	(a) verbal
	(b) visual

Short-term memory (span)

The most widely used procedure for assessing STM or memory span is the digit span task. The Wechsler Adult Intelligence Scale (WAIS), the WAIS-Revised, and both versions of the WMS provide digit span tasks. Forward digit span is clearly a measure of immediate memory, but it is less clear what backward digit span is measuring. Backward digit span has been used in the assessment of attention, which is often impaired after right-hemisphere lesions, and may be dependent on mental imagery or spatial abilities for success.

Visual span can now be readily assessed by the visual memory span tasks in the WMS-R. Both forward and backward visual span tasks (analogues to digit span) are supplied. The tester taps a number of squares on a card in sequence and the testee is required to tap the same squares in the same order. An alternative is to use the Corsi blocks test (described by Milner, 1971), in which nine blocks are randomly attached to a wooden board. These are tapped in a certain order. The principle is the same as the visual memory span task from the WMS-R. The Corsi test appears easier to administer than the visual memory span because the tester can see numbers on the back of the blocks, whereas on the WMS-R cards the tester has to remember which squares correspond to the numbers in the sequence to be reproduced. Unfortunately, norms for the Corsi test are difficult to find. They are readily available for the WMS-R.

Other ways of testing STM can be employed. They include:

1 the presentation of lists of words to be freely recalled. If the last word(s) from such a list are consistently recalled (that is, if a recency effect is shown), then the conclusion to draw is that the subject has an intact STM

2 pattern recognition tasks such as those used by Phillips (1974)

3 the Token Test (De Renzi and Vignolo, 1962), normally used as a test of comprehension, but also sensitive to deficits of STM.

Such tests will probably be applied only in certain circumstances: when, for instance, a tester wishes to check a particular hypothesis with a certain subject who shows STM deficits.

Long-term episodic memory

Long-term episodic memory can be subdivided into (a) verbal recall and recognition, and (b) visual recall and recognition. Verbal recall tasks are perhaps the most frequently used of all memory tests. The prose recall or logical memory passages from the WMS and WMS-R are amongst the most sensitive of tests for detecting organic impairment (Sunderland et al., 1984). The 'newspaper item' passages from the RBMT and the stories from the AMIPB are alternatives to the Wechsler passages. In each case, the subject is required to listen to a piece of prose of five or six lines, then tell back as much as can be remembered immediately after the reading aloud, and again after a delay of 20–30 minutes. There is a modified version of the RBMT for 5–10-year-old children, which includes prompt questions for the story recall (Aldrich and Wilson, 1991; Wilson et al., 1991).

Verbal recognition can be assessed in a number of ways. A list of words is typically presented to the subject, who, after a delay, is shown a further list of words, some of which appeared in the original list. The subject is required to indicate which words have been seen earlier. The most widely used recognition memory test in Britain today is probably Warrington's (1984) Recognition Memory Test. This has both a verbal and a visual recognition section, the latter using faces instead of words.

Baddeley et al. (1994) include verbal and visual recognition memory tests in their recently published memory battery. In the verbal task the subject is shown the name of a person, for example, 'JAMES FITZJOHN', and later has to identify this name amongst a set of four comprising 'JAMES FITZWIL-

LIAM', 'JAMES FITZGEORGE', 'JAMES FITZJOHN' and 'JAMES FITZGERALD'. In the visual task the subject is shown a coloured photograph of a door and later has to identify this door from a set of four. Baddeley et al.'s recognition memory test differs from Warrington's in two major ways. First, they provide four alternatives rather than two. Second, they have two versions: an easier test suitable for patients with substantial deficits, and a harder version to tax even the best memory. Thus both 'floor' and 'ceiling' effects can be avoided.

Perhaps the best-known visual recall tests are the Rey–Osterreith Complex Figure (Rey, 1959), the Benton Visual Retention Test (BVRT: Benton, 1974), and the Visual Reproduction tests from the WMS and WMS-R. The AMIPB also includes a complex figure analogous to that of the Rey–Osterreith. In the first named, subjects are required to copy a complex figure and then recall it by redrawing it after a delay. Subjects with visuo-spatial problems may have difficulty with the original copy. This, in turn, could affect their recall of the figure. Amnesic subjects, on the other hand, typically copy well but remember nothing after a delay. The usual delay period is 40 minutes, but sometimes a 10- or 20-minute delay is substituted. Scoring the Rey–Osterreith figure is not entirely straightforward and at least two scoring methods exist, with total scores equalling 36 and 47 respectively (see Lezak, 1983). Another possible disadvantage of the Rey figure is that it can be verbalized. For example, the overall figure looks something like a flag; one section includes a circle with dots and resembles a face; the extreme left-hand section can be likened to an elongated cross; and so on.

Four forms exist for the BVRT. In the most frequently used form (A), subjects are shown a design (comprising one, two or three elements) for 10 seconds. The design is then removed and the subject has to draw the design as accurately as possible. Form (B) is similar but has a 5-second exposure. Form (C) is a copying task to ensure poor performance is not due to poor copying ability. For patients suspected of poor constructional or motor ability, it is desirable to administer Form (C) first. Form (D) requires the subject to delay the response for 15 seconds after the 10-second exposure.

Norms exist for Forms (A), (B) and (C). Form (C) also has norms for children. Scoring details are fairly explicit and the test is sensitive to unilateral visual neglect (Lezak, 1983). A multiple-choice version of the BVRT exists for those subjects unable to copy (Benton et al., 1977). However, the norms for adults are inadequate.

The visual reproduction tests from the WMS and WMS-R require the subject to look at a design on a card for 10 seconds and then recall as much as possible in a drawing. There are three designs in the original and four in the revised version. The revised version also requires a delayed recall of the figures as well as immediate. Scoring details are explicit, particularly for the revised version. However, like the Rey, the designs are easy to verbalize.

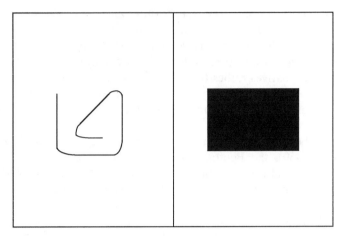

Figure 9.1 A visual paired associate stimulus similar to those used in the WMS-R

Baddeley *et al.* (1994) have designed an alternative visual recall test by getting subjects to copy different-shaped crosses and later recalling these by drawing, so, although the subjects can verbalize 'cross', this is of limited help when all the material consists of crosses. This test is part of the Doors and People Test assessing visual recall, visual recognition, verbal recall and verbal recognition.

The Graham–Kendall Memory for Designs test (Graham and Kendall, 1960) was developed as a single test for organicity. It consists of fifteen designs of increasing complexity, but Lezak (1983) considers it to be inferior to the BVRT.

New (episodic) learning

New (episodic) learning can also be subdivided into verbal and visual (or visuo-spatial). The WMS-R includes subtests for both these areas. For verbal learning there is a Paired Associate learning task. Eight pairs of words are presented with four being easy or logical (such as 'fruit–apple'), and four being difficult or arbitrary such as 'school–grocery'). Six trials are allowed in the learning phase, although only the first three trials are scored. Trials 4–6 are administered only to subjects who fail to recall any words successfully. One delayed trial is also given near the end of the test. In the visual version the subject is shown six symbols, each of which is paired with a colour. Administration is similar to the verbal paired associate learning task (described immediately above). Figure 9.1 provides an example of visual paired associate stimulus similar to those used in the WMS-R.

A number of other verbal paired associate learning tasks are available. The Randt *et al.* (1980) test described earlier includes an easier task which is less distressing for some severely memory impaired people. The Inglis (1957) and Walton and Black (1957) paired associate learning tests are also used fairly frequently. Of course, not all new verbal learning tasks use paired associates. The Rey Auditory Verbal Learning Test (RAVLT: Rey, 1964) and the California Verbal Learning Test (CVLT: Delis *et al.*, 1987) are both readily available and useful tests to include in one's repertoire. In both these tests the subject is required to listen to a list of fifteen or sixteen words and repeat back as many as possible in any order. The list is repeated four more times. Each time free recall is required. There is then a distraction list followed by recall of the original list. The CVLT (Delis *et al.*, 1987) has some advantages over the RVLT. For example, it includes a short delayed recall and a long (20 minutes) delayed recall. It also provides category cues to aid recall. For example, 'Tell me all the clothing items' (or 'tools items'). Finally, the CVLT allows the tester to score several different aspects of memory.

Tests (other than the WMS-R) to assess non-verbal (episodic) learning are harder to find. Wilson, Cockburn and Baddeley (1989b) describe a test of new learning in which subjects are given three trials to learn a six-step task. The subject has to put date and time into an electronic memory aid. All fifty normal control subjects learned the task in three trials (and most in one trial), whereas less than 44 per cent of brain-injured subjects learned the task in three trials.

Another non-verbal learning task which is easy to administer is a visual span-plus-2 task. This can be given either with Corsi blocks or with the visual tapping task of the WMS-R. Once span has been established in the usual way, the tester adds two more blocks or squares. If, in these conditions, span is five, the learning sequence of seven is administered until the subject can reproduce it correctly or until twenty-five (or even fifty) trials have been given. Although norms do not appear to exist, most non-brain-injured subjects would learn this in three trials, and certainly within five, whereas severely amnesic subjects fail to learn in fifty trials.

Finally, the RBMT includes learning a new route (both immediate and delayed). This subtest combines visuo-spatial and verbal learning as it attempts to replicate real-life learning of new routes.

Procedural or implicit learning

It has been known for a number of years that densely amnesic subjects may show unimpaired learning on certain tasks (Warrington and Weiskrantz, 1968; Brooks and Baddeley, 1976). This has been termed 'procedural or implicit learning'; that is, learning without awareness. Of great interest to researchers into theoretical models of memory, procedural learning is not frequently assessed by clinicians. This may be due to the fact that standardized assessments are not available, so each battery or test has to be made separately or obtained from colleagues working in the area. Another reason for the haphazard inclusion of these tasks is that it is now clear how implicit learning relates to everyday problems or to rehabilitation goals. However, Baddeley and Wilson (1988) suggest that impaired procedural learning in memory-disordered subjects is a poor prognostic sign. Procedural learning is unlikely to prove to be a unitary concept, however, and a number of different tasks have been used to demonstrate preserved learning in amnesic people. One of the best known is the pursuit rotor task, a visual-motor tracking task. Amnesic people typically improve the percentage of time on target despite being unable (in many cases) to recognize that they have been tested on the task previously (Brooks and Baddeley, 1976). Warrington and Weiskrantz (1968) used a fragmented-pictures task to show that providing partial information in the form of a degraded picture led to successful identification of the picture even though subjects were unaware they had seen it earlier. Stem-completion tasks are also frequently performed well by amnesic people. Subjects are shown lists of words such as 'BEACON', 'CHEMICAL', etc., and then given three letters, such as 'BEA', 'CHE'. Subjects are asked to say the first word that comes to mind. 'Beacon' and 'chemical' are more likely to be recalled than a high-frequency word such as 'bean' or 'cheese'. Baddeley (1990a) provides a good discussion of procedural or implicit learning. Considerable research is taking place, so we look forward to a procedural learning battery in the near future.

Remote memory

This is another aspect of memory functioning which is rarely assessed routinely in clinical practice despite having important implications for real-life problems. Baddeley and Wilson (1986) suggest that impaired autobiographical memory can result in anxiety, depression or other problematic behaviours. In order to know who we are, we must have a past. People with long periods of retrograde amnesia (RA) are frequently bewildered or angry by what seems to them an unexpectedly high cost of living, or radical changes in their environment, or the 'loss' of five or more years from their lives.

Famous faces, names and events from different decades are the materials most often used in assessing RA. Butters and Albert (1982) devised an interesting RA battery, but this, together with other tests of RA, has major disadvantages, including cultural specificity, differences in levels of interest, problems of overlearning, exposure time and difficulties in updating. Wilson and Cockburn (1988), in an attempt to overcome some of these problems, devised the Prices Test. Subjects have to estimate the current price of ten everyday items such as a first-class stamp or a pint of milk. The estimated price is deducted from the actual price and divided by the standard deviation. It is possible to work out the average number of years subjects are out of date, and this test has some advantages over existing tests of RA.

In particular, it reduces the effects of exposure and learning time, as most people acquire information about prices incidentally; it is more sensitive to short periods of RA, as prices change quickly; it is easy to update; and it is suitable for a wide range of subjects of different ages. Disadvantages connected with the Prices Test include overestimation of prices by subjects with frontal-lobe damage, and difficulties establishing a temporal gradient because prices change at different rates and some items cost more in certain parts of the country. Nevertheless, it is a quick and useful test of RA.

Autobiographical memory is one aspect of remote memory, and although people with RA typically show poor recall of both public and private events, it is possible to find a double dissociation, with occasional subjects showing impaired recall of private but not public events, and others showing the reverse (Kapur, 1993). Kopelman *et al.* (1990) suggest that it is important to assess autobiographical memory in brain-injured people for at least three reasons: first, to understand the nature of the memory deficit; second, to allow more adequate counselling; and third, to provide an individual focus for treatment. Baddeley and Wilson (1986) found that subjects who are very similar on intelligence and memory test scores may differ markedly on ability to recall events from their own past life. Kopelman *et al.* (1990) have developed an Autobiographical Memory Interview (AMI) to provide an assessment tool to autobiographical memory. This semi-structured interview schedule encompasses two major areas of autobiographical memory. The first assesses recall of facts and the second assesses recall of specific events or incidents in earlier life. Each assesses memories across three broad time bands: childhood, early adult life and recent times (the past year). The development of the AMI is described in Kopelman (1989) and Kopelman *et al.* (1989).

Prospective memory

Prospective memory refers to the ability to remember to carry out or perform certain tasks or actions, many of them considered as part of the normal everyday routine of living. One of the commonest complaints of memory-impaired subjects is that they forget to do things, yet there is only one test, the RBMT, which includes prospective memory items. Three of the twelve subtests of the RBMT assess prospective memory:

1 remembering to ask, at the end of the test, for a belonging that has been placed out of sight

2 remembering to ask for an appointment when an alarm rings

3 remembering to deliver a message to a predetermined place during the immediate and delayed recall of a new route

These prospective memory items in the RBMT appear to account for some of the sensitivity of the test. Cockburn and Smith (1989), for example, found that these items significantly discriminated between two groups of elderly subjects living in the community: a 'young' old group aged between 55 and 70 years, and an 'old' old group aged between 71 and 90 years.

As a screening test, the RBMT covers prospective memory adequately. However, a more detailed assessment of this aspect of memory would require items that tapped the following three main areas:

1 remembering to do things at a specified time

2 remembering to do things within a certain interval

3 remembering to do things after a certain period has elapsed

Figure 9.2 shows a 7-year-old girl and a man with Down's syndrome finding the hidden belonging in the children's version of the RBMT.

Orientation

Erickson and Scott (1977) suggest that all memory assessments should include an assessment of orientation. The WMS, WMS-R, RBMT and the Randt *et al.* (1980) test all include orientation questions. Again, there are three kinds of item: time, place and person. Amnesic subjects are oriented for person and will almost always be able to provide their date of birth, but they are typically not oriented for place or time and may not therefore know their age (unless given the current date – from which they can work out their age).

Semantic memory

Semantic memory is the system we use to store knowledge about the world. Tulving (1972) suggested that semantic memory is separate from episodic memory. If we test a subject on information acquired before onset of memory impairment then it is very likely that the subject will show an intact semantic memory (Wilson and Baddeley, 1988). However, that same subject may have difficulty adding to the semantic store after the onset of the memory disorder. Amnesic subjects are, for example, unlikely to learn new facts relating to work or new vocabulary terms once they have become amnesic.

Tests of semantic memory include the vocabulary subtest of the WAIS and WAIS-R, and certain verbal fluency tests such as that designed by Benton and Hamsher (1976). Baddeley *et al.* (1992) include a quick and sensitive test of speed of retrieval from semantic memory as part of their

Figure 9.2 Remembering the 'hidden belonging': a 7-year-old girl and a man with Down's syndrome

test of the Speed and Capacity of Language Processing. This is based on earlier work by Collins and Quillian (1969). Subjects have to decide as quickly as possible whether a particular statement is true or false. A mean decision time per item and an error score is calculated. Baddeley *et al.* (1987) showed that the test is sensitive to age and to brain injury.

Semantic memory is not, of course, restricted to verbal information. We have a vast store of information as to what things look like, sound like, smell like and feel like; and these may also be affected adversely by brain injury. Warrington (1975), for example, suggests that visual object agnosia is a deficit of the visual semantic memory system. Furthermore, Warrington and Shallice (1984) demonstrated that there are category-specific deficits, so that some agnosic patients have lost the ability to recognize living things but are able to recognize non-living things; others cannot recognize certain categories such as fruit and vegetables. Baddeley (1990a) provides a good review of semantic memory. Hodges, Salmon and Butters (1992) discuss semantic memory impairment in Alzheimer's disease, and Hodges, Patterson, Oxbury and Funnell (1992) describe progressive aphasia, which they call semantic dementia. They include an outline of a test of semantic memory which Hodges and his colleagues are currently developing in Cambridge.

Clinicians are unlikely to use sophisticated assessments of semantic memory unless their memory-impaired patients have language or perceptual disorders in addition to memory deficits.

SUMMARY

This chapter has attempted to describe the characteristics of memory-impaired people and to consider the major purposes of assessment. It has reported on some screening tests for the detection of memory problems, and also outlined aspects of memory which should be assessed in people found to have organic impairment.

REFERENCES

Aldrich, F. and Wilson, B. A. (1991). *Rivermead Behavioural Memory Test for Children: a preliminary evaluation. British Journal of Clinical Psychology*, 30, 161–8.

Baddeley, A. D. (1990a). *Human Memory: Theory and Practice*. Hove: Lawrence Erlbaum.

Baddeley, A. D. (1990b). 'The MRC Applied Psychology Unit'. *MRC News*, 47, 14–17.

Baddeley, A. D. and Hitch, G. J. (1974). '*Working memory*'. In G. A. Bower (ed.), *The Psychology of Learning Motivation*, vol. 8. New York: Academic Press.

Baddeley, A. D. and Wilson, B. A. (1986). 'Amnesia, autobiographical memory and confabulation'. In D. Rubin (ed.), *Autobiographical Memory*. Cambridge: Cambridge University Press.

Baddeley, A. D. and Wilson, B. A. (1988). 'Frontal amnesia and the dysexecutive syndrome'. *Brain and Cognition*, 7, 212–30.

Baddeley, A. D., Emslie, H. and Nimmo-Smith, I. (1992). *The Speed and Capacity of Language Processing*. Bury St Edmunds: Thames Valley.

Baddeley, A. D., Emslie, H. and Nimmo-Smith, I. (1994). *Doors and People: A Test of Visual and Verbal Recall and Recognition*. Bury St Edmunds: Thames Valley.

Baddeley, A. D., Harris, J. E., Sunderland, A., Watts, K. and Wilson, B. A. (1987). 'Closed head injury and memory'. In H. S. Levin, J. Grafman and H. M. Eisenberg (eds), *Neurobehavioural Recovery from Head Injury*. New York: Oxford University Press.

Benton, A. L. (1974). *The Revised Visual Retention Test* (4th edn). New York: Psychological Corporation.

Benton, A. L. and Hamsher, K. (1976). *Multilingual Aphasia Examination*. Iowa City: University of Iowa.

Benton, A. L., Hamsher, K. and Stone, F. B. (1977). *Visual Retention Test: Multiple Choice*. Iowa City: University of Iowa.

Brooks, D. N. and Baddeley, A. D. (1976). 'What can amnesics learn?'. *Neuropsychologia*, 14, 111–22.

Butters, N. and Albert, M. S. (1982). 'Processes underlying failures to recall remote events'. In L. Cermak (ed.), *Human Memory and Amnesia*. Hillsdale, NJ: Lawrence Erlbaum.

Cockburn, J. and Smith, P. (1989). *The Rivermead Behavioural Memory Test. Supplement 3: Elderly People*. Bury St Edmunds: Thames Valley.

Collins, A. M. and Quillian, M. R. (1969). 'Retrieval time from semantic memory'. *Journal of Verbal Behavior*, 8, 240–7.

Coughlan, A. K. and Hollows, S. E. (1984). 'The use of memory tests in differentiating organic disorder from depression'. *British Journal of Psychiatry*, 145, 164–7.

Coughlan, A. K. and Hollows, S. E. (1985). *The Adult Memory and Information Processing Battery*. Leeds: St James University Hospital/A. K. Coughlan.

Delis, D., Kramer, J. H., Kaplan, E. and Ober, B. E. (1987). *California Verbal Learning Test*. San Antonio: Psychological Corporation.

De Renzi, E. and Vignolo, L. A. (1962). 'The Token Test: to detect receptive disturbance in aphasics'. *Brain*, 85, 665–79.

Erikson, R. C. and Scott, M. L. (1977). 'Clinical memory testing: a review'. *Psychological Bulletin*, 84, 1130–49.

Erickson, R. C., Poon, L. W. and Walsh-Sweeney, L. (1980). 'Clinical memory testing of the elderly'. In L. W. Poon, J. L. Fozzard, L. S. Cermak, D. Arenberg and L. W. Thompson (eds), *New Directions in Memory and Ageing*. Hillsdale, NJ: Lawrence Erlbaum.

Graham, F. K. and Kendall, B. S. (1960). 'Memory for designs test'. *Perceptual and Motor Skills*, 11, 147–88.

Hodges, J., Salmon, D. and Butters, N. (1992). 'Semantic memory impairment in Alzheimer's disease: failure of access or degraded knowledge?'. *Neuropsychologia*, 30, 301–14.

Hodges, J., Patterson K., Oxbury, S. and Funnell, E. (1992). 'Semantic dementia: progressive fluent aphasia with temporal lobe atrophy'. *Brain*, 115, 1783–1806.

Inglis, J. (1957). 'An experimental study of learning and "memory function" in elderly psychiatric patients'. *Journal of Mental Science*, 103, 796–803.

Kapur, N. (1993). 'Focal retrograde amnesia in neurological disease: a critical review'. *Cortex*, 29, 217–34.

Kopelman, M. D. (1989). 'Remote and autobiographical memory, temporal context memory and frontal atrophy in Korsakoff and Alzheimer patients'. *Neurophychologia*, 27, 437–60.

Kopelman, M. D., Wilson, B. A. and Baddeley, A. D. (1989). 'The autobiographical memory interview: a new assessment of autobiographical and personal semantic memory in amnesic patients'. *Journal of Clinical and Experimental Neuropsychology*, 11, 724–44.

Kopelman, M. D., Wilson, B. A. and Baddeley, A. D. (1990). *The Autobiographical Memory Interview*. Bury St Edmunds: Thames Valley.

Lezak, M. D. (1983). *Neuropsychological Assessment*. 2nd edn. New York: Oxford University Press.

Mayes, A. (1986). 'Learning and memory disorders and their assessment'. *Neuropsychologia*, 24, 25–39.

Milner, B. (1971). 'Interhemispheric differences in the localisation of psychological processes in man'. *British Medical Bulletin: Cognitive Psychology*, 27, 272–7.

Phillips, W. A. (1974). 'On the distinction between sensory storage and short term visual memory'. *Perception and Psychophysics*, 16, 283–90.

Randt, C. T., Brown, E. R. and Osborne, D. P. (1980). 'A memory test for longitudinal measurement of mild to moderate deficits'. *Clinical Neuropsychiatry*, 2, 184–94.

Rey, A. (1959). *Le Test De Copie De Figure Complexe*. Paris: Editions Centre de Psychologie Appliquée.

Rey, A. (1964). *L'examen Cliniques en Psychologie*. Paris: Presses Universitaires de France.

Sunderland, A., Harris, J. E. and Baddeley, A. D. (1984). 'Assessing everyday memory after severe head injury'. In J. E. Harris and P. Morris (eds), *Everyday Memory, Actions and Absentmindedness*. London: Academic Press.

Tulving, E. (1972). *Episodic and Semantic Memory: Organization of Memory*. New York: Academic Press.

Walton, D. and Black, D. A. (1957). 'The validity of a psychological test of brain damage'. *British Journal of Medical Psychology*, 30, 270–9.

Warrington, E. K. (1975). 'The selective impairment of semantic memory'. *Quarterly Journal of Experimental Psychology*, 27, 635–57.

Warrington, E. K. (1984). *The Recognition Memory Test*. Windsor: NFER-Nelson.

Warrington, E. K. and Shallice, T. (1984). 'Category specific semantic impairments'. *Brain*, 107, 829–54.

Warrington, E. K. and Weiskrantz, L. (1968). 'New method of testing long-term retention with special reference to amnesic patients'. *Nature*, 217, 972–4.

Wechsler, D. (1945). 'A standardised memory scale for clinical use'. *Journal of Psychology*, 19, 87–95.

Wechsler, D. (1987). *The Wechsler Memory Scale – Revised*. San Antonio: Psychological Corporation.

Wilson, B. A. (1987). *Rehabilitation of Memory*. New York: Guilford Press.

Wilson, B. A. (1991). 'Long term prognosis of patients with severe memory disorders'. *Neuropsychological Rehabilitation*, 1, 117–34.

Wilson, B. A. and Baddeley, A. D. (1988). 'Semantic, episodic and autobiographical memory in a postmeningitic amnesic patient'. *Brain and Cognition*, 8, 31–46.

Wilson, B. A. and Cockburn, J. (1988). 'The Prices Test: a simple test of retrograde amnesia'. In M. Gruneberg, P. Morris and R. Sykes (eds), *Practical Aspects of Memory: Current Research and Issues*, 2. Chichester: John Wiley.

Wilson, B. A. and Ivani-Chalian, R. (1995). 'Performance of adults with Down's syndrome on the Children's Rivermead Behavioural Memory Test'. *British Journal of Clinical Psychology*, 34, 85–8.

Wilson, B. A., Cockburn, J. and Baddeley, A. D. (1985). *The Rivermead Behavioural Memory Test Manual*. Bury St Edmunds: Thames Valley.

Wilson, B. A., Cockburn, J. and Baddeley, A. D. (1989a). 'Assessment of everyday memory following brain injury'. In M. E. Miner and K. A. Wagner (eds), *Neurotrauma: Treatment, Rehabilitation and Related Issues*, 3. London: Butterworth.

Wilson, B. A., Cockburn, J. and Baddeley, A. D. (1989b). 'How do old dogs learn new tricks? Teaching a technological skill to brain injured people'. *Cortex*, 25, 115–19.

Wilson, B. A., Ivani-Chalian, R. and Aldrich, F. (1991). *The Children's Rivermead Behavioural Memory Test*. Bury St Edmunds: Thames Valley.

Wilson, B. A., Cockburn, J., Baddeley, A. D. and Hiorns, R. (1989). 'The development and validation of a test battery for detecting and monitoring everyday memory problems'. *Journal of Clinical and Experimental Neuropsychology*, 11, 855–70.

Wilson, B. A., Forester, S., Bryant, T. and Cockburn, J. (1990). 'Performance of 11–14-year-olds on the Rivermead Behavioural Memory Test'. *Clinical Psychology Forum*, 30, 8–10.

Part III

10

LEGAL ISSUES

Jamie Furnell

The development of the gamut of topics covered in previous chapters has evolved largely through a combination of academic interest and necessity of clinical practice. Increasingly, however, legal practitioners have become aware of psychology's contribution to the formulation and presentation of individual cases (see, for example, Muller *et al.*, 1984). Gudjonsson (1985) indicated demands from courts for expert psychological testimony to be increasing in both volume and range of topics. Any comment on the frequency of psychologists' legal involvement must also acknowledge the proportion of civil cases in which the parties eventually agree an outcome prior to (albeit on the morning of) a formal court hearing. A sizeable number of all such cases will be claims for compensation, and these include complaints based on alleged head injury or neurological impairment which require the skills of a neuropsychologist. A Working Party Report of the Medical Disability Society (1988) estimated there to be 85 survivors of head injury in Britain each week and that in every average health district of 250,000 people, there would be on average 230–345 disabled survivors, with 20 new severely and 44 new moderately severely brain-injured patients each year. Historically, the state has shown little interest in the plight of the head-injured – either for victims or their families. However, adequate compensation can mean the difference between subsistence and some financial security. Financial compensation can greatly enhance the availability of assistance and potential rehabilitation. At present, various systems exist in Britain by which financial compensation may be claimed by the victim of an accident. These are as follows:

1 *The Social Security System* As noted by Rogers (1989), this is 'extraordinarily complicated' at present. For non-industrial injuries, the primary short-term benefit for sickness or injury is paid, at least in the first instance, by employers. An employee who is unfit for work may claim from his or her employer a sum for a maximum of twenty-eight weeks in any tax year. Employers may later recoup statutory sick payments by deduction from National Insurance contributions. The claimant who is not entitled to

statutory sick pay may draw twenty-eight weeks of 'sickness benefit', which at the end of the period is replaced by 'invalidity benefit'. In addition, industrial injuries are covered by the Industrial Injuries Scheme, which provides for payment of 'disablement benefit' to an injured worker, or, in the case of fatal accidents, of 'industrial death benefit' to his or her dependents. With injury, the basic condition of award is that it was caused by accident 'arising out of, and in the course of, employment'.

2 *The Criminal Injuries Compensation Board* The Board (Duff, 1991) assesses and pays compensation from state funds to victims of crimes of violence. It is not required that the offender has been convicted or even traced. Compensation is not payable for small claims (the current minimum value for most types of claim is £400), and the Board may refuse or reduce compensation in certain circumstances, such as unreasonable delay in reporting the incident to the police. However, the Board will treat an incident as a crime and, if appropriate, pay compensation even though the offender is too young for criminal liability, or can plead 'insanity'.

3 *Private insurance and occupational pensions* Life insurance, personal accident insurance and permanent health insurance give protection against accidental death or injury. The first is, without doubt, the most important; the latter two are less common. Of more significance are employers' sick-pay schemes, which may go well beyond statutory minima, providing all or part of lost income for a maximum period often related to length of service. In cases of long-term injury leading to premature retirement, a payment may be made under an occupational pension scheme. The chance of receipt of any one or more of the above benefits is heavily influenced by the social class of the victim and the nature of his or her employment.

4 *The Tort and Delict principles of the English and Scots legal systems respectively* In general, the actions of one person or group of people will from time to time cause or threaten damage to others and most will involve some form of negligence. Damage may take many forms including injury to the person. Whenever a person suffers damage he or she may look to the law for redress. In the great majority of tort or delict actions coming before the courts, the plaintiff or pursuer is seeking monetary compensation ('damages') for the injury he or she has suffered. Such cases have been described as 'justice by redistribution'.

The Pearson Commission Report (1978) provided the most comprehensive readily available statistics on personal injury in the United Kingdom. It indicated that the vast majority of deaths and injuries were accidental, the largest category being accidents on the road, at home and at work. Of a total paid in various forms of compensation for such injuries, more than half came from the Social Security System, with the balance being shared more or less equally between tort and delict systems and other, predominantly private, sources such as occupational sick pay and private insurance. Overall, therefore, the tort and delict system accounted for no more than a quarter of all compensation paid. However, the relationship is rather different if particular categories of accident are examined. In the field of motor accidents, tort and delict payments considerably exceed social security payments, although the position is reversed with regard to work and other accidents. In a large number of cases of minor injury, the victim will not think it worth his or her while to pursue a tort or delict claim, potentially through the courts.

For the neuropsychologist asked to express an opinion on an injured person for the purposes of any of the above compensation systems, the approach, methods of investigation and conclusions drawn are likely to be very similar. However, for convenience, and also because it may require the most exhaustive detail, the function of the neuropsychologist within the tort or delict systems will be discussed.

As noted above, damages are compensation; when one person causes harm (including head injury or neurological impairment) to another person, the normal remedy the law gives (if in the circumstances of the case it gives right of action at all) is a right to recover damages. The law on the nature of damages has been stated in somewhat varying terms by eminent judges (see, for example, Munkman, 1989). Viscount Dunedin in *Admiralty Commissioners v. S.S. Valeria* (1922) 2 AC 242 at 248 stated: 'the true method of expression, I think, is that in calculating damages you are to consider what is the pecuniary consideration which would make good the sufferer, as far as money can do so, the loss which he has suffered as the natural result of the wrong done to him'. Similarly, Lord Blackburn in *Livingston v. Rawyards Co.* (1880) 5 APP CAS 25 at 39 stated: 'where any injury is to be compensated by damages, in settling the sum of money to be given, you should as nearly as possible get at that sum of money which will put the person who has been injured in the same position as he would have been if he had not sustained the wrong'. Thus, if the original position cannot be restored (and in many cases of serious head injury or neurological impairment, it cannot), then the law must endeavour to give a fair equivalent in money, as far as possible, to compensate for pain and physical consequences.

Such assessment may be difficult; however, damages paid for personal injuries are not punitive, nor are they a reward. They must be full and adequate, but are assessed once and for all, usually at the time of the trial, and cover both loss and injury already experienced and also what may develop at a future date. A variation on the once-and-for-all settlement is the structured settlement, which involves a capital sum and regular payments. Clearly it is in the interests of the lawyer acting on behalf of the client to obtain the very best information available about his or her client's

157

condition. The practical lawyer has to supply the bricks with which the case is built.

PROCEDURAL STAGES

In general terms, two separate stages may arise in consideration of an individual case. These are as follows:

1 *Did the fault of the defendant or defender lead directly to the damage suffered by the plaintiff or pursuer?* The injured party must show a casual connection between the actions of the defender (be he or she employer who provided an unsafe workplace, medical practitioner who carelessly administered wrong drug dosage, or motorist who drove so as to cause injury) and the damage suffered. In many cases, this may be obvious and admitted. There are, however, 'pure' accidents which involve a victim but no fault by any other person or agency, where the concept of 'damages' does not arise. The neuropsychologist may be asked to estimate ante- and carry out post-trauma assessments (physical, cognitive, social and emotional) of an individual and comment in comparison on the causation of potential or apparent differences. The caution necessary in such procedures will not be lost on experienced practitioners.

2 *If so, what are the damages?* Judges try to take into account all relevant changes of circumstances which have been caused by the accident, and some elements are common to many, if not all, claims for personal injuries. The relevant combination will vary with each case, but questions from the lawyer or comment from the neuropsychologist may cover the following:

Kemp (1975) considered features 'heads' of damage to fall within two principal categories: (1) 'non-pecuniary' or loss not involving money, and (2) 'pecuniary', where loss had direct financial implications. Each will be considered in turn.

Non-pecuniary loss

This covers several specific factors.

Pain and suffering

'Pain' is used to describe the physical pain caused by, or consequent on, the injury, while 'suffering' relates to the mental element of anxiety, fear, embarrassment and similar feelings, and also the effect of distress on the family. Section 1 of the Administration of Justice Act 1982 indicated that damages shall take into account any suffering caused by awareness of the victim that his or her expectation of life had been reduced by his or her injuries. An award of damages under this head depends upon the plaintiff or pursuer's personal awareness of pain and the capacity of the suffering (see, for example, Lord Scarman in *Lim Poh Choo* v. *Camden and Islington Area Health Authority* (1980) AC 174 at 188). In addition, suffering need not be caused solely by the plaintiff or pursuer's concern for himself or herself. In the case of *Rourke* v. *Barton* (*The Times*, 23 June 1982), the injured plaintiff was distressed by her subsequent inability to care for her husband when he was home. In Scotland, recompense for pain and suffering is termed 'solatium'.

Loss of amenities

This head embraces everything which reduces the plaintiff or pursuer's enjoyment of life, considered apart from any material loss. What matters is the fact of deprivation of an amenity rather than whether the injured person is aware of such deprivation. Thus, an injured person rendered permanently unconscious, or whose awareness of his or her loss is otherwise impaired, is entitled to a full award. Relevant items under this head would seem to be reduction in, or loss of prospects of, marriage for young persons, loss or impairment of any of the five senses, interference with the plaintiff or pursuer's sex life, loss of the pleasure and pride a craftsperson takes in his or her work, loss of enjoyment of a holiday, or perhaps particularly the loss of a favourite or regular hobby.

Pecuniary loss

The fact of a head injury or neurological impairment may also result in direct financial implications of various sorts.

Family care

As Brooks (1984) has indicated, the adverse effects of traumatic brain injury can impose physical and mental stresses on the family. Psychosocial changes including disinhibited moods and behaviour, lack of insight and poor self-care are among the most devastating long-term consequences of brain injury, which may severely incapacitate the patient and place increasing burdens on relatives and friends. Noble *et al.* (1986) note that difficulties may include inability to remember the way home, leaving a burning cigarette on furniture or clothes, or switching on a kettle empty of water with subsequent fire risk. Thus part of an award of damages must include the need for care and attendance; care may involve either family or professional (both nursing and therapies) help. Extensive levels of such professional help at home will be compensated if reasonable and necessary, even if hospital care would be cheaper. The cost of professional rates will be carefully investigated. In contrast, family care is not to be valued at professional rates. This is because the wages of a qualified nurse or auxiliary reflect additional components of the earner, including tax and National Insurance, which do not apply to a plaintiff or pursuer's spouse, parent or relative. The actual value placed on family care can present practical problems; however, accurate functional assessment by a neuropsychologist may help to clarify matters.

Employment and pension loss

The quantification of past wage loss is essentially a mathematical exercise; figures are provided by past employers and an average of 'take-home' pay reached over a representative time period. The amount a plaintiff or pursuer saves by being in hospital or an institution is deducted from his or her claim for loss of income. It is likely a neuropsychologist will be asked to predict future work capacity in the light of injury so that future earning capacity and wage loss may be assessed. Also relevant may be the extent to which the plaintiff or pursuer is deprived by his or her injuries of the ability or opportunity to acquire some skill or qualifications, which would have placed him or her in a better position in the labour market to obtain either employment or more remunerative work. Subsequent pension loss will have to be taken into account.

Housing

The house of a head-injured or neurologically impaired person should be within reach of a town for shopping and social outings. It may require alterations for level access and sufficient accommodation, and adaptations of bathroom and electrical fittings. The necessity for and specific nature of these can be indicated by functional assessment. In addition, removal costs, legal fees and loss of interest on capital employed may be relevant.

Transport

Comment may be necessary on the plaintiff or pursuer's capacity to drive, or alternatively the need for a car or more specialized or adapted means of transport for some independence, albeit driven by others.

Miscellaneous

In addition, there will be concern about any particular aids or equipment such as computers which may help the victim to communicate or provide constructive activity. Intercom alarms may be appropriate. Holidays may cost more. Experts will advise on the actual costs of all these items.

Thus, lawyers' requests to neuropsychologists may cover the generality of all the above topics, including cognitive, motor, perceptual, emotional and social functioning before and after the injury or impairment, with emphasis on the precise nature and extent of any current difficulties, and if possible prediction a long time into the future with prognosis for relative recovery. Clearly, specific questions and combinations of areas of concern will depend upon circumstances of individual cases. From the perspective of the lawyer, what is required is flexible application of psychological knowledge and skills with rigour to meet the demands of the specific client.

A SEVERE VERSUS MINOR HEAD INJURY

In cases of compensation involving head injury, a distinction tends to be made between, first, severe head injury and, second, cases of transient or minimal physical and neurological import but with emotional sequelae for the victim.

First, in cases of severe head injury, lawyers acting for victims have realized that such claims require a view similar to that previously used in paraplegic cases, and have adjusted that approach in order to extend the available heads of damages. The pain and suffering (or solatium) aspect of such awards may now represent a relatively small portion of the award. For example, in *King* v. *Waterns-Howel* (1989) 2 ALL ER 375, a 34-year-old single woman suffered brain damage as the result of a negligently administered anaesthetic. The anaesthetic caused blood pressure to fall, with subsequent cardiac arrest. She was unconscious for three days, and spent two further months in hospital regaining use of her senses and limbs. However, she demonstrated loss of higher intellectual function, emotion, volition, memory and in consequence her ability to plan courses of action. She showed an adverse reaction to being placed in a residential home, and was depressed, agitated, aggressive and at times suicidal. The incapacity was permanent. A total award of £266,000 was made comprising, *inter alia*, pain and suffering at £42,500, past attendance costs at £16,000, future attendance costs at £86,000 and future wage loss of £61,000.

Similarly, in the case of *Hodgson* v. *Trapp* (1989) AC 807; (1988) 3 ALL ER 870, a 33-year-old married woman was reduced to a 'vegetative' state as a result of a road traffic accident. She suffered defective short-term memory and severe mental impairment, requiring twenty-four-hour attendance. The implications for her family were that her husband was required to give up work, and the children were sent to boarding school while he looked after her. It was held that some reduction in her life expectancy due to infection was possible, but she might live until old age. An award of £431,840 was made, including £53,871 for cost of care to the date of trial with £154,000 for future costs and £73,123 for future loss of earnings. A sum of £25,000 was allowed for cost of alterations to the family home and £1,200 for special items of furniture. Solatium of £65,000 was awarded.

In contrast, in *Carswell* v. *British Railways Board* (1991) SLT 73, a 25-year-old track man suffered slight head injuries and some anxiety and sleeplessness as a result of a fall while walking along a railway line. He had tripped and fallen, striking his head on a rail, and alleged that he subsequently suffered headaches and severe nightmares. The pursuer sustained head injury and shock with some post-traumatic mental upset. The acute phases of the problem were short lived. Solatium was assessed at £1,750. Hence mental upset was the major feature in that case upon which subsequent compensation was founded.

Update services exist to keep lawyers appraised of the components and amounts of contemporary awards; Goldrein and de Hass (1992) proved an example.

Emotional reactions

As the above cases show, the emotional after-effects of situations in which accidents have occurred may, in the midst of complex and sophisticated neuropsychology, be relevant to damage settlements. The emotional effects of the experience of the accident may compound with immediate physical or neurological sequelae and affect both non-pecuniary and pecuniary items. In the past, both English and Scots law tended to take what most mental health professional workers might regard as a rather naive view of distress, based upon narrow concepts of 'mental illness'. In the 'nervous shock' case of *Bourhill* v. *Young* (1943) A.C. 92, a claim for damages was rejected on its facts, but the House of Lords gave clear recognition to the legitimacy, in principle, of such claims. In *Hinz* v. *Berry* (1970) 1 ALL ER 1074, a robust lady saw her husband killed and her children injured in a motor accident. The court held that, on the facts, if she had not seen the accident she would have stood up to the situation, though grief stricken. She suffered from morbid depression, and an award currently worth £30,000 was made for that suffering.

In the case of *McLoughlin* v. *O'Brian* (1982) 2 ALL ER 298, Lord Wilberforce commented helpfully:

> whatever is unknown about the mind/body relationship (and the area of ignorance seems to expand with added knowledge) it is now accepted by medical science that recognisable and severe physical damage to the human body and system may be caused by the impact through the senses of external events on the mind. There may thus be produced what is as identifiable as illness as any that may be caused by direct physical impact.

Particularly, the concept of post-traumatic stress disorder elucidated in DSM-III-R (American Psychiatric Association, 1987) has been developed.

A thorough discussion of 'nervous shock' and similar concepts has appeared in a report on the Zeebrugge arbitration (see 'Post traumatic stress disorder – the Zeebrugge arbitration', 1989). The implication for the clinician appears to be that the emotional reactions caused both directly by the circumstances of an accident and subsequent upon the eventual results of the accident require comment.

THE EXPERT WITNESS

The functions and techniques of the 'expert' witness are increasingly documented and understood. In general, the 'expert' may express opinion as well as speak to matters of fact (Wilkinson, 1986). The skills and format of report writing have been examined by Haward (1981), Ziskin (1981) and Cooke (1990). From the point of view of the legal practitioner, experts' reports which have any bearing on liability must be, first, comprehensive, with thorough review of background and present possible evidence, and, second, pertinent, by a practitioner of sufficient specialized expertise and seniority at least commensurate with any specialist who may be led by the other side. Further, Haward (1981) and Cooke (1990) have addressed preparation for court attendance and strategies for dealing with examination, cross-examination and re-examination as a witness. Any tendency by neuropsychologists to complacency in such an arena may be counteracted by quiet contemplation of Evans's (1983) work on training of advocates.

Finally, for those neuropsychologists who venture into the forensic process, there may be increased professional and financial dangers (Furnell, 1991), particularly concerning potential professional negligence claims, and suitable professional indemnity insurance would seem a sensible precaution.

ACKNOWLEDGEMENTS

I wish to thank David Sandison of Lawford Kidd and Co., Edinburgh, for his helpful comments on a draft of this chapter, and also Laura McLean of the same firm for calm typing of successive versions of the document.

REFERENCES

American Psychiatric Association (1987). *Statistical Manual of Mental Disorders.* Washington DC: American Psychiatric Press.

Brooks, D. N. (ed.) (1984). *Closed Head Injury: Psychological, Social and Family Consequences.* Oxford: Oxford University Press.

Cooke, D. J. (1990). 'Do I feel lucky? Survival in the witness box'. *Neuropsychology*, 4, 271–85.

Duff, P. (1991). *Criminal Injuries Compensation.* Edinburgh: Butterworth.

Evans, K. (1983). *Advocacy at the Bar: A Beginner's Guide.* London: Financial Training Publications.

Furnell, J. R. G. (1991). 'The child psychologist and the law: are we fools rushing in?'. *Proceedings of First BPS Division of Criminological and Legal Psychology Annual Conference. Canterbury 1991*, II, 73–81.

Goldrein, I. S. and de Haas, M. R. (1992). *Butterworths Personal Injury Litigation Service*. London: Butterworth.

Gudjonsson, G. H. (1985). 'Psychological evidence in court: results of the BPS Survey'. *Bulletin of the British Psychological Society*, 38, 327–30.

Haward, L. R. C. (1981). *Forensic Psychology*. London: Batsford Academic and Educational.

Kemp, D. A. McI. (1975). *The Quantum of Damages in Personal Injury and Accident Claims*. London: Sweet and Maxwell.

Muller, D. J., Blackman, D. E. and Chapman, A. J. (1984). *Psychology and Law*. London: Wiley.

Munkman, J. (1989). *Damages for Personal Injuries and Death*. London: Butterworth.

Noble, P., Hellyer, B. and Fanshawe, E. (1986). *Disability and Compensation Claims*. London: Sweet and Maxwell.

Pearson Commission Report (1978). *Compensation for Personal Injuries*. Cmnd. 7054. London: HMSO.

'Post traumatic stress disorder – the Zeebrugge arbitration' (1989). *Personal and Medical Injuries Law Letter*, 5(5), 37–42.

Rogers, W. V. H. (1989). *Winfield and Jolowicz on Tort*. London: Sweet and Maxwell.

Wilkinson, A. B. (1986). *The Scottish Law of Evidence*. Edinburgh: Butterworth.

Working Party Report of the Medical Disability Society (1988). 'The Management of Traumatic Brain Injury'. *Lancet*, 11 June, 1350.

Ziskin, J. (1981). *Coping with Psychiatric and Psychological Testimony*. 3rd edn. California: Law and Psychology Press.

11

DEVELOPMENTS IN ASSESSMENT TECHNIQUES

Sarah L. Wilson and Graham E. Powell

INTRODUCTION

This chapter will review some of the newer developments in assesment techniques which can provide invaluable information for the neuropsychologist. These developments are technology-based and include computer-based assessment, computerized transaxial tomography (CT), positron emission tomography (PET) and magnetic resonance imaging (MRI). This chapter will also examine a relatively new issue in the practice of neuropsychology; that is, the assessment of patients in coma.

COMPUTER-BASED ASSESSMENT

Although work in this field began in the 1960s, it was not until the arrival of the microcomputer that interest began to proliferate, and the work referred to will be mostly microcomputer-based. Computers can be used both to administer and to score tests. In most applications both functions are employed, but in some, just one.

The benefits and problems of computer-based assessment in general have been amply reviewed elsewhere (Wilson and McMillan, 1991, 1992). There are advantages which are of particular consequence to the neuropsychologist, however; these relate especially to clients with impaired communication abilities. In the assessment of individuals whose responses are slow or difficult to comprehend, it is easy to prompt unconsciously by changes in body language, as by leaning towards the client and widening the eyes when it appears that the correct answer is emerging. Computers, of course, have no body language. Another major advantage is for those clients whose ability to use the conventional forms of communication required by tests is limited or non-existent. It can be relatively easy and inexpensive to provide response media for use with the computer-based testing system, which can enable the assessment of individuals with very severe physical disabilities.

The disadvantages of the use of computer-based assessment are mostly related to the sophistication of the available technology. For example, the complexity of graphic material used in tests is limited by the screen resolution of the computer system (see Bartram *et al.* (1987) for recommendations on this). If it is required that the software should score as well as present the test and record responses, then there is a limitation to tests with answers that can be precisely defined, such as spellings or multiple-choice questions. This difficulty may be overcome by the development of 'expert' systems which can cope with natural language, but the extent to which such a system could be applied in testing would be dependent on the lexicon available to it (Wilson, 1988). System portability can also be a problem, since monitors can be heavy, but not if the test software can be administered by a laptop computer. The biggest disadvantage for the neuropsychologist is, however, the limitation to the use of test material in two dimensions only. There is too the important point that in a neuropsychological assessment, although the actual answers to test items given by the patient are important, valuable information can also be gained by observing the way in which the patient deals with the test items, and the use of computer-based tests could constrain this.

Box 11.1 provides an indication of some of the research and development in computer-based neuropsychological assessment. As space is limited, interested readers should refer to the papers cited for details such as hardware used, specific client populations, evaluative data, etc. There is also a fuller review in Wilson and McMillan (1992). The tests are divided into the following functional areas: general psychometrics, memory and attention, perception and orientation, executive functions and novel procedures.

IMAGING THE BRAIN

Neuro-imaging is the assessment of some aspect of brain tissue in order to produce a picture of brain structures that can be inspected visually for abnormalities, or from which measurements such as the size or density of a structure can be made for comparison purposes.

This section will cover computerized transaxial tomography (CT scans), positron emission tomography (PET), single-photon emission computed tomography (SPECT) and magnetic resonance imaging (MRI). It will not cover pure measures of function such as tachistoscopic and dichotic listening methods, evoked potentials or regional electroencephalogram (EEG), although it is recognized that computers have had a significant impact upon their nature and use. In particular, the computerized analysis of power in the different EEG frequencies (particularly the alpha band) has enabled the observation of the correlation between cognitive and neural processes in real time. As a subject undertakes a range of different psychological tasks, one can observe how different regions of the brain become more or less activated (e.g. Collins *et al.*, 1990). The interested reader is referred to

Box 11.1

Computer-based assessments

Test category	Test	References
General psychometrics	Mill Hill Vocabulary Scale (1982)	Beaumont and French (1987); Watts *et al.* (1982)
	Standard Progressive Matrices	Beaumont and French (1987); Calvert and Waterfall (1982); Watts *et al.* (1982)
	Eysenck Personality Inventory	Beaumont and French (1987); Ridgway *et al.* (1982)
Memory and attention	Digit Span	Beaumont and French (1987); Wilson (1987)
	Corsi blocks	Morris *et al.* (1988)
	Delayed matching to sample	Morris *et al.* (1988)
	Visual spatial memory	Acker (1982); Carr *et al.* (1986)
	Digit Symbol	Acker (1982)
Perception and orientation	Little Man Test	Acker (1982)
	Road Map Test	Beaumont and French (1987)
	Perceptual Maze	Elithorn *et al.* (1982)
	Line Bisection	Halligan and Marshall (1989); Wilson (1990)
Executive functions	Tower of London	Morris *et al.* (1987)
	Stroop Test	Iregren *et al.* (1986)
	Wisconsin Card Sorting Test	Acker (1982); Beaumont and French (1987); Davidson *et al.* (1987)
Novel procedures	Continuous Attention Test	Tiplady (1988)
	Animated tracking task	Davidson *et al.* (1987)
	Detection of shunt blockage	Grant (1986)

Beaumont (1983) for reviews of the principles involved. However, in terms of the 'image' of the brain produced by regional EEG, it is still greatly lacking in resolution compared with CT and the other measures mentioned, as it is generated from relatively few sites (that is, from the twenty or so electrodes used to collect the signal).

Computerized transaxial tomography (CT)

A CT scan is a three-dimensional representation of the brain based upon an analysis of X-rays. In essence, a narrow beam of X-rays is passed through the brain and radiation not absorbed by the brain and skull tissue is absorbed by radiation detectors on the other side of the head. The amount of radiation is recorded in about 160 positions equally spaced along a line, and then the X-ray source is rotated by 1° and the procedure is repeated. The source is then rotated by another degree and so on, until it has been moved through 180°. There are therefore typically 160 × 180 equations to perform to produce a dot matrix of that size. New machines can have a dot matrix of as large as 512 × 512 (Ramsey, 1987). Eight or so of these sections are printed out, corresponding to different planes of the head, and each slice is routinely 8 mm thick, but 4 mm or 2 mm can be achieved.

Following the pioneering work of A. M. Cormack and G. N. Hounsfield, for which they received the Nobel Prize for physiology and medicine, the CT scanner has become a familiar and widespread neuroradiological technique since 1972, used for both clinical and research purposes. It reveals much more detail than ordinary X ray, is non-invasive, takes a relatively short time (twenty-five minutes or so), and has a wide field of application including the detection of tumours, cerebrovascular accidents, severe head injuries, intracranial lesions in general and many forms of atrophy. Overnight, CT scans effectively replaced many prolonged, dangerous and unpleasant investigations (Raichle, 1987).

One of the main drawbacks of the technique is that it only discloses structure, and cannot detect many neurological abnormalities of a functional nature, as in certain kinds of epilepsy, for example. In addition, its resolution of soft tissue is not sufficient to detect minor or small changes, such as occur after mild head injury (Eisenberg and Levin, 1989). It is better at detecting grosser damage; for example, CT scans show abnormalities in about a quarter of moderate head injury cases. A further problem are the artifacts and blurring that can be caused by the patients moving their heads, or the interference produced by surgical clips and metallic plates. The movement artifacts are being dealt with by developing second-, third- and fourth-generation machines, some of which require less than five seconds of actual scanning time (Ramsey, 1987).

Positron emission tomography (PET)

Whereas CT scans measure structure only, PET scans reflect both structure and function. Typically, the subject is given a radioactively labelled form of glucose, such as fluorodeoxyglucose, which contains fluorine 18 with a half-life of 17 minutes. Isotopes such as this can be substituted for the stable atoms which make up the biological system without changing the biological characteristics of the traced molecule (Leenders et al., 1984). The radio-actively labelled glucose is therefore metabolized by the brain in the normal way, and the concentration of radioactivity is recorded by special detectors. This concentration is a fairly direct measure of brain activity, since there is a link between local neuronal activity and increased blood flow that has been known about since the last century. An active area of brain is supplied with more glucose via increased blood flow, and so the concentration of radioactivity increases.

An element is unstable if there are more protons than electrons. Excess protons are released as neutrons and positrons, and if positrons collide with electrons they annihilate each other to produce two gamma rays moving in exactly opposite directions (that is, two high-energy annihilation photons at 511 kiloelectron volts). These two gamma rays are able to pass through the brain, skull and surrounding air, to be picked up by detectors around the patient's head. Detection of an event is by a coincidence circuit; that is, an event is recorded only when two annihilation photons strike diametrically opposite detectors at exactly the same time. Other, non-coincident, gamma rays are just part of normal background activity or 'noise'. The origins of the gamma rays are then mapped and converted by the computer into a map or picture of the brain, which comes in horizontal sections similar to those produced by CT (Raichle, 1983).

The application of PET depends in part upon the element that is traced. Radioactively labelled glucose or oxygen (oxygen-15 with a half-life of 2 minutes) both enable metabolic activity to be mapped. For example, the oxygen-15 steady-state inhalation model is widely used to measure regional cerebral blood flow (rCBF), oxygen extraction rate (rOER) and oxygen utilization (rCMRO$_2$: Frackowiak et al., 1980). After breathing oxygen-15 for about fifteen minutes, the tissue concentration of H$_2$^{15}O reaches equilib-rium (delivery of H$_2$^{15}O is balanced by its washout), and the measurements can be made. On the other hand, one can radioactively label a particular drug with known pharmacological properties in order to map neurotransmit-ter function. Phelps and Mazziotta (1985) review this work with labelled compounds such as haloperidol, L-dopa, imipramine and morphine. For example, the administration of a labelled antipsychotic drug will enable the mapping of dopamine receptors.

Clinical applications include assessing changes of blood flow with age and dementia (Leenders et al., 1990); the evolution of central ischaemia (Wise et al., 1983); epilepsy (Brooks, 1991); cerebrovascular disease (Brooks, 1991); and movement disorder (Leenders et al., 1984).

The advantages of PET are obviously that it permits an in vivo examina-tion of the relationship between physiology and anatomy, and that it can pick up areas of function that have been altered because of a disruption of normal relationships with regions that are damaged. However, its development is limited by the need to have a nearby cyclotron to produce short-lived isotopes. There are also some drawbacks with the technique itself. In particular, the spatial resolution is poor – not much better than 6 mm. The temporal resolution is also poor, as it can take two hours to obtain a scan (which also means one cannot test restless or unco-operative patients). For this reason, methods based on the measure of blood flow after a single inhalation of $C^{15}O_2$ or ^{15}O are being developed.

Single-photon emission computed tomography (SPECT)

This technique uses the technology of CT scan reconstruction, employing single photons rather than X-rays. It is different from PET and has less resolution, in that the tracer only emits a single photon, so that measurement by coincidence circuits cannot be used. However, there are commercially available tracers that do not require a local cyclotron, and so the technique is less expensive than PET (Kolb and Whishaw, 1990). SPECT will have a major impact upon clinical decision-making when it becomes more widely available, but as yet examples are limited. A recent one is provided by Delecluse *et al.* (1990). They used a ^{133}Xenon inhalation technique on a case of suspected primary progressive dementia. As well as finding the expected left-temporal hypo-perfusion, there was also a 'vast' area of subclinical injury to include most of the ipsilateral hemisphere and frontal lobes.

Magnetic resonance imaging (MRI)

This technique is based on principles elucidated by Felix Block and Edward Purcell, who shared the Nobel Prize for these advances in 1952. MRI is based on the fact that certain atoms, such as hydrogen, phosphorus, sodium and carbon, behave like tiny spinning magnets (dipoles). Normally these are oriented randomly, but they will line up in parallel if placed in a strong magnetic field – usually generated by a permanent magnet, resistive electromagnet, or superconductive magnet cooled by liquid helium or nitrogen.

The atoms wobble as they spin and the nuclei of the different elements wobble at different frequencies because each element has a different weight. If radio waves are beamed across aligned atoms at right angles to the magnetic field, then they can be caused to wobble synchronously, if the radio frequency is exactly right.

When the radio waves are turned off, the atoms 'recover' or return to their original state. As they do so a voltage is induced in the magnetic field ('magnetic resonance') and a radio frequency signal is given off (the return to the ground state can only be made by dissipating excess energy to the lattice), which can be picked up by a coil of wire around the tissue (that is, an ariel). T_1 is the relaxation time, or time taken to return to equilibrium following a radio-frequency disturbance (also known as 'spin-lattice relaxation time'). Solids, and liquids like CSF (cerebrospinal fluid), have long T_1 values. The location of the different atoms is analysed by the computer and reconstructed as an image, usually in the form of a 1-cm slice (varying from millimetres through to several centimetres).

MRI shows the make-up of cells and their surroundings, and is much more sensitive than CT scans, producing pictures of 'exquisite anatomical details' (Raichle, 1987). It is particularly good at discriminating grey and white matter. It is certainly a machine of the future, but in the meantime is very expensive both to buy and to run, has a long scanning time, and is contraindicated in a substantial number of cases (such as those with metal clips or plates, or with heart pacemakers, or who are unable to remain still for a sufficient period of time), although this last problem may be dealt with simply and inexpensively (Wilson et al., 1992).

There is a growing clinical and experimental literature on MRI. Recent examples in neuropsychology include Eisenberg and Levin's (1989) work on head injury. Twenty patients with minor to moderate head injury were assessed on CT and MRI and on a psychological test battery. Both CT and MRI revealed that frontal and temporal lesion predominated, but their true extent was only apparent on MRI, which yielded volumetric measures that correlated with psychological test performance. A second example is provided by Kesselring *et al.* (1990). MRI was used to try and distinguish between acute disseminated encephalomyelitis (ADEM) and multiple sclerosis (MS). Twelve patients with ADEM were given serial measurements to examine the theory that, although both ADEM and MS are demyelinating diseases of the CNS (cerebrospinal fluid), they differ in that they are monophasic and multiphasic respectively. In line with this, Kesselring *et al.* found that ADEM patients did not show further degenerative changes after the first episode, but normally showed a degree of resolution of brain function, though not complete.

Future developments in imaging

The drive will be towards developing a better three-dimensional image (currently obtained from slices). It will need better spatial resolution, perhaps down to 1 cubic mm, a temporal resolution in milliseconds, and a total averaging time of 10 or 20 minutes. To do this, electron spin resonance and impedance resonance will be explored (Holder, 1986). In addition, more direct images of neuronal functional activity are needed, which directly relate to neural discharge rate – at the moment we can only measure metabolism, and this has an uncertain relationship with underlying neural electronic activity. The aim will be to measure individual spikes – an enormously exciting prospect.

171

ASSESSMENT OF PATIENTS IN COMA

Coma and vegetative state

The assessment of patients in a comatose state is an area of increasing interest to neuropsychologists, who are most likely to be concerned with patients when they are medically stable but have not reached a state where they are recognized as being aware. The areas of concern for the psychologist are most likely to be monitoring recovery and examining the effects of treatment.

Jennett and Teasdale (1977) define coma as a state where the patient gives no verbal response, does not obey commands and does not open the eyes, either spontaneously or to a stimulus; this definition is widely accepted. The initial acute or sleep-like stage of coma can last in general for up to 4–6 weeks after onset; after this time the patient begins to awaken regardless of the severity of the injury (Plum and Posner, 1980). In the condition that ensues, there are periods of wakefulness when the eyes are open and move; responsiveness is limited to primitive postural and reflex movements of the limbs, and the patients never speak. Respiration and heart beat are spontaneous. This syndrome was originally described by Jennett and Plum (1972), who named it 'persistent vegetative state'. Subsequent authors have preferred to use the term 'vegetative state' unless the condition persists for more than a year (Bricolo *et al.*, 1980). The term 'prolonged coma' (Bricolo *et al.*, 1980) has also been used, but this terminology appears to include the very small proportion of patients who die without opening their eyes. More recently the terms 'prolonged post-comatose unawareness' (Sazbon and Groswasser, 1991) and 'reflexive state' (Andrews, 1993) have been suggested.

There are a number of syndromes similar in outward manifestation to vegetative state which are distinct from this condition (Jennett and Teasdale, 1981). These are: 'locked-in' syndrome, in which the patient is tetraplegic and mute but responsive and sentient; akinetic mutism; complete aphasia; and psychiatric states including schizophrenic catatonic stupor and hysterical coma. In brain death, the patient is dependent on a ventilator and, however much is done, the heart always stops beating spontaneously within a week or so, usually after a few days. Once this is established there is a progressive dissolution of the organs, beginning with the brain no matter how much artificial support is provided. In brain death, a flat or isoelectric EEG is obtained.

Behaviour scales

Apart from the electrophysiological and scanning techniques mentioned earlier in this chapter, there are a number of behavioural measures which

172

can be used with these patients. These have the advantage, particularly when considering assessment on a daily basis, of being quicker and much less expensive to apply, and easier to interpret.

The most widely used assessment for comatose patients is the Glasgow Coma Scale (GCS: Jennett and Teasdale, 1977, 1981). This consists of three subscales: eye opening, best motor response and verbal response. Each subscale indicates improving levels of function; for example, the eye-opening scale starts at none, then goes to pain, then to speech and finally to spontaneously. The subscales can also be scored, starting with 1 for the lowest level of function, and the scores can be totalled. Patients scoring 9 or more on this scale are deemed to be out of coma. The GCS is primarily applicable to patients in acute coma; patients in vegetative state, however, will score the maximum on eye opening and may show little change on the other two scales over a long period, yet may have obviously improved in other ways, so behaviour scales that include other areas of function are more appropriate.

A number of behaviour scales that are appropriate for use with vegetative-state patients have been published. They vary in sophistication and sensitivity and most can be scored and totalled to give an overall score – as with the GCS, the larger the better.

De Young and Grass (1987) published a relatively brief response scale which examines the following functions: visual, olfactory, gustatory, auditory, tactile and range of motion. Ansell et al. (1989) produced the Western Neuro Sensory Stimulation Profile (WNSSP), consisting of the following subscales: arousal/attention, auditory response, expressive communication, visual response, tactile response, olfactory response. The WNSSP manual presents evaluative data on reliability and validity, as does the manual for the Sensory Stimulation Assessment Measure (SSAM: Rader and Ellis, 1989). SSAM has subscales for audition, vision, olfaction, gustation and touch. Freeman's (1987) assessment examines the following: vigilance, emotion, drive, vision, audition, touch, limb and body movement, hand function and vocalization. Each of the sensory and motor functions is divided into a hierarchy of five levels. The Coma/Near Coma Scale (CNC) assesses eight different parameters of behaviour: auditory, command responsivity, visual, threat, olfactory, tactile, pain and vocalization. Scoring is according to the number of times a specified response is evoked (Rappaport et al., 1992). An extensive review of behaviour scales is given by Horn et al. (1993).

Behaviour sampling

Another approach to the assessment of comatose patients is the use of behaviour sampling. This method has been applied (Wilson et al., 1991, 1993) in studies of the efficacy of sensory stimulation for patients in a vegetative state, but can equally well be used to monitor changes in patients within days, between days or over longer periods of time (Wilson *et al.*, 1991, 1993). Observations were made at 10-second intervals over a 10-minute period.

CONCLUDING REMARKS

In this chapter, some developments in assessment techniques have been reviewed, which the neuropsychologist is likely to encounter either directly or indirectly during the course of his or her practice.

REFERENCES

Acker, W. (1982) 'A computerised approach to psychological screening: the Bexley–Maudsley Automated Psychological Screening and the Bexley–Maudsley Category Sorting Test'. *International Journal of Man–Machine Studies*, 17, 361–9.

Andrews, K. (1993). 'Should PVS patients be treated?'. *Neuropsychological Rehabilitation*, 3(2), 109–19.

Ansell, B. J., Keenan, J. E. and de la Rocha, O. (1989). *Western Neuro Sensory Stimulation Profile*. Tustin, CA: Western Neuro Care Centre.

Bartram, D., Beaumont, J. G., Cornford, T., Dann, P. L. and Wilson, S. L. (1987). 'Recommendations for the design of software for computer-based assessment (CBA)'. *Bulletin of the British Psychological Society*, 40, 86–7.

Beaumont, J. G. (1983). 'The EEG and task performance: a tutorial review'. In A. W. K. Gaillard and W. Ritter (eds), *Tutorials in ERP Research: Endogenous Components*. Amsterdam: North-Holland.

Beaumont, J. G. and French, C. C. (1987). 'A clinical field study of eight automated psychometric procedures: the Leicester/DHSS project'. *International Journal of Man–Machine Studies*, 26, 661–2.

Bricolo, A., Turazzi, S. and Feriotti, G. (1980). 'Prolonged post-traumatic unconsciousness: therapeutic assets and liabilities'. *Journal of Neurosurgery*, 52, 625–34.

Brooks, D. J. (1991). 'PET: its clinical role in neurology'. *Journal of Neurology, Neurosurgery, and Psychiatry*, 54, 1–5.

Calvert, E. J. and Waterfall, R. C. (1982). 'A comparison of conventional and automated administration of Raven's Standard Progressive Matrices'. *International Journal of Man–Machine Studies*, 17, 305–10.

Carr, A. C., Woods, R. T. and Moore, B. J. (1986). 'Developing a microcomputer-based system for use with psychogeriatric patients'. *Bulletin of the Royal College of Psychiatrists*, 10, 309–12.

Collins, D., Powell, G. E. and Davies, I. (1990). 'The reliability of task induced asymetrics as indicators of individual variability in cognitive strategies'. *Personality and Individual Differences*, 11, 205–7.

Davidson, O. R., Stevens, D. E., Goddard, G. V., Bilkey, D. K. and Bishara, S. N. (1987). 'The performance of a sample of traumatic head-injured patients on some novel computer-assisted neuropsychological tests'. *Applied Psychology: An International Review*, 36, 329–42.

Delecluse, F., Andersen, A. R., Woldemar, G., Thomsen, A. M., Kjaer, L., Lassen, N. A. and Postigliona, A. (1990). 'Cerebral blood flow in progressive aplasia without dementia'. *Brain*, 113, 1395–1404.

De Young, S. and Grass, R. B. (1987). 'Coma recovery program'. *Rehabilitation Nursing*, 12, 121–4.

Eisenberg, H. M. and Levin, H. S. (1989). 'Computed tomography and magnetic resonance imaging in mild to moderate head injury'. In M. S. Levin, H. M. Eisenberg and A. L. Benton (eds), *Mild Head Injury*. New York: Oxford University Press.

Elithorn, A., Mornington, S. and Stavrou, A. (1982). 'Automated psychological testing: some principles and practice'. *International Journal of Man–Machine Studies*, 17, 247–64.

Frackowiak, R. S. J., Lenzi, G. L., Jones, T. and Heather, J. D. (1980). 'Quantitative measurement of regional cerebral blood flow and oxygen metabolism in man using ^{15}O and positron emission tomography: theory, procedure and normal values'. *Journal of Computer Assisted Tomography*, 4, 726–7.

Freeman, E. A. (1987) *The Catastrophe of Coma*. Buderim: David Bateman.

Grant, D. W. (1986) 'Cats and fishes: an automated neurological self-administered program for hydrocephalic children'. Paper presented at Innovations in the Application of Microcomputers to Psychological Assessment and Therapy, Royal Hospital and Home, Putney, May.

Halligan, P. W. and Marshall, J. C. (1989). 'Two techniques for the assessment of line bisection in visuo-spatial negelect: a single case study'. *Journal of Neurology, Neurosurgery, and Psychiatry*, 52, 1300–2.

Holder, D. S. (1986). 'Future perspectives in imaging human brain function; a theoretical analysis of techniques that could be used to image neural firing in the human brain'. In L. Battistin and F. Gerstenbrand (eds), *PET and NMR: New Perspectives in Neuroimaging and in Clinical Neurochemistry*. New York: Liss.

Horn, S., Shiel, A., McLellan, L., Campbell, M., Watson, M. and Wilson, B. (1993). 'A review of behavioural assessment scales for monitoring recovery in and after coma with pilot date on a new scale of visual awareness'. *Neuropsychological Rehabilitation*, 3 (2), 121–37.

Iregren, A., Akerstedt, T., Anshelm Olson, B. and Gamberale, F. (1986). 'Experimental exposure to toluene in combination with ethanol intake'. *Scandinavian Journal of Work and Environmental Health*, 12, 469–75.

Jennett, B. and Plum, F. (1972). 'Persistent vegetative state after brain damage'. *Lancet*, i, 734–7.

Jennett, B. and Teasdale, G. (1977). 'Aspects of coma after severe head injury'. *Lancet*, i, 878–81.

Jennett, B. and Teasdale, G. (1981). *Management of Head Injuries*. Philadelphia, PA: F.A. Davis.

Kesselring, J., Miller, D. M., Robb, S. A., Kendall, B. E., Moseley, I. F., Kingsley, D., Du Boulay, E. P. G. H. and McDonald, W. I. (1990). 'Acute disseminated encephalomyelitis: MRI findings and the distinction from multiple sclerosis'. *Brain*, 113, 291–302.

Kolb, B. and Whishaw, I. Q. (1990). *Fundamentals of Human Neuropsychology*. New York: H. Freeman.

Leenders, K. L., Gibbs, J. M., Frackowiak, R. S. J., Lammertsma, A. A., and Jones, T. (1984). 'Positron emission tomography of the brain: new possibilities for the investigation of human cerebral pathology'. *Progress in Neurobiology*, 23, 1–38.

Leenders, K. L., Perani, D., Lammertsma, A. A., Heather, J. D., Buckingham, P., Healy, M. J. R., Gibbs, J. M., Wise, R. J. S., Hatazawa, J., Herfold, S., Beaney, R. P., Brooks, D. T., Spinks, T., Rhodes, C., Frackowiak, R. S. J. and Jones, T. (1990). 'Cerebral blood flow, blood volume and oxygen utilization: normal values and effects of age'. *Brain*, 113, 27–47.

Morris, R. G., Eveden, J. L., Sahakian, B. J., and Robbins, T. W. (1987). 'Computer-aided assessment of dementia: comparative studies of neuropsychological deficits in Alzheimer-type dementia and Parkinson's disease'. In S. Stahl, S. Iversen and E. Goodman (eds), *Cognitive Neurochemistry*. Oxford: Oxford University Press.

Morris, R. G., Downes, J. J., Sahakian, B. J., Eveden, J. L., Heald, A. and Robbins, T.W. (1988). 'Planning and spatial working memory in Parkinson's disease'. *Journal of Neurology. Neurosurgery, and Psychiatry*, 51, 757–66.

Phelps, M. E. and Mazziotta, J. C. (1985). 'Positron emission tomography: human brain function and biochemistry'. *Science*, 228, 799–809.

Plum, F. and Posner, J. B. (1980). *Diagnosis of Stupor and Coma*. Philadelphia, PA: F. A. Davis.

Rader, M. A. and Ellis, D. W. (1989). *Sensory Stimulation Assessment Measure: Manual for Administration*. Camden, NJ: Mediplex Rehab.

Raichle, M. E. (1983) 'Positron emission tomography'. *Annual Review of Neuroscience*, 6, 249–68.

Raichle, M. E. (1987). 'Images of the brain in action'. In R. L. Gregory (ed.), *The Oxford Companion to the Mind*. Oxford: Oxford University Press.

Ramsey, R. G. (1987). *Neuroradiology*. 2nd edn. Philadelphia, PA: Saunders.

Rappaport, M., Dougherty, A. M. and Ketting, D. L. (1992). 'Evaluation of coma and vegetative state'. *Archives of Physical Medicine and Rehabilitation*, 73, 628–34.

Ridgway, J., MacCulloch, M. J. and Mills, H. E. (1982). 'Some experiences with administering a psychometric test with a light pen and a microcomputer'. *International Journal of Man–Machine Studies*, 17, 265–78.

Sazbon, L. and Groswasser, Z. (1991). 'Editorial: prolonged coma, vegetative state, post-comatose unawareness: semantics or better understanding'. *Brain Injury*, 5, 1–2.

Tiplady, B. (1988). 'A continuous attention test for the acute behavioural effects of drugs'. *Psychopharmacology Bulletin*, 24, 213–16.

Watts, K., Baddeley, A. and Williams, M. (1982). 'Automated tailored testing using Raven's Matrices and the Mill Hill Vocabulary tests: a comparison with manual administration'. *International Journal of Man–Machine Studies*, 17, 331–44.

Wilson, S. L. (1987). 'The development of an automated test of immediate memory and its evaluation on severely physically disabled adults'. *Applied Psychology: An International Review*, 36, 311–28.

Wilson, S. L. (1988). 'Direct use with clients: automated assessment treatment and decision making'. In B. Glastonbury, W. LaMendola and S. Toole (eds), *Information Technology and the Human Services*. Chichester: John Wiley.

Wilson, S. L. (1990). 'Psychological assessment in severe physical disability'. In R. West, J. Weinman and M. Christie (eds), *Microcomputers, Psychology and Medicine*. Chichester: John Wiley.

Wilson, S. L., Finney, J. S., Powell, G. E. and Andrews, K. (1992). 'Problems in magnetic resonance imaging in patients with severe brain injury and a solution to one of them'. *Brain Injury*, 6(1), 75–7.

Wilson, S. L. and McMillan, T. M. (1991). 'Microcomputers in psychometric and neuropsychological assessment'. In A. Ager (ed.), *Microcomputers in Clinical Psychology*. Chichester: John Wiley.

Wilson, S. L. and McMillan, T. M. (1992) 'Computer-based assessment in neuropsychology'. In J. Crawford, D. Parker and W. W. McKinlay (eds), *A Handbook of Neuropsychological Assessment*, Hove: Lawrence Erlbaum.

Wilson, S. L., Powell, G. E., Elliott, K. and Thwaites, H. (1991). 'Sensory stimulation in prolonged coma: four single case studies'. *Brain Injury*, 5(4), 393–400.

Wilson, S. L., Powell, G. E., Elliott, K. and Thwaites, H. (1993). 'Evaluation of sensory stimulation as a treatment for prolonged coma: seven single experimental case studies'. *Neuropsychological Rehabilitation*, 3(2), 191–201.

Wilson, S. L., Thompson, J. A. and Wylie, G. (1982). 'Automated psychological testing for the severely physically handicapped'. *International Journal of Man–Machine Studies*, 17, 291–6.

Wise, R. J. S., Bernarchii, S., Frankowiak, R. S. J., Legg, N. J. and Jones, T. (1983). 'Serial observations on the pathophysiology of acute stroke: the transition from ischaemia to infarction as reflected in regional oxygen extraction'. *Brain*, 106, 197–222.

ASSESSMENT PROCEDURES
AND TESTS

Tests which are cited in the text and have published materials are listed here, with the authors, year of publication and publisher. In those instances where the text citations are published articles, the tests are not listed here, but can be found in the references at the end of each chapter. A list of names and addrresses of the more frequently occurring test publishers is given at the end of the list, otherwise the publisher's address is given in the main body of the list. However, in the case of a test being published in book form the publisher's address is not given in full.

Adult Memory and Information Processing Battery (1985)
Coughlan, A. K. and Hollows, S. E.
Available from A. K. Coughlan, St James University Hospital, Beckett Street, Leeds LS9 7TF.

Assessment of Motor and Process Skills (1993)
Fisher, A. G.
Occupational Therapy Department, Colorado State University, Fort Collins CO, USA.

Autobiographical Memory Interview (1990)
Kopelman, M. D., Wilson, B. and Baddeley, A. D.
Thames Valley.

Bender Visual-Motor Gestalt Test (1946)
Bender, L.
NFER-Nelson and Psychological Corporation.

Benton Visual Retention Test (BVRT) (5th edition 1992)
Benton, A. and Sivan, A.
Psychological Corporation.

Burt–Vernon Graded Spelling Text (2nd edition 1974)

Burt, C., revised by Vernon, P. E.
Hodder and Stoughton.

Boder Test of Reading–Spelling Patterns (1982)
Boder, E. and Jarrico, S.
Psychological Corporation.

Boston Diagnostic Aphasia Examination (1972) (Revised edition 1983)
Goodglass, H. and Kaplan, E.
The Assessment of Aphasia and Related Disorders.
Lea and Febiger, Philadelphia, PA.

British Ability Scales (BAS) (1983)
Elliot, C. D., Murray, D. J. and Pearson, L. S.
NFER-Nelson.

British Picture Vocabulary Test (1982)
Dunn, L., Dunn, L., Whetton, C. and Pintilie, D.
NFER-Nelson.

Bruininks–Oseretsky Test of Motor Proficiency (1978)
Bruininks, R.
NFER-Nelson.

Bus Story Test (1969)
Renfrew, C. E.
Available from the author at North Place, Old Headington, Oxford.

California Verbal Learning Test (1987)
Delis, D., Kramer, J., Kaplan, E. and Ober, B.
Psychological Corporation.

Category Test: Computer Version (1992)
DeFlippis, N. A.
Psychological Assessment Resources.

Chessington Occupational Therapy Neurological Assessment Battery (1986)
Tyerman, R., Tyerman, A., Price, H., Hadfield, C. *et al.*
Nottingham Rehabilitation Ltd, 17 Ludlow Hill Road, West
Bridgeford, Nottingham NG2 6HF.

Children's Category Test (CCT) (1993)
Boll, T.
Psychological Corporation.

179

Children's Paced Serial Addition Task (CHIPASAT) (1991)
Johnson, D. A., Roethig-Johnston, K. and Middleton, J.
Children's Head Injury Trust, c/o The Radcliffe Infirmary, Woodstock
Road, Oxford OX2 6HE.

Children's Rivermead Behavioural Memory Test (1992)
Wilson, B. A., Ivani-Chalian, R. and Aldrich, F.
Thames Valley.

City University Color Vision Test
Fletcher, R.
Keeler Instruments, 456 Park way, Lawrence Park Industrial District,
Broomall, PA, USA.

Communicative Assessment for Daily Living (1980)
Holland, A.
Baltimore, University Park Press.

Contributions to Neuropsychological Assessment (1983)
Benton, A., Hamsher, K., Varney, N. and Spreen, O.
NFER-Nelson.

Doors and People: A Test of Visual and Verbal Recall and Recognition (1994)
Baddeley, A. D., Emslie, H. and Nimmo-Smith, I.
Thames Valley

Edinburgh Functional Communication Profile (1984)
Skinner, C., Wirz, S., Thomson, I. and Davidson, J.
Buckingham, Winslow Press.

Fagan Test of Infant Intelligence (1988)
Infant Test Corporation
11000 Cedar Avenue, Cleveland OH, USA.

Farnsworth–Munsell 100 Hue Test
Munsell Color.
Munsell Color, Macbeth, 2411 North Calvert Street, Baltimore, MD
21218, USA.

Finger Tapper (1970)
Psychological Assessment Resources.

First Steps: Screening Test for Evaluating Preschoolers (1993)
Miller, L. J.
Psychological Corporation.

Functional Communication Profile (1969)
Sarno, M. J.
Institute of Rehabilitation Medicine, New York University Medical Center, 400 East 34th Street, New York NY 10016, USA.

Graded Arithmetic – Mathematics Test (2nd edition 1976)
Vernon, P. E. and Miller, K. M.
Hodder and Stoughton norms supplement available from NFER-Nelson.

Graded Word Spelling Test (1971)
Vernon, P. E.
Hodder and Stoughton.

Grooved Pegboard (1948)
Psychological Assessment Resources.

Halstead–Reitan Neuropsychological Test Batteries (1969, 1974)
Reitan, R. *et al.*
Reitan Neuropsychological Laboratory, 1338 E. Edison Street, Tucson AZ 8571, USA.

Hand Dynamometer (1947)
Psychological Assessment Resources.

Ishihara's Test for Colour Blindness
Ishihara, S.
Kaneham, distributed by Tötmus Optical Inc., Petersburg VA, 23803, USA.

Kaufman Infant and Preschool Scale (1968)
Kaufman, H.
Stoetling.

Kendrick Cognitive Tests for the Elderly (1972)
Kendrick, D.
NFER-Nelson.

Kinaesthetic Sensitivity Test (1985)
Laslo, J. and Bairstow, P. J.
Holt, Rhinehart and Winston, Eastbourne.

Language Modalities Test for Aphasia (1961)
Wepman, J. and Jones, L.
Educational Industry Service, Chicago.

Luria–Nebraska Neuropsychological Battery (1980)
Golden, C., Hammeke, T. and Purisch, A.
NFER-Nelson.

Miller Assessment for Preschoolers (1988)
Miller, L. J.
Psychological Corporation.

Minnesota Test for the Differential Diagnosis of Aphasia (1965)
(Revised edition 1973)
Schuell, H.
University of Minnesota Press, Minneapolis, and NFER-Nelson.

Mossford Assessment Chart for the Physically Handicapped (1983)
Whitehouse, J.
NFER-Nelson.

Movement Assessment Battery for Children (Movement ABC) (1992)
Henderson, S. E. and Sugden, D. A.
Psychological Corporation.

Multilingual Aphasia Examination (1976)
Benton, A. L. and Hamsher, K.
Department of Neurology, University of Iowa Hospital, Iowa City
IA 52243, USA.

National Adult Reading Test (2nd edition 1982)
Nelson, H. and Willison, J.
NFER-Nelson.

Neale Analysis of Reading Ability (Revised British edition 1989)
Neale, M., Christophers, U. and Whitton, C.
NFER-Nelson.

Peabody Picture Vocabulary Test (PPVT) (Revised edition 1981)
Dunn, L. and Dunn, L.
American Guidance Service (available from NFER-Nelson).

Perceptual-Motor Behaviour: Development Assessment and Therapy (1985)
Laszlo, J. I. and Bairstow, P.
Holt, Rinehart and Winston, Eastbourne.

Psycholinguistic Assessments of Language Processing in Aphasia (1992)
Kay, J., Lesser, R. and Coltheart, M.
Lawrence Erlbaum, London.

Purdue Pegboard (1948)
Tiffin, J.
Psychological Assessment Resources.

Raven's Progressive Matrices and Vocabulary Scales (2nd revision 1985)
Raven, J.
NFER-Nelson.

Recognition Memory Test (1984)
Warrington, E. K.
NFER-Nelson.

Renfrew Action Picture Test (1966)
Renfrew, C.
Available from the author at North Place, Old Headington, Oxford.

Revised Edinburgh Functional Communication Profile (1990)
Wirz, S. L., Skinner, C. M. and Dean, E. C.
Communication Skill Builders, 3830 East Bellevue, Box 42050, Tucson AZ, USA.

Rivermead Behavioural Memory Test (RBMT) (1985)
Wilson, B., Cockburn, J. and Baddeley, A.
Thames Valley.

Rivermead Perceptual Assessment Battery (RPAB) (1984)
Whiting, S., Lincoln, N., Bhavani, J. and Cockburn, J.
Thames Valley and NFER-Nelson.

Sensory Integration and Praxis (1991)
Fisher, A. G., Murray, E. A. and Bundy, A. C.
F. A. Davis and Co, Philadelphia, PA.

Sensory Integration and Praxis Tests (1988)
Ayres, A. J.
Western Psychological Services, 12031 Wiltshire Boulevard, Los Angeles, CA 90025, USA.

Sensory Stimulation Assessment Measure (1989)
Camden, N. J., Rader, M. A. and Ellis D. W.
Medplex Rehab.

Speed and Capacity of Language Processing (1992)
Baddeley, A. D., Emslie, H. and Nimmo-Smith, I.
Thames Valley.

Test for Reception of Grammar (TROG) (1983)
Bishop, D.
Available from the author at MRC Applied Psychology Unit, 15 Chaucer Road, Cambridge CB2 2EF.

Test of Language Competence (1985, 1987)
Wiig, E. H. and Secord, W.
Harcourt Brace Jovanovich, 757 Third Avenue, New York NY 10017, USA.

Test of Motor Impairment (TOMI) (Revised edition 1984)
Stott, D. H., Moyes, F. A. and Henderson, S. E.
Psychological Corporation.

Token Test for Children (1962)
DiSimoni, F.
DLM Teaching Resources, One DLM Park, Allen TX 75002, USA, and NFER-Nelson.

Trail Making Test (1944)
Army Individual Test Battery and Reitan, R.
Reitan Neuropsychological Laboratory, 1338 E. Edison Street, Tucson AZ 85719, USA.

Visual Object and Space Perception Battery (VOSP) (1991)
Warrington, E. K. and James, M.
Thames Valley.

Visual Retention Test: Multiple Choice (1977)
Benton, A. L., Hamsher, K. and Stone, F. B.
Department of Neurology, University of Iowa Hospital, Iowa City
IA 52243, USA.

Vulpe Assessment Battery Revised (1994)
Vulpe, S. G.
Slosson Educational Publications Inc., PO Box 280, East Aurora NY
14052, USA.

Wechsler Adult Intelligence Scale (WAIS-RUK) (Revised UK edition 1986)
Wechsler, D.
Psychological Corporation.

Wechsler Intelligence Scale for Children (WISC-III UK) (Revised UK edition
1992)
Wechsler, D.
Psychological Corporation.

Wechsler Memory Scale (Revised edition 1987)
Wechsler, D.
Psychological Corporation.

Wechsler Preschool and Primary Scale of Intelligence (WPPSI-RUK)
(Revised edition 1990)
Wechsler, D.
Psychological Corporation.

Western Aphasia Battery (1982)
Kertesz, A.
Harcourt Brace Jovanovich, 757 Third Avenue, New York NY 10017,
USA.

Western Neurosensory Stimulation Profile (1989)
Ansell, B. J., Keenan, J. E. and de la Rocha, O.
Western Neurocare Center Inc., Tustin CA, USA.

Wide Range Achievement Tests (1965) (Revised editions 1980s)
Jastak, S. and Wilkinson, G. S.
Psychological Assessment Resources.

Wisconsin Card Sorting Test (1948) (Revised edition 1981)
Grant, D. A. and Berg, E. A.; revision, Heaton, R. K.
Psychological Assessment Resources and NFER-Nelson.

Word Finding Test (1969)
Renfrew, C.
Available from the author at North Place, Old Headington, Oxford.

NAMES AND ADDRESSES OF PUBLISHERS

Hodder and Stoughton
Mill Road
Dunton Green
Sevenoaks
Kent TN13 2YA

NFER-Nelson
Darville House
2 Oxford Road East
Windsor
Berks SL4 1DF

Psychological Assessment Resources
PO Box 998
Odessa
Florida 33556
USA

Psychological Corporation
24–28 Oval Road
London NW1 7DX

Stoetling Co.
1350 S. Kostner Avenue
Chicago
Illinois 60623
USA

Thames Valley Test Company
7–9 The Green
Bury St Edmunds
Suffolk IP28 6EL

NAME INDEX

Acord, L. D. 62
Adams, C. B. T. 17
Adams, K. M. 13
Alberman, E. 34
Albert, M. L. 104, 105
Albert, M. S. 144
Aldrich, F. 140
Allen, D. A. 35, 36
Andrews, K. 172
Andrews, T. K. 24
Annett, M. 25, 34
Ansell, B. J. 173
Ashworth, B. 85
Ayres, A. J. 82, 86, 90, 91

Baddeley, A. D. 135, 140–1, 142, 143,
    144, 145, 146, 147–8
Baer, R. A. 22, 56
Bagnato, S. J. 25
Bairstow, P. 41, 82, 86
Barker, D. D. 62
Barley, W. D. 51
Barnes, M. 24
Bartram, D. 166
Basser, L. S. 17
Bauer, R. M. 101
Bayes, K. 130
Baxter, D. M. 128, 131
Beardsall, L. 52
Beardsworth, E. D. 17, 52, 54
Beaumont, J. G. 4, 6, 8, 13, 167
Beauvois, M-F. 100, 129
Beck, N. C. 51, 52
Beech, J. 36, 38, 122
Bell, B. 88
Benson, F. D. 57
Benton, A. L. 102, 141, 146
Berti, A. 105
Bigler, E. D. 12, 57, 60

Bishop, D. V. M. 37
Bisiach, E. 104, 107
Black, D. A. 143
Bleiberg, J. 9
Bornstein, R. A. 52
Bourgeois, B. F. D. 32
Bowers, D. 102
Boyle, G. J. 55
Braff, D. L. 62
Brain, Lord 9
Brayne, C. 52
Bricolo, A. 172
Britton, P. G. 59
Brooks, D. N. 56, 57, 58, 121, 143, 144,
    159
Brown, J. 117
Brown, R. A. 85
Bruce, V. 102
Bruininks, R. H. 34
Bruyer, R. 102
Brust, J. C. M. 130
Bub, D. 128, 131
Bullard-Bates, C. 17
Bunge, M. 6
Buschke, H. 25
Butters, N. 61, 64, 144, 148

Caine, E. D. 47
Caramazza, A. 131
Casey, R. 24
Chapey, R. 119, 120
Chelune, G. J. 22, 56
Chomsky, N. 111
Christensen, A. L. 9
Cockburn, J. 138, 144, 146
Cohen, S. 62
Collins, A. M. 148
Collins, D. 166
Coltheart, M. 38, 126, 130

187

Stein, D. G. 17
Stott, D. H. 40
Stratton, P. 23
Stuart, M. 38
Stuss, D. T. 57
Sugden, S. E. 40
Sullivan, E. V. 60
Sunderland, A. 137, 140
Swift, A. 31

Tart, R. 61
Taylor, A. M. 100
Taylor, E. 30, 31
Taylor, H. G. 30
Taylor, N. 90
Teasdale, G. 172, 173
Temple, C. M. 18, 35, 37, 40
Tharp, B. R. 31
Thompson, P. J. 62, 63
Tobin, W. 83
Trimble, M. R. 62, 63
Tulving, E. 146
Tzavaras, A. 103

Van Dongen, H. R. 122
Van Gorp, W. 63
Vanderwart, M. 99
Vicente, P. J. 6
Vignolo, L. A. 140
Vincent, E. 38
Volpe, J. J. 17
Vulpe, S. G. 91

Waber, D. P. 20
Walsh, K. W. 6, 8
Walton, D. 143

Walton, J. 58
Ward, M. 40
Warrington, E. K. 8, 98, 99, 100, 101, 102, 103, 104, 127, 128, 130, 131, 143, 144, 148
Wechsler, D. 48, 58, 138
Weiskrantz, L. 7, 144
Wepman, J. 117
Whishaw, I. Q. 170
Whitehouse, J. 88
Whitbourne, S. K. 120
Whittle, A. 83
Wig, E. H. 36
Wilcox, M. J. 119, 121
Wilson, B. 20, 50, 51, 88, 105, 137, 138, 140, 143, 144, 145, 146
Wilson, S. L. 165, 166, 171, 173, 174
Wilkinson, A. B. 163
Wingfield, A. 98
Wirz, S. L. 121
Wise, R. J. S. 169
Wolfson, D. 55
Wood, P. 83
Woods, R. T. 59

Young, A. W. 14, 97, 98, 99, 101, 102, 104, 105, 106, 107, 118
Young, J. A. 85
Ysseldyke, J. E. 19
Yule, W. 38

Zettin, M. 101
Zev Rymer, W. 84
Zihl, J. 98
Zillmer, E. A. 55
Ziskin, J. 164

SUBJECT INDEX

Miller Assessment for Preschoolers 87, 90, 182
mind–body problem 6
Minnesota Test for the Differential Diagnosis of Aphasia 112, 182
Mossford Assessment Chart for the Physically Handicapped 182
motor impairment 24, 40–1, 88–9; tests of 34, 89–90
motor responses, in infant tests 22–3
Movement Assessment Battery for Children (Movement ABC) 40, 90, 182
multi-infarct dementia (MID) 59, 60
Multilingual Aphasia Examination 182
muscle tone 83–5
myelination 18

name retrieval problems 99, 101
National Adult Reading Test (NART) 51, 52, 53–4, 182
National Institute of Mental Health (NIMH) 63–4
Neale Analysis of Reading Ability 182
neglect dyslexia 125, 130–1
neurodegenerative diseases 31
neuro-imaging 166–71
neurological examinations 10–11
neuronal ceroid lipofuscinosis (NCL) 31
neuropsychological function, models of 6–7
new learning 142–3
non-fluent aphasia 113–14
non-pecuniary loss 158–9
non-verbal learning 143
non-verbal memory tests 20
norm-referenced testing 19
nystagmus 75, 77–8

object recognition 98–100
observation, assessment by 25, 83, 84, 88, 89, 120
occupational pensions 156
occupational therapists 83
optic aphasia 100
optokinetic nystagmus 77–8
orientation 146–7

pain, compensation for 158–9, 161, 162
paired associate learning 20, 22, 142–3
parallel distributed processing 8
parents, assessment of and infant development 23

Parkinson's disease 59–60
passive movement 84
Peabody Picture Vocabulary Test 36, 182
Pearson Commission Report 156–7
pecuniary loss 159–60
pension loss 160
Performance IQ 49, 56–7, 59, 62
phonological dyslexia 129
physiotherapists 83
plain X-ray 11–12
plasticity 17–18
positron emission tomography (PET) 12, 168–70
post-traumatic amnesia (PTA) 24, 57
post-traumatic stress disorder 162–3
praxis 90–1
prediction 23
Prices Test 144–5
private insurance 156
procedural learning 143–4
prognosis 5; for dementia 58; of language development 37
propositional language 112
prosopagnosia 101–2
prospective memory 145–6
Psycholinguistic Assessments of Language Processing in Aphasia (PALPA) 118
Psychological Disability Scale 31
psychological intervention 5
psychometric tests 48
psychophysiological measures 23
Purdue pegboard 34, 183

RAF Near Point Rule 75
Raven's Coloured Matrices (RCM) 53, 60–1
Raven's Progressive Matrices (RPM) 53, 62, 183
reading ability 37–8
reading without semantics 129–30
reasoning, assessment of 53
Recognition Memory Test 140, 183
recovery 17, 24, 25, 121–2
regional equipotentiality 7
remote memory 144–5
Renfrew Action Picture Test 25, 36, 183
retrograde amnesia 136, 144, 145
Rey Auditory Verbal Learning Test 143
Rey–Osterreith Complex Figure 20, 141
right hemisphere damage 49, 53, 59, 62, 100; dyslexia and 125, 130–1